CASSOCKS IN THE WILDERNESS

REMEMBERING THE SEMINARY AT SPRINGWOOD

CHRIS GERAGHTY

Spectrum Publications, Melbourne 2001

First published in Australia in 2001
Reprinted February 2002, 2018
by Spectrum Publications Pty Ltd
PO Box 75, Richmond, Vic, 3121
Tel: +61 (13) 00 540 736
Fax: + 61 (13) 00 540 737
Email: spectrum@spectrumpublications.com.au

Copyright 2001 Chris Geraghty
All rights reserved.
No part of this publication may be reproduced
in any manner without prior
written permission of the publisher.

Cover design: Spectrum Publications
Typesetting by Spectrum Publications
Typeface: Goudy

ISBN 9780867863161
0867863161

To our boys

Patrice and Pascal

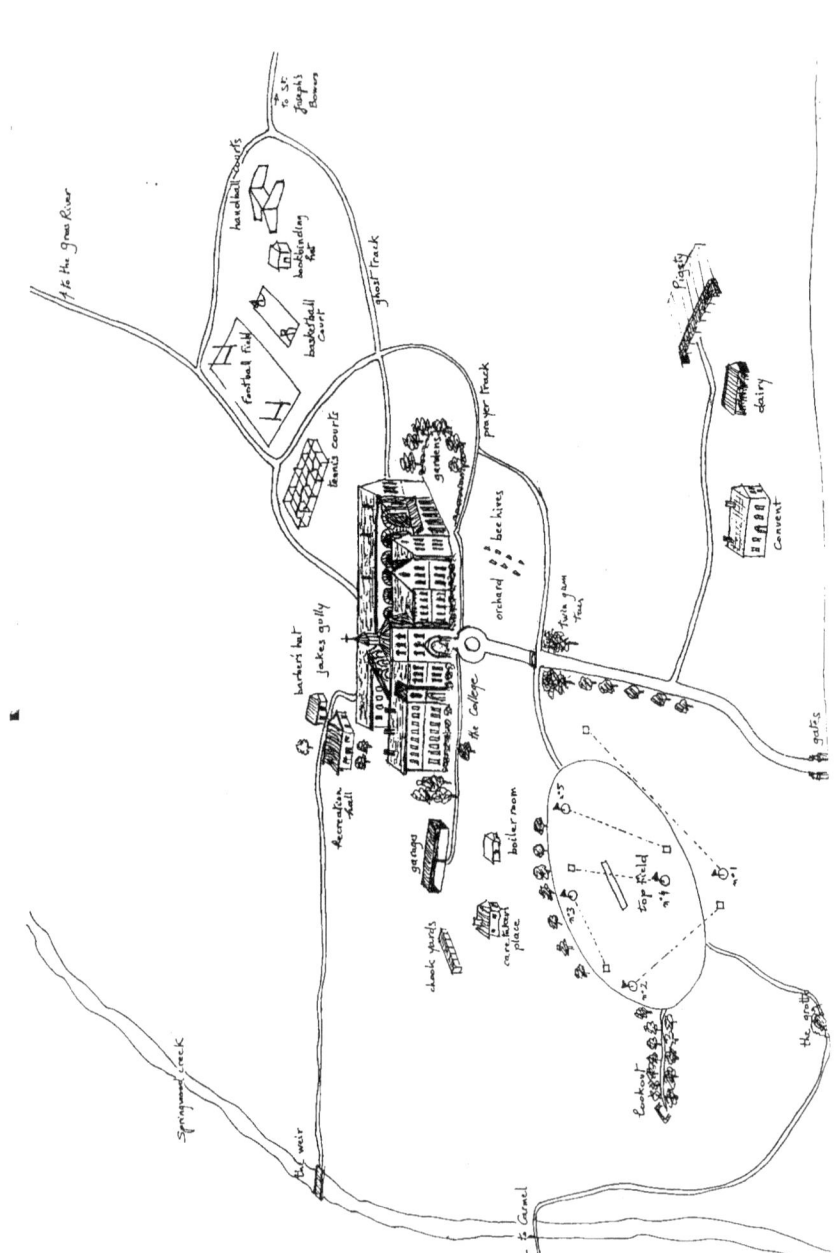

Contents

Foreword	vii
Preface	xi
The timetable	xiii
Leaving the family	1
Sparrow fart in the seminary	21
Breakfast and a bit of freedom	39
The system at work	63
Classes and more prayers	93
Life in the afternoon	121
Chapel again and study	151
High points and celebrations	171
Epilogue	189
Class lists 1951-1957	194

Foreword

Chris Geraghty writes about a clerical system which seemed intent on dehumanising those who ventured into it. It was even bent upon distorting the human face of God. It was very, very important that at the end of this long process, like tin soldiers, everyone should emerge the same. Conformity, symbolised by dress, clerical mannerisms, piety and a form of education, was all important. The priest had to be 'all things to all men', unquestioningly obedient and compliant to his superiors. Provided such conformity was apparent, other defects of immense proportions could simply be ignored.

I entered this system in 1966, and reached the end of the process in 1972. During my years in the seminary, there were many changes to that system which Chris remembers. My early years at Springwood were, however, actually as described in this book. There were many moments of the absurd, instances of complete hilarity, and acts of unbelievable cruelty.

My first contact with Chris Geraghty was in those early years at Springwood when I was a humble student. He had completed the process and had been turned out as an ordained priest. He had been elevated to the rank of professor in the seminary system. He was cool and aloof, but without absolute frigidity. In those days, he was a fine looking young man with charisma and a hint of humanity. However, any attempt to touch him would result in instant withdrawal. I remember clearly that, like the other professors, he wore a shoulder cape on his black soutane as a symbol of importance, as a badge of professorial conformity, to create distance from the student body. I hated those symbols and was not attracted to those who adopted them. Needless to say, there was no friendship between us at that stage.

In that cold institution, Chris Geraghty taught me liturgical studies, a subject in which I had absolutely no interest. He discoursed on the importance of ancient Jewish sacrifices and the relevance of symbolism for the Church. He spoke with enthusiasm about the theories of communal participation in sacred mysteries. He identified in me a complete lack of interest in what he was lecturing about. In fact, he now claims I was the only person ever ordained a priest in Sydney who could not read. I was certainly not inspired to read about ancient Jewish sacrifices! In fairness to Chris however, I was not inspired by any of the other lecturers or professors at Springwood. Doc Joiner, who is mentioned in this book, taught me in biology, lecturing verbatim from notes undoubtedly prepared years before. Why we were doing biology I do not know. While I dreamt of freedom, rugby and Randwick, Doc spent tedious hours lecturing us on the 'interstitial fluid', a mysterious substance of great importance. To this day I have no idea what Doc was talking about. The inhumanity of this seminary system is best exemplified by the circumstances surrounding our leaving the priesthood.

After we left, our friendship began, and is now a close bond. Chris had spent twelve long years in the seminary system, as a student. He then worked for a short number of years in a parish, studied for a doctorate in theology, before his appointment as a professor in the seminary at Springwood where he remained for approximately five years. There he was entrusted with the education of priests for the archdiocese of Sydney. He was thought highly of by the authorities who encouraged him to undertake further liturgical studies overseas. He spent two years in France before returning to the seminary system at St Patrick's College at Manly. Though he had made a major contribution to the education of the clergy and to the archdiocese as a whole, after leaving the ministry, he received no official contact from the church authorities. No letter was sent; no telephone call made; not even a Christmas card. This man had failed to conform and was treated as if he had died – no, as if he had never existed.

I was treated better than Geraghty, as he is quick to remind me. After having left the ministry in 1976, I lived in a small one-bedroom flat for a number of years. One evening in 1980, I was sitting in my squalid little flat, watching television and drinking beer, when the phone rang. I answered it. 'Father Marr?' 'Yes' I said instinctively, and in shock. 'This is Father Roche. I am in charge of the sick priest's fund. I have noticed that you are behind in your contributions to the fund. It is not good to get behind as health can leave us at any moment. You should attend to this issue.' – 'Yes Father. How much do I owe?' 'You are $127.11 in arrears.' 'I will send a cheque immediately.' 'Good, fine, God bless you now.' This was my one and only official contact with the Church, and one more than Chris Geraghty.

Geraghty is well placed to describe the seminary system. He had been part of it for so many years. His memory is strikingly accurate, his eye sharp, his observation sometimes acid, but often amusing. As I read, I smiled knowingly and often enjoyed a good belly laugh. Geraghty's honesty is refreshing.

Cassocks in the Wilderness is an entertaining read for anyone who wishes to learn what the seminary system, and the Church behind it, was like in the fifties. It is compulsive reading for Catholics who lived through the harsh, ironclad system, for generous men and women who thought they had a vocation and tested it in fire, and of course for the many boys who took the train trip to Springwood station and then the old rattlers to the college.

We share an institutional background which is not easily shared with those who have not experienced such absurdity. We studied law together at night, while both of us held down jobs during the day. Chris worked for the Health Commission after his blossoming career as a taxi driver collapsed. I worked as a cleaner of hotel public bars and lavatories. Our daytime paths often crossed at North Sydney as I drove my rusty red truck to another cleaning job and Chris waited in a bus queue to be transported to his office. A blast of the horn was always met with a wave of the hand and hearty laughter. In later life Chris and I became good friends. We ride horses together. We often laugh together. It is for both of us a long way from the incense and Gregorian chant, the solemn silence and lectures about ancient Jewish sacrifices and 'interstitial fluid'.

Peter Marr
Solicitor, Grafton

Preface

St Columba's College, Springwood, was a junior seminary in the Blue Mountains where I lived from 13 February 1951 to early December 1957. The institution had begun its life in 1909, and was closed down at the end of 1977, when it was converted into a high school for the children of local mountain residents. Those aspiring to become priests had come and gone in heavy numbers. The priests who had staffed the college had also varied over the years - rectors, teachers, bursars and spiritual directors. Later in my life, I was destined to become one of the teachers for a few years. Like any institution, the buildings, the grounds, the rules and routine, the staff and atmosphere changed as the years passed.

I have not attempted to construct a history of the institution, or even to write the story of my life beyond the seven years of my internship at Springwood. There are many ghosts who still wander the corridors of the college and who do not appear in these pages. Many of my own personal memories, the highs and lows of my life, do not feature here. For both of us, the college and me, there is a bigger story to be told, a story overflowing the boundaries of the years 1951-1957, and beyond the limitations of my memories.

As for the institution, let someone less egocentric construct the narrative which officially began with Cardinal Moran and concluded with Cardinal Freeman. He might even attempt to explain what Springwood and the minor seminary were about.

This is my story, but only part of my story, a small part, an important part. Others would have judged the Springwood experience differently – perhaps more gently, more favourably, or more harshly, with less sympathy for a system based on routine, obedience, discipline and authority. I have written down my memories of this place in the mountains principally for my two boys in the hope that they may come to understand their father better when they begin to wonder who he was and where he came from. I have also recorded my story for my fellow interns, to amuse them, to summon up memories for them, and for those who have lived in similar worlds, men and women alike. I also hope that this little book, its photographs and lists might contribute to a historical record of a world now gone. These pages might also enlighten those who would seek insight into the Catholic clergy, perhaps to help soften their criticism, or explain, at least in part, the crises, personal and institutional, which have spoilt the image of a noble message of liberation and, by association, the lives of many good men.

In the fifties, we clerics and would-be-clerics were inhabiting a pre-modern world, living in an age of innocence, of ignorance, in our own, isolated realm. As we enter the third millennium, it now seems such a distant, mystifying world. What the hell did they think they were doing!

I wish to express my gratitude and appreciation to Joan Schultze for her untiring assistance in recording my memoirs. She now knows how demanding and impatient I can be. I thank her for her fortitude, her dry, earthy sense of humour, for her uncomplaining support. I pay warm tribute to the interest and professional skill that Maryna Mews has shown in the editing of my manuscript. Finally, I owe a debt to my wife and to our boys who have remained tolerant and patient throughout the months I have devoted to recalling my memories of a distant life. They have contributed to my declericalisation. Though Adele has never visited the Springwood complex, under my instructions and with the aid of an aerial photograph she produced the layout of the college which appears at the front of this book. Finally, a word of thanks to the estate of James McAuley and to Bruce Dawe for permission to reprint passages from their poetry.

In recording my memories, I have not intentionally set out to be cruel to anyone. I have tried to record my impressions accurately, honestly, though I have sometimes varied the names of the characters who appear. Like myself, all my fellow students of years past must surely have changed and may now wish to preserve their anonymity. I would not like to be the cause of any embarrassment or hurt. If they recognise themselves, as I am sure they will, I hope they will smile as they remember.

Timetable

CLASS-DAYS

6.00	Rise
6.30	Morning Prayers and Meditation
7.00	Mass and Thanksgiving
7.45	Beds made
8.00	Breakfast – Recreation
9.00-11.00	Classes – Recreation
11.15-12.25	Classes – Recreation
12.40	Examination of Conscience
12.45	Dinner – Recreation
1.40-3.40	Classes
3.40	Coffee – Recreation
5.20	Visit to the Blessed Sacrament and Spiritual Reading*
5.40	Study
6.15	Benediction (on days noted in the Calendar)
6.30	Tea – Recreation
7.20	Rosary (during October Devotions, Spiritual Reading)
7.35	Study
9.15	Walk
9.30	Night Prayers and Meditation Points
10.00	Lights extinguished

* On certain days, marked in the Calendar, Benediction takes the place of the Visit. On Wednesdays the Spiritual Conference, and on Fridays the Stations of the Cross, take the place of the Spiritual Reading.

SUNDAYS AND FEAST DAYS

6.30	Rise
7.00	Morning Prayers and Meditation
7.30	Mass and Thanksgiving
8.15	Breakfast – Beds made – Recreation
9.30	Solemn High Mass or Missa Cantata – Recreation
10.30-10.45	Rector's Conference (Sundays only) – Recreation
12.40	Spiritual Reading – Examination of Conscience
1.00	Dinner – Recreation
2.00-3.00	Private Reading, Letter Writing, etc.
4.30-5.30	Study
5.45	Vespers and Benediction
6.30	Tea – Recreation
7.20	Rosary – Study
9.15	Walk
9.30	Night Prayers and Meditation Points
10.00	Lights extinguished

(In October: 5.15 p.m., Vespers; 6.00 p.m., Rosary and Benediction)

THURSDAYS

6.30	Rise
7.00	Morning Prayers and Meditation
7.30	Mass and Thanksgiving
8.15	Breakfast – Beds made – Recreation
12.55	Examination of Conscience
1.00	Dinner – Recreation
2.00-2.30	Choir Practice
2.30-3.15	Private Reading, Letter Writing, etc.
5.00	Visit to the Blessed Sacrament and Spiritual Reading*
5.20	Study
6.15	Benediction (on days noted in the Calendar)
7.20	Rosary (October, Spiritual Reading) – Study

* On days when there is Benediction, Benediction takes the place of the Visit.

Snap-frozen in some seminary,
the word, secured against the ubiquitous shock
of honest air or breath, rots as it thaws.

At Mass, Bruce Dawe

Leaving the family

A STRANGE BED

I was alone for the first time since leaving my mother's womb, alone in a gigantic room under a cathedral ceiling, with forty other boys all strangers to me, each curled up in bed, under grey army blankets. It was a warm summer night and a dazzling necklace of diamonds hung low over the Blue Mountains. The bush birds were asleep. The possums and rock wallabies were discreetly feeling their path through the prickly bush. All was still and silent as the young men who surrounded me, tried to sleep. Gradually the breathing grew more regular, despite some snorting, snoring and an occasional passage of foul, personal wind.

St Columba's dormitory was a large, spacious hall on the second floor, encased inside and out in honey-coloured sandstone, with giant windows down one side to admit the warm summer air and the curious, thirsty mosquitoes. It looked out over a valley of rough country and scrawny trees that drew life from Hawkesbury stone. I lay in bed. I hated the heat. It always made me itchy and restless. I was not free to throw off the blankets as I had not been told whether that was allowed. No sound of traffic, no buzz of humanity. I could not hear my father rattling cupboards in the kitchen, talking to himself. No city noises. The clatter of the tram which used to pass by our home in Florence Street was absent. A warm silence filled the space inside the thick walls. High up into the rafters and the heavenly ceiling, it came in through the open windows from the valleys, the cliffs, rocks, the sharp, itchy scrub. Silence floated over the unseen wildflowers, the flannel flowers and the regal waratahs, all covered in darkness, waiting patiently for the dawn of another day.

The wall of flats outside my Cremorne cell in Florence Street had disappeared. The paling fence, the narrow concrete passageway, the shaded light in John Nicholls' bachelor room had suddenly been exchanged for stars in the heaven, nervous creatures in the night, lizards, sleeping bush butterflies and possums in trees in a vast, endless space. My final ritual prayer for the night -

> *Gentle Jesus, meek and mild, look on me a little child.*
> *Jesus, take my heart and bless it, nothing evil may possess it.*

My little mind wandered back over the day – packing, Central Station, the farewells to family (the significance of which I had not realised), the steam train up the mountains, the bruised and weary buses, the refectory meal. How had I come to be there? I was twelve years of age – a tender twelve, a child's twelve, drawn away from my mother and father, separated from my sisters and brother. I had been railroaded. Circumstances beyond my control (all circumstances were then beyond my control) had conspired to snatch me from the nest. I drifted off to sleep at last, and woke in a strange bed.

A loud penetrating noise was clanging on and on, insistently. I was accustomed to the soft rustle of my mother's nightie, a hand on my shoulder, or the whispered voice of my sister as she called me to accompany her each morning through the dark streets of Cremorne to the local church. A boy in a black cassock was walking through the passage between the rows of beds, working a large brass bell. The room was full of teenagers, males only, some still curled up disobediently in their narrow, wire beds, others on their knees, heads buried in regulation blankets. Others were rushing out, down the worn steps to the row of cold basins with wooden surrounds like toilet seats, or to the smelly shower block and toilet cubicles, to deliver a powerful jet of morning urine. They were all older than I was, all forty-odd of them, already teenagers. And some of them seemed to know the routine. Towels over the shoulder or circling the waist to cover the shameful bits, toothbrush in hand, everyone at different stages of undressing and dressing under the modest cover of a dressing-gown.

No one was speaking, not even in whispers. I followed the lead of those who seemed in the know. I washed, dressed in my short pants, and made my way with the others to the chapel. I wondered what was for breakfast. I was nervous. I was self-conscious, and excited. I had begun a long journey, confident in the knowledge that the cardinal and my parish priest had judged that I was worthy.

A CALLING FROM GOD

Father John Lander died in September 1993. To the end we remained unreconciled. We had not spoken for years, since my fatal rejection of the princely life of priesthood. In the late forties and early fifties he had been the honoured curate assisting Eris O'Brien (subsequently Archbishop) at our Neutral Bay parish. He had been a holy man. Perhaps not so much holy, but rather extremely pious. I remember him spending hours in the parish church in private prayer before the Blessed Sacrament, and wondered what he said, how he filled in the time. In my altar boy days, he appeared friendly, paternal and uncomplicated. As I grew older, I came to understand that he was unworldly, simple, scrupulous. He was clinging in a storm to the soggy log of a disappearing church, to the quaint religious world of Pius XI and XII.

Johnny Lander had been ordained in 1934 from Manly seminary, as priest No.562. Before he had been sent to our little parish on the edge of Sydney harbour, he had worked the Lord's vineyard in the Bathurst diocese and later among the inmates of Long Bay gaol. I wonder what the criminals had made of such a pale, pious, unsophisticated man. He had said routine masses for them and heard confessions more interesting than those of convent school children's artificial peccadillos. For most, he had been part of the screws' oppressive systems. Archbishop Eris O'Brien, who had been in nominal charge of our parish at Neutral Bay, had worked him hard. Eris used to read well into the night and always appeared late for morning mass, yawning, with sleep in his eyes, so Johnny Lander was the workhorse in our parish.

In later years Father Lander became the parish priest of Brighton-le-Sands where I and others used to visit him in that fervent period after our ordination in 1962. As fledglings let out from Manly College, one of the raw newly ordained priests used to visit his parish each weekend to celebrate a parish Eucharist, and to initiate himself into the ritualistic grind of Saturday confessions. He used to welcome me with special warmth as he had had a hand in my calling from God. I was surprised to discover that John Lander had a full set of Charles Dickens's works. I was impressed. I had never known him to be interested in anything but pious devotions, Our Lady, benediction, altar boys, the rosary, the Sacred Heart, housie, in ritual and religious routine. He had another life beyond the world we inhabited together. I thought he might leave his books to me in his will, but I was too shy to show my hand. Then when I divorced the diocese, he remained loyal to the other party and never spoke to me again.

From the mid-forties I had been one of his red-and-white altar boys at Neutral Bay where he had demanded discipline and obedience, and a hushed, respectful silence, even outside the church. But he was never harsh, or militaristic. We were required to conduct ourselves with due decorum, to preserve an odour of silence in the sacristy, to refrain from drinking the altar wine, from hiding in the cupboards among the ornate vestments and tangle of brass candelabras, from riding our bikes round and round the church.

Every year he would take us on a picnic, usually to the northern beaches, providing the sandwiches, the cakes, and the soft drinks from the Shelleys factory, always wearing his black suit, black hat, and Roman collar, though, at least for a few moments, we would glimpse his pure alabaster, somewhat flabby hairless body, exposed in a pair of black, woollen, ample togs. It was during one of these bland excursions, when I was young and innocent (a condition which lasted a long time) that I first saw a couple making love in the sand dunes at Avalon. I did not understand what they were doing but I remember my puzzling fascination. I recall the intensity of their struggle, the violent rolling and thumping, and my private struggle to achieve custody of the eyes. I had never seen anything like it.

I had attended the nuns' school in the local parish until the end of fourth class, and despite some financial difficulties, my parents had later dressed me in a grey, short-pants suit and sent me off to the Marist brothers at Mosman where I finished my primary schooling. During the Marian year in 1950, we had been visited at school by a vocations collector, an elderly Marist brother who was affectionately known by the boys as Brother 'Spitballs' because he used to salivate all over the class while talking to us. He was short, elderly, rather rotund, with cold, frameless glasses, a dirty, tattered black cord around his fat stomach, and powdered chalk dust mingled with dandruff on his shoulders.

Brother Andrew (Spitballs) used to visit each classroom, addressing the boys, asking each to fill out a printed form to indicate whether he was even vaguely interested in becoming a religious brother. I was a rather serious little fellow. Others used to lead Spitballs along, pretending interest, but having absolutely no sense of calling. Such duplicity was foreign to me. When I indicated interest by a single tick in the 'yes' box, I found myself in a serious one-to-one conference with Brother Andrew, being encouraged to say my prayers to the holy founder of his order, and to reflect (at the age of eleven) so as to discern the will of God. Suddenly things had become serious. He told me to discuss my vocation with my parents, and to request a character reference from my local parish priest. I was on the way. The next stop would be the minor juniorate of the Marist brothers at Bowral where there happened to be room for me.

Throughout the Catholic boys' schools of Sydney, Brother Andrew was involved in the same fishing and trawling exercise as Father Kevin McGovern, though Kevin's job was to attract suitable candidates to the archdiocesan minor seminary at Springwood. In the forties and fifties, these drives were surprisingly successful. Many fish were netted. The seminaries and juniorates throughout the nation were full of keen, pious, obedient, eager, Catholic boys. Now the tidal wave has passed, leaving nothing but dry sand, a sense of wonder at what it used to be like and confusion about what actually happened.

That night I told my parents what had happened at school. I do not recall any serious opposition. A vocation was a blessing in a working-class Catholic household. My father's attitude in later years was that I could always come home whenever I chose. In the meantime, the education I would be receiving was better than any I might have expected at Mosman. But in the kitchen that night, Dad showed no surprise, no displeasure or encouragement. What was happening was 'par for the course' in a good Catholic family. My parents had been friends of the local nuns, on smiling, bowing terms with the priests since the children had begun to attend the parish school.

Obediently, puffed up a little with religious pride that I had been chosen, I approached Father Lander for the reference as Brother Spitballs had advised. There was no discussion. He simply said 'Oh, no. You're not going to Bowral. You're off to Springwood. No Marist brothers juniorate for you. I will arrange for you to go to the seminary.' And that was it.

The application forms arrived by post. I completed them in my careful, schoolboy handwriting, anxious to avoid mistakes. I declared I had had pneumonia at the age of five, that Mum was a convert, and that my father would be responsible for paying an annual fee of twenty pounds for my board and keep, though full board was eighty. On the reverse side of my application I recorded all my examination results for fifth and sixth classes. Brother Gregory, the headmaster at Mosman who would teach me some years later in the seminary, provided a certificate of character and my end-of-year examination results. I was fourth in a class of forty-eight:

> *His teachers during his time here testify to his excellent character and conduct, both in and out of school. In class he works well, although he had not won very high positions in the term tests.*

In November, my mother forwarded my application to the college accompanied by a handwritten letter in which she told the man in charge that I had not yet received the sacrament of confirmation, that she hoped I would be successful in my undertaking and that she constantly prayed for my success. She was then thirty-four years of age (twenty-two when I was born as her third child).

Things were happening behind my back. Father Lander wrote off to Springwood to support my application. He said he had known me for three years and had had the chance to observe me closely:

> *I have always found him a splendid type of Catholic boy. He has a strong manly demeanour. He is honest and truthful, respectful to parents and elders, and particularly respectful to ecclesiastical superiors and religious teachers. For more than three years he has*

served as an altar boy, and has always discharged the duties with a marked piety, promptness and regularity.

In another letter, Father Lander described me as 'splendid material for the priesthood'. He recommended that I receive financial assistance – 'his father being but a wharf labourer – incidentally a splendid type of Irishman'. He observed that I was vacillating in my decision between the priesthood and the Marist brothers because, as I had said, 'to be a priest costs too much'. What prescience! 'My only fear is that the course might seem too long to him and the goal too far away for his dynamic disposition.' Even as a young boy, I was impatient and impetuous.

CHOSEN FOR HIGHER THINGS

Some weeks later, in my short grey pants and school tie, I visited St Mary's Cathedral with my father. In the spacious, cold, marble sacristy, His Eminence Norman Cardinal Gilroy decorated in his shining red regalia, Bishop (later Archbishop) James Carroll in his purple, and the cardinal's private secretary, Father Mick Baulman, interviewed me. Formal episcopal questions – child-like answers – all very satisfactory. My father would be asked to pay only what he could afford, a token contribution. He was a waterside worker, a wharfie, and received only modest and irregular wages. He could not afford much, but he agreed to pay something for my keep: twenty-five pounds a year, I believe he agreed to, but he could never afford any more than ten.

What could a little boy say to persuade two prelates and their assistant that he had a vocation to the priesthood? I told them I was good at my catechism, that I went to mass every day with my sister, that I said my prayers regularly, that I attended a Catholic school, that I was an altar boy and could recite the Latin. That seemed to make them happy. At least they nodded approval.

What were they looking for? Another crowd to swell the chapel at Springwood? Young lambs to feed into the seminary sausage machine? Keen workers to keep the wheels of religious industry turning? Neophyte soldiers for Christ? Loyal, obedient, working-class boys who could be machined and moulded, tried and tested, and turned out like sets of stamps, or like new Holdens off the assembly line? They had an insatiable institution to feed. They were confident that just about anyone would do, so long as he could present a birth certificate to prove he was legitimate and had balls, and a baptismal certificate to prove he had been saved in the one, holy, Catholic, apostolic Church. I was chosen – from on high.

My mother purchased my singlets, underpants, shirts, twelve handkerchiefs, four towels and several pairs of socks. In retrospect, these new items must have strained the family finances, but the sacrifices were generously made as I had embarked on a great adventure – one not uncommon among Catholic families in the early 1950s – and I had the approval of my father's hero, Archbishop O'Brien. Maybe I was a bit young, but time would cure that, and I would be with other boys on the same journey.

On occasions, rare occasions in later life, my father used to reminisce about my first trip to Springwood. He had a clear recollection of my

Cardinal Gilroy

boarding the train at Central Station, jostled and shouldered out of the way by more senior, bigger students with their luggage. I was there in short pants, with a large suitcase, and a very innocent young face. It was the beginning of a life.

It is now nearly fifty years since I travelled with my family by tram from Neutral Bay Junction to Central Station. February 1951, on a humid, sultry day, a motley crowd gathered on the platform. There were perhaps a hundred and fifty students present, all ages and sizes, with brothers and sisters, aunts, parents, to wave us goodbye on our journey to Springwood seminary. A working-class crowd mainly. The women were not wearing brand-name dresses, only rack frocks, with standard shoes and purses. Australia had not yet entered the world of fashion.

I was in grey serge pants, neat grey long socks, my old school shoes, shirt and tie. My father had put ten bob in my pocket and it was held down with a clean handkerchief with my name printed on one corner. My clothes, all purchased from Gowings, were neatly and lovingly packed in a battered suitcase held together with an old leather strap. In obedience to the printed advice we had been sent, each item of clothing had been stamped in black ink, 'C.J. Geraghty', but the industrial washing machines at Springwood would soon fade these marks. My mother would have to order expensive, stitch-on labels from the haberdashery section of McDowells to replace them and spend a few hours sewing. The suitcase also held a new, red tartan dressing-gown, a cheap pair of sandshoes which were certainly not aerodynamically designed, and an ample washing bag sewn up by my mother with a drawstring through a narrow fold around the top. This bag had been the topic of some discussion in the family as none of us could guess why I would need such an item. We were not accustomed to imagining the problems of laundering for multitudes.

I felt quite out of place on the platform at Central Station. Only a few boys were wearing short pants – John Langtry, Bill Challenor, Bob Spackman, Terry Hynes and myself. Some of them had smooth faces, and hairless legs, though most were more mature in their long pants. I was the youngest by at least twelve months, and close to the smallest, though Spackman and Langtry were also tiny. Everyone wore short, neat hair plastered in place with Brylcream. It was the fashion. Big boys were everywhere. Most seemed familiar with the procedure, as they had made the journey before, some four, five, or six times. I stood awkwardly with my mother and father, knowing no one, embarrassed in my short pants, conscious of my worn luggage. I waited to be told what to do.

In later life, my father sometimes recalled, always with a chuckle and a sense of pride, how I had burrowed in between the other students as we all crowded into the train, my suitcase in hand, leaving home for the first time, and then staked out a seat for myself in the compartment. His eyes would moisten, his voice tremble as he remembered my departure from Central Station on that day.

My father was a soft, sentimental Irishman. He had come to Australia with almost nothing – no education, no money, and only one reference, which was addressed to Mr Lohan of Rose Bay. We were very working class, but he was also proud, as Irishmen can be, and determined that his family would succeed. He was proud of his heritage, of his lovely auburn curly hair, of his beautiful wife, of his strong proletarian background, and of his children, who would bring status or shame to him by what they would do.

The whole world revolved around my father. His brother William would prove to be the same when we met him in Ireland years later. Dad worked hard for us and held not one penny for himself. He used to leave his pay packet unopened on the kitchen table each week for rent, food, clothes, for meagre school fees, and receive his tram fares each day from Mum. Although he soled our school shoes, gardened, mowed, washed dishes, and boiled the potatoes, none the less he seemed to live in a world of his own.

The radio was tuned to Dad's station (the ABC) whenever he wanted to listen to the news. We were all silent and attentive when the waterside workers' pick-up numbers were broadcast on 2KY. When television arrived and we could afford a set, he watched the news on Channel 2 at seven o'clock each evening. After the family had purchased a car and since he never learnt to drive, he was driven to work over the bridge and picked up again in the evening. His needs were simple and basic, but we attended to them.

Leaving the Family

Dad never told us how he felt, or discussed his problems with us. He never shared with us the details of his family life in Ireland, of his journey to Australia, of what it was like as an Irish migrant during the Depression in Australia, of how he courted Mum or of how he felt about his first son's death. He was awkwardly private, like miners, or rouseabouts, like most labourers. He lived his life in the present, without reflection, one day at a time, from one pay packet to the next, bill after bill, working as much overtime as he was offered. But we knew when Dad was angry, or worried, or under pressure. We knew by instinct what pleased him, what displeased him. He loved his family, and Ireland, and his simple faith, though he would not have known more than a few basic facts about Christianity and the Church, and did not even know the words of the Our Father or the Hail Mary, or the mysteries of the rosary.

Dad was worldly-wise and canny. He knew a thing or two about politics, about unions, and he was a shrewd judge of people. Others related to him on his terms. While Mum listened to others and went out to support and serve them, Dad was only interested in his family. People outside his home came to him and dealt with Mr Geraghty. He maintained an aloofness, a dignity, a distance, a vagueness, a certain dreamy demeanour. But he was soft and gentle, and while liable to burst suddenly into fire, the flames would quickly die down. Experience and adversity had given him a deep understanding of the world and the needs of mankind.

They waved me off, Mum and Dad, Maureen, Sean, and my sister Colleen who was the spoiled baby of the family. The warmth and intimacy of my family life were gone. I was leaving home at a tender age to make my way among clerics, bishops, cardinals and rough and tumble priests. I would never return to the bosom of my family except as a seminarian, a priest, as a stranger, trained by the system to be pure, distant, aloof, in the world but not of it, an outsider. I was on my own. The projection of my life had been laid down for me, by nuns and priests, by my trusting family, as narrow and as tight as the parallel, steel rail tracks which began there at Central Station, passed through the Western suburbs and disappeared into the distance.

Journey's End and a Beginning

The trip in the steam train out through the flat bushland to Penrith, up through the mountains to Springwood, took about three hours. I felt too new, too young, too foreign to participate in the teasing and horseplay the other more experienced students were enjoying. They hung coats out of open windows, threatening to drop them in the tunnel. A jet of spittle was projected out of one window to be sucked in through the opening of another compartment. One student playfully thumped another. They all seemed so pleased to be together again, on their way back to the consecrated location in the mountains. I sat quietly in the corner, observing all but not yet free to share in the fun and laughter. I was in foreign territory. Perhaps I would never be sufficiently at ease to become part of this world.

Three dilapidated buses met the train at Springwood. It was already dark. Each student, almost to a man, drew desperately on his last cigarette – an Old Chum, an Ardath, Craven 'A', Peter Jackson – as we boarded the buses with our year's luggage. They were crowded and overflowing. Slowly grinding through their gears, they made their familiar way to the college as though unaided. My rattly bus was full of males, standing room only, bodies crowded together, lurching and swaying, full like a mission session at Mosman or one of the early Sunday masses at Neutral Bay in the fifties – jam-packed to overflowing. The bus was already out-of-date, but it would last a few more years. It was, like the Church, on its last set of tyres, with dints in the bodywork. In need of a re-bore and some new duco, with worn clutch and brake pads, it was slow off the mark, functional, but almost worn out. It was a suitable vehicle to convey aspirants to the priesthood back to the seminary.

As we passed through the stone gates of the college, the older students burst into boisterous song. I recognised the language they sang from reciting formulae at mass each morning at Neutral Bay. They were singing the college hymn *Columba Penna* in Latin, two or three verses (no one knew the fourth!) slurring the words, mumbling the second and third verses as people do with our national anthem. [the four verses are to be found at the end of this chapter]

The road in from the gates was about a mile. In later years this drive was asphalted, but in 1951 we travelled over unsealed, dusty red clay. At the top of the drive, guarding the college, stood two stately gum trees which I came to know as the 'Twins'. Over the years ahead I would often sit in silence during hot, tedious days of retreats, my back against one of the Twins. I would listen to the buzz of bees, brushing persistent flies away from the eyes and nostrils, trying to think (I thought I was thinking a thought in those days, but now know I was struggling to have anything to think about). I would try to pray (I never really got on top of this practice either), poking sticks down holes that cicadas had crawled out of in summer, to sing in the Twins' branches for their few short weeks of life. These grand eucalypts were to become part of my daily landscape.

The bus rattled across a ramp grill, slowed down, passing between narrow cultivated beds of roses on either side of the drive, and swung around the grassed circle in front of the golden sandstone college. It was a balmy night. The stars were sparkling bright in the sky – much brighter than in the city. In a lit up area at the entrance, students pushed and shoved as they dragged suitcases from the weary buses. Beyond the illumined circle of restless humanity, in the shadows, lay the dark bush, silent and mysterious. We had arrived and as the family at home were sitting down to their tea, I wondered where I was.

A NEW CHUM SETTLING IN

I was hungry. It was time for dinner, or tea as we came to call it there. A hot dinner was always served by the nuns in the middle of the day, just as in Europe. At half past six each evening, we wolfed down a light meal, invariably insufficient to take the sharp edge off the hunger pains which I used to suffer for perhaps two hours before the meal.

On this first night we took our seats at random in the refectory, as our places at table had not yet been allocated. Since I knew no one, it did not matter where I sat, though the boys returning to familiar territory scrambled to sit together. A priest in a cassock recited grace in Latin, chairs thundered, and one hundred and fifty seminarians sat down to eat. There was no shortage of troops. This was a long way from our kitchen in Cremorne.

Down the centre-aisle rumbled a wooden trolley on wheels, top and bottom layers crowded with commercial, shining silver teapots, bigger than I had ever seen. Eleven students to each table, eleven settings of heavy-duty cups and saucers, and a quarter-pound of butter to be divided evenly between eleven. Someone at one end of the table began carving stale bread into thick, unrefined slices. A mean, thin spread of butter or jam (but not both together) on thick dry bread was washed down with gulps of tea. This was my first seminary meal. And there were many to follow.

We marched two abreast from the refectory in silence (I was sliding easily down into the military routine of seminary life) through the long wide corridor to the chapel, where again, just for today, we sat at random. A few muttered words of welcome from the priest in charge, Monsignor Charlie Dunne, followed by general words of warning. We new boys remained for a more intensive dose of warnings as we attended to some of the fundamental facts of life – total, angelic silence in the chapel, no coughing, no nose-blowing, no sniffing – these were forbidden. No banging of kneelers. To and from the refectory and the chapel in silence. No hands in pockets. No shouting, laughing loudly, or boisterous behaviour. Those already in the know escaped to examine the noticeboard and determine the identity of the prefects for the year, the head prefect, the prayermen in the chapel, the sacristan, the master of ceremonies – in short, how the life of the institution would be ordered for another year, and by whom.

The information I needed that first night was not so sophisticated. I only needed to know what dormitory I was to sleep in, where I would be sitting in the chapel, what table I would be eating at in the refectory, and later, where I would attend classes and study periods. There seemed to be a lot of confusion in the corridors, some boisterous teasing, plenty of settling-in noise. Eventually I was taken to St Columba's dormitory upstairs and told where I was to sleep. A single bed, a pile of blankets, rough, calico sheets, a tiny wardrobe with three drawers, some hanging space, a tilting mirror and next to the bed, a wooden boot-box.

My mother had bought a new shoe-polishing kit which included both tan and black polish (though I had never owned tan shoes), a bright, clean, folded yellow buffing rag, a fresh brush, all neatly packed within a leather container. I unpacked my things carefully. My new sandshoes, and the shoe-kit went straight into the boot-box beside my bed. My red checked dressing-gown, also new, was hung in the cupboard. I arranged my handkerchiefs, socks, underpants, shirts, singlets, in the three drawers just as I thought my mother would have done for me at home. I was ordering my new world.

The dormitory was alive with merriment. Terry Sharpe was obviously an old-boy, every bit of fifteen. He had been at Springwood a number of years already and was accepted as one of the larrikins, too established to be bothered with a new boy without hair in all the important places. He would be sleeping on my left, within two or three feet of my face. Dudley Lennox was on my right, close enough to hold hands in the night. Paul occupied a lumpy sunken bed and a duchess (our term for a wardrobe) over by the window. We were located on the first floor, looking down through frosted windows ten feet high, across Jakes Gully (the toilet was called the jakes and all college effluent flowed into this gully) and Hawkesbury bushland.

Paul was a bushie from the Riverina and proved to be a gifted student who later became a lawyer. My clear haunting memory is watching him squeezing his facial and chest pimples as he scrutinised himself in the mirror of his duchess. Though there was no privacy, teenagers still had important rituals to perform. Paul and I, and many others, were destined to occupy this same dormitory for some years, though my pimples would not appear for some time.

I was later to learn that Paul never washed his sports clothes. Winter and summer, from half past one until about half past three, every afternoon except Thursday (and on Thursday from nine to five) he wore the same blue football jumper, the same baggy khaki shorts, and the same grey jockstrap. The only cleansing water which touched these stiff, smelly clothes was when rain fell and he happened to be playing cricket, tennis, handball or whatever. It was difficult to stand near him in the line waiting for a brief turn on the handball court. The smell of stale body odour could be rather offensive.

Every afternoon, after sport, Paul would peel his smelly, sweaty sports gear from his pale body and stuff it in his boot-box near his bed. The next day, in the afternoon, he would open the lid and the imprisoned clothes would emerge as though under their own spell, to carry him around the grounds of the college. He seemed immune to all critical, offensive remarks. He joined in the teasing fun, apparently believing nothing said was serious or true. His eyes would screw up behind thick glasses and his yellow teeth would appear in a friendly smile. After a number of years, a few desperate students raided his lethal boot-box, extracted his clothes, carried them ceremoniously on the end of a pole to the washbasin and buried them in water. When Paul came looking for them, they were hidden under a covering of dirty liquid.

There was a lot to learn and a lot to observe before I was to become part of this system. I had commenced my training. I was installed and beginning a new life. I went to bed and lay tight under the blankets. In this cathedral space, in the dark, I mumbled my prayers and began to wonder where I was and what had so suddenly happened to me.

How so young?

Some of the more senior students and some of the priests who lived at the college were perhaps wondering what a twelve-year-old boy was doing here in a seminary, away from his mother. If they were not, perhaps they should have been, yet if they were, no one said anything to me. I had no doubts. From the beginning, and like young Pius XII, I knew exactly where I was going. My eyes were fixed on my ordination goal. I knew what I wanted. It was only later in my life, when I was thirty plus, that my world would become complicated, and my simple cognitive, theological and spiritual mind-set would be thrown out of perfect heavenly balance.

There were many young foals and colts here in the forties: Bede Heather, Kevin Flynn, Dick Connolly, Pat Kenna, Bill Dougherty, Kerry Bayada and others. But by the time I arrived, there were only six of us, though there had been nineteen in first-year secondary school in 1942. I wonder why this programme of enticing young boys from school to train them at Springwood was later abandoned. Perhaps the system had not proved financially viable. Not enough starters were finishing. Economic rationalism might have been on the rise in the Church in the fifties.

Springwood was the bushland setting where young men, sometimes very young men, used to begin their training for the Catholic priesthood for all the dioceses in New South Wales. This was the junior seminary and I was destined to be here seven years – at least for my first period of service. I would return there as a 'professor' (a title used for teachers), in the mid-sixties. Our seminary in the Blue Mountains west of Sydney adopted the weekly timetable of schools and religious institutions in Rome, with Thursdays free and work on Saturdays. Our liturgical calendar was based on the seasons in the northern hemisphere. Our official language was Latin rather than English, and our loyalty was to Rome as well as to the Commonwealth and to the Queen of England. Our strong links with Rome, demanding obedience and loyalty, at least partly explain how someone so young could be enticed from the nest and transplanted in the dry, rocky ground of Springwood.

The clergy had been reduced to such a mess at the time of the Reformation and even before, that the cardinals and bishops who attended the Council of Trent in the sixteenth century had determined that a form of regulated training should be established. The seminaries, seed beds to cultivate vocations, were based on the pattern of medieval cathedral schools. They were meant to cater for young men, adolescents, even children in their most suggestive and malleable years, and especially to encourage the sons of the poor. The seminaries were a system devised to clericalise and regularise the Roman priesthood from the years of innocence. Aspirants, even from the age of twelve, were to be force-fed with clericalism. They would be tonsured, made to wear the cassock, to attend mass daily, to receive the sacraments regularly, and to submit themselves to constant scrutiny and rigorous discipline. The Code of Canon Law, promulgated in 1917 in the reign of Pope Benedict XV, prescribed that in all major dioceses there should be two types of seminaries – a major seminary for philosophy and theology students, and a minor one for boys to study letters, that is languages and literature. Canon 1353 prescribed that priests, especially parish priests, should ensure that they protect with special care young boys who showed signs of an ecclesiastical vocation, to preserve them from the evils of the world. They were to inspire these boys to practise the virtue of piety, and cultivate in them the seed of a divine mission. Father Lander had done that for me at Neutral Bay.

The Springwood minor seminary traced its origin to the Code of

Canon Law and the Council of Trent. Surprisingly, this institution was still operating in the early fifties, though not as vigorously as it had in the forties. Some parents were no longer prepared to sacrifice their children. Catholics were beginning to find a place in society. They were less isolated, more socially accepted, with greater opportunities to find office work rather than unskilled, labouring jobs. Catholics were now better educated, and more prosperous.

But the clerical world was still dragging its feet, hungering for the halcyon days of the Middle Ages when people knew little, could not read or write, and when its power and authority remained unchallenged. The elderly clerics would fight to preserve the old world, but theirs was a lost battle. A glimmer of hope would appear in the sixties, with Pope John XXIII and the Second Vatican Council, but in the eighties and nineties Rome would use bulldozers to bury the flickering light, to restore its geriatric power and to keep the ecclesiastical boat on an even keel in the dry dock. But that was all ahead of me.

I went off to Springwood at the end of the seminary process, when parents and children were still in awe of bishops and the pope. We were still docile and unquestioning. The celibate, clerical life was still accepted as a joy. I knew nothing of the pressures, the power of the bottle, of the madness which followed loneliness, much less of the scandals to come. The Geraghtys were regular churchgoers. Catholic schooling, nuns, being an altar boy, benediction, first Friday devotions, the family rosary were all taken for granted. If Father recommended it, if he said I should go, if it was ok with him, who were we to question? Off I went.

Columba penna nivea
Collo resplendens roseo,
Loca petit siderea
De claustro mundi luteo.

Hic nidum sibi posuit
In petra poenitentiae,
Devotos Christo genuit
Pullos per verbum gratiae.

Pro dulci canto querulis
Intendebat gemitibus,
Crebris adiungens sedulis
Flectus orationibus.

Sit Deo soli gloria
Qui nos post cursus stadia,
Columbae per suffragia
Ducat ad coeli gaudia.

St Columba's College
Springwood N.S.W.

16 Florence Street
Cremorne
Sydney
20.11.50.

Dear Father,
I am writing this letter to you on behalf of my son Christopher & am forwarding now the form filled in as far as we are able. I understand we are to forward the other details when Christopher has been before the board meeting. As Christopher has not been confirmed yet I will not be able to furnish that certificate but Father Lauder assures us that is in order. God send these particulars after Christopher has been before the meeting.

I hope he is successful in his undertaking & constantly pray for his success.

Would you kindly let me know Father if there is anything we have omitted to do. Thanking you in anticipation.

Yours sincerely
Lucy Geraghty

Sparrow fart in the seminary

> All shall rise promptly at the first sound of the bell, invoke the Holy Names of Jesus, Mary and Joseph, sign themselves with the Cross, and offer to the Sacred Heart the thoughts, words, actions and sufferings of the day now begun.
>
> Within the time allotted all shall wash and dress, nourishing pious reflections in preparation for Morning Prayer and Meditation. [Rule 10]

At the first sound of the bell

I was duty-bound to spring out of bed the moment the student who had been appointed for the week to ring the community bell, had walked briskly through the dormitory. He pumped a large, hand-held, brass bell. The keen students jumped up from under the multiple layers of warm army blankets and charged out of the dormitory to compete for the showers. Others wanted to be first to the washbasins, to clean teeth, to wash sleep from their eyes, some among them to lather up and shave. The recalcitrant, the sluggish, those whose fervour had lost its edge, the sybarites, would lie in bed up to twenty minutes more, listening to the warning bells summoning them to the chapel. They waited to be roused by the prefect in the dormitory, perhaps the casual Adrian Rheinberger or the kind but anxious Brian Larkey. Reluctantly, especially in winter, but obediently, I used to struggle out soon after hearing the bell.

Jimmy Salway was what we referred to as a late vocation. He was an old bushie from the South Coast, who had begun from scratch in the first year of secondary school at the age of twenty-two or so, barely able to read or write. He made no headlong rush to the washbasins. There was no need. Each basin was serviced with only one tap (a very cold one), and every morning Jimmy used to scrap and scratch his face with a blunt, cutthroat razor, slicing little pieces of skin from his tough face, making everyone's blood run even colder as we watched him operate with freezing mountain water. My face was soft and smooth, like Jacob's. It was some years before I would need a razor.

For five years I slept in various locations in St Columba's dormitory, changing from one narrow bed to another as the years passed. The mattresses were thin. Some of the beds were saggy in the middle where the exhausted spring had been stretched over the years by restless bodies. While forty or so of us dressed quickly and modestly, the same ritual was happening in other dormitories throughout the building. For several months of the year, these long dormitories were chilled by the mountain winter and unheated, except for blankets and young blood. Pyjamas were shed and replaced by underpants and singlets, all under the cover of a modest dressing-gown draped around hunched shoulders. A cleric, however young, must be forever vigilant that no one should catch a glimpse of his dangerous parts.

Many fled from the dormitories within minutes of rising. Others dragged their feet to the chapel to arrive as close to 6.30 a.m. as possible. Some lazy larrikins regularly arrived seconds after the 6.30 final bell, which meant that they had to report to the dean of discipline, maybe even to the rector, that they had been late once again for chapel. Any tardiness, any failure to be kneeling when the final bell sounded, perhaps genuflecting in mid-aisle or dipping a hand into the holy water font, was a reportable offence, an occasion for the powers (the priests in charge) to encourage lax students to greater fervour, or an occasion for correction, even punishment. I generally kept out of trouble.

Unofficial devotions

It was advisable before leaving the dormitory, to check whether one had a handkerchief, clean or soiled, in one's pocket. There could be no return to this base until after lunch when everyone would change for compulsory sport. Many a new student was caught by an alert prefect, making his way back to the dormitory to retrieve a forgotten handkerchief. Even when a student consulted the rector for permission to return to his dormitory for a handkerchief to mop up a head cold flow (these were the days before Kleenex), his request was invariably refused without explanation. The lesson had to be learnt – always to check one's pockets before leaving for morning prayers. We were being trained to think ahead.

Waves of students, mainly in cassocks, hurtling down flights of stairs, made their way to the chapel to complete their private devotions before community prayers began. The central aisle of the chapel would be choked with pious seminarians, shouldering one another, jockeying for positions in front of one or other of the fourteen stations of the cross, which hung in series around the walls and depicted various episodes of Christ's sufferings. Most students performed this ritual every day.

It was just another one of those devotional exercises which had to be done daily, preferably more than once. No matter how quickly the regime was completed, the day would not be complete without it. There would be a sense of emptiness or lack of fervour. We were reaching for the heavens, and every little bit would make a difference, especially if it was entirely voluntary, as so much was routine and compulsory. Some could complete the ritual genuflections performed in front of all fourteen stations, together with a prayer and a brief reflection before each picture, within the space of two minutes, no more! Others proceeded more piously. Some were extravagant in their double genuflections, their profound bows from the waist, deep sighs, sorrowful upturned cows' eyes. One might almost expect the really fervent to burst into bleeding stigmata, or at the very least beads of perspiration.

One of the stolid plodders (known affectionately as 'Donk') recited his rosary beads once more as he made his way round the stations. His beads were well worn as they were seldom out of his hand throughout the day. Whenever idle, while waiting in a corridor for lunch, perhaps standing at table in the refectory waiting for the grace to be recited, Donk fidgeted on his beads, reciting rapid Hail Marys on fluttering lips. He was pious indeed.

A minority of the students preferred not to join in the early morning river of devotion to the Passion of Christ. Some regularly arrived late. Some sat quietly in the chapel, deep in thought, looking at the tabernacle, or perhaps at the diminutive statue of Our Lady Help of Christians, the patron saint of the order of nuns whose vocation was to care for seminarians at Springwood and Manly. Some read another dreary chapter from *The Imitation of Christ* by Thomas à Kempis, or snatched a reflection from *The Breviary of Piety*. Few, very few were doing nothing. We were not strong on relaxation. Leisure time was inherently dangerous, and formed no part of the training programme. I was one of those who chose not to 'do the stations' before mass. The thoroughfare was too crowded and some of my fellows made the exercise seem trivial. Even as a young student I could not see the point of fast prayers, garbled words, pray, mechanical repetition, so I read a pious book or tried to pray, or just sat. Sometimes I sat and thought, and sometimes I just sat!

A five-minute warning bell sounded, and then the final 6.30 a.m. bell, to commence morning prayers. Late comers like Terry Sharpe, John Sweeney, John Conway or big Bill Meacham, made their way publicly to their pews in the chapel. A few regulars were always late. Some had not had time to do up the buttons of their cassocks. Hair was wet, not combed, still dripping, shoelaces undone. Punctuality made for a peaceful life. Tardiness for any daily exercise guaranteed regular contact with the powers upstairs.

MORNING PRAYERS AND BOREDOM

Morning prayers commenced. One of the two prayermen, kneeling in his special pew at the back of the chapel, would recite the ritual phrases. These prayermen were selected by the monsignor for the quality of their voices, and to give the seniors some practice in public chapel performance in preparation for their final, sacerdotal function. Frank Mulcahy had a strong, honeyed voice which obviously gave him status and pleasure. Happy Byron and Hos Dryden were given turns, as were later John Alt and Barry Collins, who became the bishop of the clay and dust Wilcannia-Forbes diocese in an area the size of France. He is now dead.

The assembled student body, ranked in three long rows of bench stalls on either side of the main aisle, facing one another across the chapel, acknowledged its approval with occasional 'Amens'. During these seven or eight minutes of routine public prayers, there was minimal participation. Perhaps an 'Ave', a 'Pater' and a few rushed 'Bless us' responses to follow the bullet-rattle names of an abbreviated litany of the saints. It was just as well as many of us were still sleepy. After prayers, we moved with a rustle of cassocks from our knees to our seats. The next twenty-five minutes was programmed for quiet, private meditation, but for many of us, it was a period of a little extra slumber before mass began at seven o'clock. I tried hard to do what was expected, but my flesh was weak and my eyelids heavy.

The overall period of meditation was divided into three neat segments. The second of the two official prayermen read out a short passage from a devotional meditation book which developed topics for mental prayer for every day of the year, each topic neatly expanded in three self-contained passages. Even the daily ebb and flow of reflective prayer was ordered and disciplined. We young colts were expected to focus our wandering minds and unruly hearts on the substance of the first paragraph which had been read aloud. We were encouraged to mull over the contents of the passage, explore its spiritual implications, translate our mind into mental prayer, perhaps even form some practical resolution, all within the space of seven or eight minutes before being interrupted by the next passage.

This daily period of meditation was dry, even boring. I never really acquired the technique, much less discovered the secret. That is not to say I did not try. Though these elusive exercises were part of my daily life from the age of twelve, I never managed to move beyond the dimension of a daily routine. I was performing activities, while all the time longing and waiting for the programmed period of meditation to end. Though I did not twiddle my thumbs and look into space, many precious hours were wasted. I was young and immature, but ready to learn, and anxious to answer the challenge of becoming a good, holy priest. I was a seed ready to bloom into something bright and splendid. For some years I was only a blurred member of a large amorphous group of students. In such a crowd, juniors went unnoticed. I was just beginning and the journey was as long as twelve years. No one was there to take my hand, to lead me and explain in language I could understand, how to pray. As a group, we were all told what to do, but never who to be in God's presence.

The Springwood powers were strong on regular exercises and discipline, but this institution, like the Church at large, was not sensitive to the values and needs of the individuals like me. It was more interested in continuity throughout the ages, in stable power and tight control. We were being trained like factory workers. No one guided my puerile, faulting steps, not even the official spiritual director. There was no one to assess my progress, to give the appropriate nudge, to reveal the mysteries. No working system was in place to foster each little student in his daily twenty-five minute struggle to experience the delights or the frustrations of spontaneous spiritual prayer.

One learnt by doing. It was a discipline. Prayer was a daily ritual, a routine grind whereby aspirants to the priesthood would train themselves to spend a substantial period, perhaps half an hour, reflecting on some predigested spiritual truth or insight. It was designed to produce some practical resolution to keep them on the straight and narrow, ordered, disciplined and composed within a clerical system. There were no built-in quality control mechanisms and, at least for me, the self-taught system did not work.

Every morning before mass, the assembly of students of all ranks would sit in silence in the chapel and meditate. Some slept. Others fidgeted. There was a good deal of consulting of watches. Most of us tried and failed every day. This was for real men, adults, not callow teenagers. This was work for trained experts, not unskilled beginners. It was cruel to leave such young boys with high ideals and no means to succeed to their own devices. The same system was there for all of us, young and old, the same period of time, the same meditation points, the same chapel pew. We were an army meditating in unison.

The general topics of meditation changed weekly. We might meditate for one week on various aspects of the Gospel parables of the prodigal son, of the king in his vineyard, of the rich man and Lazarus, or of the sower who found weeds among his wheat. Or we might be programmed to contemplate during another week on obscure interpretations of any one of Christ's miracles. The topics for Passion Week or the long Easter season were easy to guess.

For one memorable week each year the chapel was ablaze as I passed my allotted time unravelling the mysteries of Aridity, and trying to apply my dry, wrinkly reflections to my life. Then the next week changed the focus to the more interesting topic of Tepidity. I remember that those two long weeks each year proved a challenge to my youthful fervour. It demanded some imagination to meditate in silence for almost thirty minutes on the spiritual state of weariness, on boredom, on the feeling of exhaustion, on a type of chronic spiritual fatigue syndrome - more imagination than I was able to muster. Almost fifty years later, the subtle difference between these two important states of spiritual ennui escape me. I might be able to reflect for perhaps five minutes on both subjects, but not without laughing.

Suddenly one of the two prayermen at the back would give a loud knock on his wooden pew. This was the sign to cease dreaming, to wake up, refocus the mind, cut short the spiritual reflection and to prepare for mass. There was a brief period of rustle and bustle in the chapel which was by now warmed with the breath and bodies of the assembly. Official sacristans moved out of their pews at the top of the chapel and disappeared into the sacristy to make sure all was ready for the celebration, while the small band of Marist brothers, led by Brother Gerard, quietly and discreetly entered the chapel at the back.

Two glass and silver cruets, one filled with water, the other with wine, were placed on a table near the altar, the silver communion plate arranged on the same small table, together with several tiny pieces of starched, pressed linen. Someone strained with a long taper to light the six candles on the tall, bronze stands adorning the altar. Someone else rushed out to light the two smaller candles, six on solemn feast days. The master of ceremonies fluttered about to make sure the altar server was ready and waiting. Those in black cassocks slipped into their lace-edged, white surplices, but we juniors up the front were still confined to civvies.

Right-handed celebrants

As we waited to catch the first glimpse of the professor who was to celebrate the mass for the ensuing week, the altar server emerged from the sacristy, his hands reverently joined, his eyes cast down. He would then be followed by one of the powers, wearing vestments. George Joiner would thunder onto the altar in an impatient headlong rush. George Meredith, the spiritual director, entered in a dainty, feminine, apologetic fashion. Noel Carroll, a diminutive man, alert to his priestly dignity and inferior size, but unable to inspire a natural respect from the students, would glide into view. We could not treat him seriously. Even at the age of seventy, he was described by some of his confrères as the oldest teenager in the diocese.

Noel had studied at All Hallows in Ireland where he had been ordained to the priesthood. He had acquired a certain foreign accent, a cross between an American drawl and an Irish lilt. As a teacher, he was one page ahead of his pupils. With little bursts of discipline he could manage. He tried to cover his ignorance by a tough, smooth manner. When it was his turn to celebrate morning mass, Noel would slide onto the altar, holding the chalice stem in one hand, the other placed on top to keep the covering sacred cloth from flapping. He seemed conscious that we were all looking at him. Charlie Dunne, the rector, would also take his turn to celebrate the mysteries. He had the appearance of a human volcano about to erupt. With his face flushed, his red hair unruly, he wandered slowly onto the sanctuary as if in a trance.

The celebrant, whoever he might be for that particular week, genuflected, ascended the altar steps and tidied the coloured covering over the chalice in front of the tabernacle. He then moved to his right to open the missal, set the variously coloured ribbons in the relevant pages, and descended the steps to commence the Latin ritual. The colour of his vestments would change to suit the ecclesiastical season – white, green, rose, purple, black. Some would enunciate the prayers clearly, precisely, crisply, like George Meredith, while Joiner would rumble out the Latin like a distant, indistinct thunder roll. Charlie Dunne muttered slowly, lazily, in the hope he would not be heard and therefore could accuse server and students of inattention: *In nomine Patris, et Filii, et Spiritus*

Sancti. Introibo ad altare Dei. (In the name of the Father, Son and Holy Spirit, I will go into the altar of God.)

The chase was on. Even with an English prayer book, it was impossible to keep up with the rumble of the Latin. An extract from the Old Testament or perhaps from a letter of Saint Paul was read at a racing pace, verses from the psalms recited, and as we rose to attention in unison, without any noise, a passage from one of the four gospels was rattled off. The ritual moved on rapidly, peppered with multiple hurried signs of the cross, many slovenly genuflections and hand circles made over the chalice and bread. I kept turning pages, finding this and that in various parts of the missal, skipping a bit to catch up, happy with myself if I could maintain the pace. All the ritual movements were performed by the celebrant with his right hand. Priests were expected to be right-handed. The left hand belonged to the devil.

Within weeks of my arrival at Springwood, Charlie Dunne summoned me to his cluttered room to tell me he had noticed I cut bread with my left hand, and ate soup also left-handed. I would have to change. On this one occasion, and by way of exception, the monsignor favoured me with a reason. I had to hold myself ready to distribute communion with my right hand. The host would be raised at the solemn elevation, in the priest's right hand. Blessings were invariably right-handed. There was no room in the Lord's ranks for left-handed priests. It was unnatural, or at least unacceptable. Proper order required right-handed clergy.

From then on I was under orders to become a right-handed person. But I was happy to change, so I could conform to the norms of priestly behaviour. The order from above did not extend to the playing field. I was still allowed to play tennis left-handed, to bowl the cricket ball with my left arm whenever I was lucky enough to have a turn, and to kick with my left foot – like all good Catholics!

Apart from taking communion, but only in the form of a tiny, shiny white wafer, not from the chalice, and apart from the prayers in English after mass for the conversion of Russia (prayers which were ceased by Roman edict in the sixties) there was not much activity in the body of the chapel, only on the sanctuary. The Vatican Council was not even a dream in the fifties. No one could have envisioned such distant matters as participation in the liturgy, the use of English, communion from the cup, regular singing like the Protestants, active involvement of the whole community, even concelebrations with more than one priest officiating at the Eucharist. In those dark days, the lone priest with his altar server would say mass, doing everything himself, often at high speed, completely unconscious of the congregation. We would remain dumb, meek as church mice, either chasing the priest silently through our missals, or engrossed in our own private devotions. It was awkward for a time, but I soon learned to be right-handed in the service of the Lord.

Charlie Dunne's methods may have been brutal, but they sometimes produced results. When Geoff Mulhearn arrived at Springwood in 1956 he informed the rector, perhaps naively, that he was a serious asthmatic. A frail boy, he arrived at the college fortified with an abundance of medication to protect him against the harshness of the climate, the mountain frosts and the unheated study halls. Charlie Dunne's treatment was simple. His words were brief, and blunt. 'If you have one attack of asthma in this place, it will be your last. You will be sent straight home. Do you understand?' Geoff understood. 'Yes, monsignor.' He never had another attack. He was cured. I was suddenly right-handed. The college daily routine continued without interruption.

Always junior

For my first five institutional years, I sat at the head prefect's table in the refectory, the table closest to the one at which the clerical authorities ate. I prayed in the front pew of the chapel, right under the gaze of the celebrant and the retreat master, disturbingly within striking range of Monsignor Dunne whenever he stood on the edge of the sanctuary to deliver his disciplinary swipes. I could hear him breathe. I felt his eyes, his penetrating, critical gaze. On several occasions I was subjected to his threatening, chubby finger pointed offhandedly at me when he had noticed me fidgeting, or consulting the silver, oblong wristwatch which my father had given me as a present before I had left for the seminary. The juniors were always positioned at the front, and I was the youngest of all the juniors. That placed me at the very front since seniority ruled the world.

I waited impatiently for promotion to a chapel stall further back from the centre aisle. I also waited impatiently to be moved from the top table, away from the scrutiny of the eating, watching priests. But I never seemed to finish my apprenticeship. That feeling of juniority remained all my life. As soon as my goal was claimed, more was expected. Another goal came into view. No sooner was I a senior at Springwood than I became a junior at Manly, then as a senior in the major seminary I became a junior member of the clergy, and later a junior member of the seminary staff, and later still, a junior solicitor when I was quite senior, then a junior barrister, and finally a junior judge. I always felt that I was at the bottom of the pile, to be seen, observed, assessed, but not heard. I never seemed to be able to demonstrate my loyalty to the satisfaction of others, to join their group. I was either a bystander or an outsider, always under suspicion, oozing rebellion, waiting to be chosen as part of the team. In my fifth year, I complained to Dr George Joiner about forever being stationed at the top table in the refectory. It was in the year of my Leaving Certificate. I was sixteen, perhaps seventeen. He replied that I would be moved when he was good and ready. He reminded me of my junior status, but finally he agreed to give my request some thought.

One of the boys also working for his Leaving Certificate had become strangely tense and withdrawn. Though I was too young to understand these things, he was obviously journeying painfully through a nervous breakdown. I only observed that he was quite odd. There were sudden outbursts of anger. He used to sit alone in class, chewing the skin on his hands until they bled. His biting was not restricted to his nails, or even to the skin around his nails. He used to bite hard on the thick butt at the base of his thumb, or on the dorsum of his hand, close to his wrist. We all agreed that he was seriously disturbed, in agony before our eyes. But his pathetic condition had not escaped our superiors and it was instructive to consider how they dealt with his problem.

George Joiner summoned me to his room on the first floor, off the balcony, overlooking the quadrangle. He held the responsible position of dean of discipline, a position in which he obviously felt uncomfortable because from his youth he had been such a larrikin. I naturally assumed some infringement had been observed, that I was on the mat. It was serious because George invited me to sit down. He opened by telling me he was concerned about a boy in my class. He wanted to know whether I had noticed his behaviour, and I had to admit I had. The dean then put a proposition to me. He asked me to continue to sit at the top table in the refectory for a further few months. He planned to move the tormented aspirant onto the same table and to arrange for him to sit beside me. He wanted me to pay special attention to him. I should talk to him, show some interest in him, try to distract him, and generally befriend him. It would be appreciated if I walked sometimes with him during the day, if I tried to involve him in some friendly activity. I was to be the counsellor.

Dr Joiner must have been desperate to find some treatment for my confrère's problems. The place was staffed with a number of experienced priests, each trained to some extent in pastoral theology, and we all had the theoretical advantage of a specially appointed spiritual director. Psychiatrists and psychologists were not unknown in the fifties. I did not appreciate at the time what was happening, but looking back, this boy's treatment was somewhat ad hoc. I agreed to the dean's proposition. I sat next to my charge, watched him chewing his hands, forced him to talk to me, encouraged him to break out of his cycle of distress. And George kept his promise. After a few months, I was moved to a refectory table a little further away from the powers. Eventually the problem disappeared. The boy went home to his parents. He studied at university, married, begot children and became an expert in his profession. There is some consolation in the realisation that life is forever in flux. But I was not moved from the front pew in the chapel, from under the hairy nose of the rector.

THE AGONY OF YOUTH

The chapel was cold in winter, and the candles on the altar did nothing to heat the space. But I had other, more immediate, more embarrassing problems to contend with. My body was changing. Little straggly, lonely hairs were appearing under my arms and around those private parts. Without warning, and certainly unplanned, my member would expand almost to bursting, doubling in size. In cold weather, when private parts almost disappear, it quadrupled itself. This local swelling would happen at the most inopportune moments. It was difficult for an ignorant, bumbling teenager to know how to react. Was the expansion as obvious to the general public, to the assembled community, as it felt to the sufferer? Were my efforts to hide my unwelcome condition successful? Were others suffering the same medical condition?

The altar in the Chapel

The Chapel during Holy Week

For some of those formative seminary years, almost like clockwork, when the altar bells rang and the students in unison struck their breasts and recited *Domine non sum dignus* (Lord, I am not worthy), preparing themselves for communion, it happened. As much as I tried to suppress it, struggling to focus my mind on spiritual matters, my loins would swell, the member would stand erect and appear as a bulging ridge in the front of my serge pants. This embarrassing condition arose every morning at almost the same time. Praying, willpower and determination could not postpone the visitation, but seemed to aggravate it. In this condition I would rise from my place, join the queue of fifteen or twenty students waiting for communion, and slowly progress to the altar. I did not want to miss communion and draw attention to myself. I had always gone to communion, ever since I was a little boy. With hands joined as nonchalantly as possible across my loins to hide my condition, I hoped I could return quickly to my place, unnoticed. On reflection, perhaps the only solution which might have borne fruit, was never tried by me. Perhaps laughter or relaxed amusement would have saved me my daily distress, or tighter underpants.

Even in the hothouse isolation of the seminary, hidden in the mountains, I was a young, innocent boy in an unruly world. No one took me aside to explain what might be happening to my body. Even the purely physical mechanisms of procreation remained a mystery for longer than was proper. I had inklings from listening on the edge of conversations between other seminarians, but I generally missed the point and was unable to comprehend why some of my confrères were laughing, or whispering in that secretive way. I was deprived of the factual information essential for any young boy growing up. The seminary was staffed by five or six priests, and four religious brothers. There were students studying and living there who were old enough to have been my father. The head prefect in my first year, Jack Shanahan, had seen service in the Second World War. Allan McPherson had been a pharmacist, Tony Ryan a medical doctor, John Satterthwaite, later to become bishop of Lismore, had been an engineer. But nobody told me. The senior prefects who shepherded the juniors up and down the front drive, though they were trusted with our supervision, would not have dared to raise the horrible subject of sex.

During my time at Springwood, I was sent to the local parish church, by Charlie Dunne, to pick up the sacrament of confirmation from Archbishop Eris O'Brien. Satterthwaite had been deputised to be my sponsor. After he and I had walked the three miles into town, I received the oil of chrism on my forehead, the gentle slap on the cheek, and we walked home again. None of these people thought to enlighten my innocent mind, or to lift the worry of unexplained bodily changes. I was on my own.

George Meredith was the spiritual director appointed by the cardinal to care for the principal spiritual needs of the students. We were bound by the holy rule to consult him for fifteen minutes, at least once each month. These were trivial, formal consultations during which he was more inclined to discuss the importance of the college rules and to cultivate a petty scrupulosity than to address personal issues that were too close to the bone. George also offered us regular sessions of confessions – Thursday afternoons, during monthly half-day retreats, and every day before mass to ensure no one was tempted to approach holy communion in the state of mortal sin. There was also an external confessor who came to Springwood each week to cater for those of us who did not like George. Emile Sobb, and later Danny Fay, even the acidic, cold Father Bagot would take their turn. But all remained mysteriously silent.

I knew I should have known about the facts of life and what exactly was involved. But in truth, for a long time I had no idea, and I was too proud to ask. I was already the butt of others' jokes, condemned to hover on the fringes of their friendship, with no one considering me as special, so I was not about to expose myself to more hurtful taunts. I had to pretend I knew and hoped no one would investigate my ignorance. That meant I had to be careful to laugh at the right time when others were laughing, to avoid the give away remark, to listen carefully and to try to unravel the puzzle. I imagine those who had assumed responsibility for my education simply presumed I knew all there was to be known, or at least enough. Perhaps they thought it was better that I remain innocent and ignorant for as long as possible, preferably for the whole of my life. Maybe they too were ignorant or inadequate, despite their adult status. What would they know? Diagrams in textbooks, this snake-like member goes there and shakes out some gooey seed. Entertaining thoughts like those led to fears of hellfire and torment. A boy's life could be ruined by thinking about occasions for sin.

How many others were locked up in the same ignorance, I had no idea. These matters were unmentionable. Candles, chapel, silences, Latin prayers, processions, the daily conscience examination, the soutanes, the stillness of the mountains, the removal from families, the lack of warmth and friendship, ensured I shared no common humanity. I remained ignorant for a long time. On the fringe of groups, I half heard conversations which I thought might be naughty, even impure, but without understanding fully what was being said. I had to cope with the regular swelling in the chapel, waking at night to find a clammy dampness in my pyjamas and on the sheets, waiting for a hot surge to subside before rising from under the blankets at six o'clock in the morning, all without the calm which comes after knowledge.

ITE, MISSA EST

Once I was safely back in my chapel stall, I could relax. I would spend a few minutes thumbing through my prayer leaflets, reciting prayers of praise, of adoration, love, thanksgiving, petition, of reparation. I had a handy, well- thumbed leaflet of four or five pages, setting out prayers before and after communion. My sister Maureen and I had used them religiously from childhood, every morning at early mass at Neutral Bay. They were conveniently stored behind the front cover of my missal, with my prized holy card collection.

When the tiny round white wafers of blessed bread had been distributed and the priest had washed up the cup and plate (known to us as chalice and paten), a few concluding prayers were recited in Latin. The first chapter of St John's Gospel was rattled off as the last gospel. Three Hail Marys were said in English for the conversion of Russia, and mass was finished. Everything happened quickly. It was all over in a rush. The performance would be repeated at the same time the next day and the day after, month after month, for the seven years I was an inmate at St Columba's.

A few moments of silent, private prayer followed. The length of time was measured by devotion or compulsion. No one wanted to leave too soon for fear inordinate haste might be interpreted as lack of piety, but most of us had had enough. I waited, moving from one knee to the other, glancing towards the back of the chapel furtively, waiting my time to escape. A few of the more self-confident boys would begin leaving their places. They hurried a genuflection. Under my downcast eyes, I listened to them leave the chapel by the back door. The sacristans and master of ceremonies were on the move, extinguishing candles, removing the cruets and the communion plate from the altar, and generally cleaning up. The routine of the day was picking up its pace.

The side-altar private masses were hurried to conclusion. In the 1950s concelebrated masses were unknown. One of the staff-priests celebrated the community mass each morning, while the others seemed to rattle off very private masses on the side-altars in the chapel, or on the one hidden behind the main altar directly under the colourful, devotional window. Clergy visitors, parish priests, monsignors, also slotted into the small, self-contained, side-altars, to perform their public act in private.

Some of these visitors were as rough as pigs' guts. Monsignor McCosker from Ryde who used to visit his clergy mates perhaps four or five times a year, would delight in shocking us young neophytes. He used to race into the sacristy, throw on the vestments and before emerging to take up his position on one of the side-altars, he would offer a bet to his pious server that he could complete his religious observance before the celebrant of the community reached a nominated stage in the proceedings. He always won his wager. The monsignor was speedy, slipshod and crass.

Within a few minutes the trickle of students leaving the chapel became a torrent, until the chapel was empty. We were still in silence. Not a word had been uttered by conscientious students since night prayers the evening before. We were still tongue-tied by the rules: 'Silence shall be strictly observed at the prescribed times…. The time from Night Prayer until after Holy Mass is to be spent as in Retreat.' [Rule 12a, 12c] There were fifteen minutes before breakfast at eight o'clock, just sufficient time to attend to some personal, private needs: gulping a few mouthfuls of water at the bubbler at the bottom of the stairwell, a short walk outside the library or perhaps a decade of the rosary before we lined up in silence against the wall, along the length of the corridor, waiting for the sign to break our fast.

DR. M. J. FITZPATRICK
205A BEN BOYD RD.
NEUTRAL BAY AND
81 RANGERS AVE.
CREMORNE

PHONE X~~Y~~ 2839.

20th December, 1950

This is to certify that I have this day examined Master Christopher Geraghty who is ~~suffering from~~ in my opinion, medically fit to take up duties as a student of Springwood College

~~he/she will not be fit for work for at least days/weeks~~

Breakfast and a bit of freedom

Food at last

At eight o'clock, the chimes in the grandfather clock which stood on duty just off the corridor, outside the priests' downstairs common room, would sound. The student body moved in unison away from the cold wall and formed a column two abreast down the centre of the corridor. The refectory doors on the right at the top of the polished hallway were solemnly opened by the head prefect. In silence we made our way to our allotted places at tables, almost as regular as an army.

The refectory was a hall where the students and the sacerdotal staff used to take their meals. It contained fourteen or fifteen large tables, set at right angles to a central aisle. At the top of the hall stood the main professorial table, just inside the entrance double door and beneath a large, worn canvas on which a third-rate artist had depicted the coronation of the Virgin in heaven. The main table was decorated by the nuns with silver salt and pepper shakers, crested plates and starched napkins. There were even special knives and forks with which to peel and eat fruit. I was later to master the quaint art of eating fruit (apples, oranges, peaches), with a knife and fork. We were being trained to be middle-class Victorian gentlemen.

At the bottom of the refectory, beyond the students' plain, industrial tables, stood a wooden rostrum or lectern, a type of pulpit, from which one of the senior students would read to us. Beyond was the kitchen area where the faceless nuns worked at industrial sinks, huge ovens, commercial washing machines, and large, walk-in refrigerators. It was years before I was senior enough to venture into the kitchen area where Mothers Teresa or Philomena used to rule their domain in grey religious silence.

Like my home in Cremorne, like any institution, a camp, a hospital, a prison, food was an essential part of our daily routine at Springwood. We were growing, hungry youths. I was ravenous most of the time. No matter how much bread I stuffed into my stomach, no matter how rapidly I wolfed whatever was provided, the supply of food was never enough. The three main meals (such as they were) were supplemented on ordinary workdays by afternoon tea. The timetable varied somewhat over the years, as the secondary schooling began to disappear, so that towards the end of my period of confinement, we would gather in the refectory after fifteen minutes of community reading in the chapel. The prayerman would read aloud some pages of a spiritual book, concluding at 3.45 p.m. Study in the study halls commenced at four o'clock. Our afternoon tea filled up the intervening quarter hour. Each student drank a cup of a peculiar hot milk substance, something like cocoa or Milo, but with a somewhat bitter taste. In summer we drank cold, insipid cordial. The liquid washed down two half-slices of stale bread, barely garnished with a smear of lemon butter spread. It was hardly worth the effort. The quantity was never enough to suppress those gnawing hunger pains, especially in winter.

Breakfast varied. Sometimes cornflakes or Weet-Bix, sometimes a few spoonfuls of baked beans or weary tinned spaghetti. Stale bread was always in plentiful supply. The rare freshly baked bread would only appear when the bursar had miscalculated his order and found the supply of stale bread unexpectedly depleted. Fresh bread caused problems. Students used to eat double the quantity, gulping down thick slices of steaming hot, doughy mouthfuls. When forced into an empty stomach, the dough and gastric juices combined to create explosions at both ends. Fresh bread caused me many bouts of painful indigestion, but I still did not learn to eat slowly, to savour and enjoy the pagan taste of food. Our Springwood fare, like prison food, or any institutional fodder, was basically tasteless. Eating habits established in one's early years are difficult to eradicate. I continue to suffer from the hungry habits established years ago at Springwood. Food is devoured, not savoured. I always seem to complete my meal well before my fellow guests. Meals consist in the shovelling of as much bulk as possible, within as short a time, for survival. Unless I pay attention and concentrate, food is not a pleasurable experience, much less some social event.

The seminary breakfast provided scarcely sufficient food to carry me through until lunchtime when the main meal of the day would be served. At one o'clock I could expect a bowl of warm soup, two sausages, or maybe a cannonball made from minced meat, or perhaps a few spoonfuls of watery mince, known as 'dog'. At other times there was a shoulder of mutton to be shared between eleven, not leaving much once the greasy fat had been sliced away. The meat dish came with mashed potato, mashed pumpkin, perhaps some carrots, sometimes parsnip or turnip. Dessert might consist of a steamed pudding covered with Golden Syrup, known as a 'sinker', a bowl of creamed rice, or yellow tapioca. There was nothing I would not eat, nothing I did not eat.

There was, however, one exceptional occasion. In winter, we were often served a steaming bowl of porridge at breakfast. This lumpy, gluggy substance was generally pretty terrible, but once the porridge was even more disgusting than usual. No one among the hundred and fifty-odd hungry students could bring himself to swallow it. It had been served up in large, aluminium containers, slopped into plates, sprinkled with sugar and floated in milk. One taste and each student decanted his portion back into the dish, to be poured into the pig buckets in the kitchen. Out of curiosity, a number of us followed the pig-man in his soutane to the sty, to watch what the pigs did with the revolting porridge. We were vindicated. The pigs turned up their snouts at the trough and walked away!

Even in the darkness of winter when the evenings were freezing, and it was often drizzling with rain, the final meal of the day was sparse. Each of us might receive a slice of Devon and a quarter tomato, or alternatively, a quarter of a fruit bun each. Everything had to be divided and shared. No one seemed to be blessed with one whole anything. A quarter of a pound of butter was shared between eleven students. Sometimes each student received a heaped teaspoon of plum or apricot jam from a small container. We could, however, eat as much bread as our butter and jam would allow, and the tea was plentiful.

I often left the refectory on winter nights, still hungry at 6.50 p.m., with nothing more to eat until eight o'clock the following morning. Rations were limited. Breakfast would take about fifteen to twenty minutes a day. Except on rare occasions such as major feast days of the pope, or St Columba's Day, or the feast of St Patrick, we ate breakfast in silence, or, more accurately, there was no general conversation. Knives, spoons and plates crashed and clashed. There was constant movement up and down the central aisle. Throughout it all, above the din, a luckless student whose meal was postponed until after breakfast, would read aloud to the assembly.

At the evening meal we were also entertained with public reading, again except on those rare occasions when we were permitted to relax and talk among ourselves. Some of the priests who presided over our meals were generous. Others never seemed to tinkle the small bell on the top table or announce: '*Benedicamus Domino*', to which we would reply with gusto, '*Deo gratias*', the sign to chatter. Some clerics were more ascetic than others, more discipline-conscious, more tight-arsed.

The same book would last for months. Imagine how many weeks and months it took to read *The Rise and Fall of the Third Reich* at full voice, night after night, for a thousand pages of grinding reading. Our morning readings tended to be more pious. We listened to the life of the Curé of Ars, or of St Charles Borromeo, also to John Henry Newman's novel *Callista*, or Robert Hugh Benson's *Come Rack, Come Rope*. Nothing too modern. Nothing too exciting. Evening books were secular, like *Across the Nullarbor* or *Kings in Grass Castles*. But for fear the student body might not see life as serious, might breathe easy, relax and show signs of flippancy, the evening eaters were also offered a somber chapter of *The Imitation of Christ* by Thomas à Kempis as soon as they were seated.

Except during Passiontide (which occurred just before Easter and during which we commemorated the passion and death of Christ), the midday meal was generally devoured amid a storm of loud conversation. However, this limited human contact could not be a joy unalloyed by some seriousness, as this meal was also the occasion for the solemn proclamation of the martyrology. Fortunately at Springwood this book was read to us in English. It presented the names and brief historical details of the saints who celebrated their feast on that day, particularly the martyrs who had been admitted to paradise on that very day. As a rule, there was about one page of martyrological details to be read aloud before we could begin. We all waited inattentively, soup spoons poised, anxious to begin our conversations and our eating.

Someone always seemed to be reading to us at Springwood. Meditation points were publicly proclaimed in the chapel, during night prayers, in preparation for our meditation session the next day, and again in the morning. We gathered in the chapel after sport each day for spiritual reading. And Monsignor Dunne would read parts of the college rule book every Sunday. Long hours passed each day, sitting in a large group, listening to passages read aloud.

But these mealtime readings were only half heard. The cafeteria din rose and fell as plates were distributed. Containers of food were wheeled in on two-tiered, wooden trolleys, as a table prefect dusted off the breadboard and hurried to the massive breadbin in the bottom corner of the refectory to replenish the table's supplies. A mixture of human noises ebbed and flowed while the reader on the rostrum competed for space on the airwaves. Sometimes the whole meal would be eaten and not a word of reading heard. Frank Mulcahy's loud, mellow, Shakespearean voice could always dominate the noise. Tom Keneally rose to the occasion to make the reading audible, and entertaining, using every opportunity to hone his dramatic skills. But these were the exceptions. No one thought to suggest a microphone, megaphone or loudspeaker. We knew instinctively that each of us was being trained like a Redemptorist preacher of the Word. It was clear some would never make the grade.

When the background noise became unbearable, Charlie Dunne would grow even redder and more petulant as his blood pressure rose. He was convinced the student body of over a hundred could eat in almost total silence, that the ambient noise must have been deliberate. There need be no noise whatsoever. If a chair was scraped, a plate dropped, a spoon fell on crockery, the rector would glare menacingly at the culprit, signalling him out for special attention with his fat, middle finger, for disciplinary activity if the offence was committed more than once. He had us all bluffed. Even the experienced senior students, the late vocations, appeared cowed and nervous. We were going to be disciplined priests, with unswerving self-control.

Tradition had handed down, from one generation to the next, a simple system of hand signs which we used when we were meant to be listening to the reading. There was a sign for more bread, for jam, tea, milk, sugar, for salt, but pepper was not provided. With these hand gestures, which were mastered in the first few weeks of training and which were like a deaf-and-dumb code language, we managed to communicate our basic requirements. There was no need for whispers.

If Charlie noticed someone eating with his mouth open, or his elbows spread too widely, or holding his knife incorrectly, or putting too much food in his mouth, he was immediately admonished. Second offences were not tolerated. According to the huffing and puffing monsignor, a slice of bread was to be cut into eight regular portions, each buttered, and a thin spread of jam applied. When ready, a gentleman slowly placed each piece in his mouth, masticating slowly and thoroughly before discretely swallowing the morsel. Of course it was bad form to eat and drink together, but everyone knew that. These instructions were delivered with an authoritative, deadpan seriousness.

We were expected to behave like nineteenth-century gentlemen. *Christian Politeness and Counsels for Youth*, written by the Christian brothers, was read at breakfast each Sunday. According to this authority a gentleman always travelled with his back to the horses (presumably to shield the lady from any unwanted blast of foul wind), and always walked close to the kerb, to protect the lady from mud and slush splashed up by any passing carriage. This same public book provided advice to us about table manners and etiquette.

When the level of noise became intolerable, the monsignor would lean across the table, punch the small table bell to attract immediate attention and, breathing fire, command, in short, puffy, dragon breaths that we all eat in silence and attend to the reading. We always obeyed. It was our vocation. Rarely would some recalcitrant aspirant deliberately drop a teaspoon, just to annoy the vigilant powers. Invariably the perpetrator would be sitting towards the back of the refectory and would refuse to own up when the community was challenged to deliver up the culprit. No one would dob.

Prefects of course were dobbers by profession, for they had been appointed to the task by the powers. The rebellious refectory noise would have been made out of sight of the prefect sitting at the end of the table, otherwise one could expect retribution. The secret was kept safe by those witnessing, lest tomorrow, or soon, they themselves be subjected to investigation.

Rogues' gallery

After twenty minutes rapid shovelling down of food, Monsignor Dunne, or whoever was the senior power at table, tapped the bell to end the ceremony. Momentary silence, a thunder of moving chairs, and further silence during which the rector slurred a casual thanksgiving prayer in Latin. The students chorused 'Amen', and we processed in silence to the chapel at the other end of the corridor which had been polished to glow by one of the industrious nuns.

> *In passing from the Chapel to the Refectory, and vice-versa, the Students shall walk two and two in processional order in their respective divisions or classes. [Rule 12 (a)]*

> *On these and on like occasions each student shall attend to the proprieties of ecclesiastical demeanour: the hands are to be held in a becoming manner, and the eyes kept under prudent control. [Rule 12 (b)]*

On my journey down the tunnel, I passed portrait photographs of episcopal old boys. There was Bishop John Toohey of Maitland, looking deceitfully youthful. His family were in pubs and owned impressive real estate on Pittwater at Palm Beach. He was like an old-fashioned union-boss – big-boned, large hands, sharp eyes, used to wheeling and dealing. A Jim Healy, a Martin Ferguson. Toohey presided like a lord at his table in the bishop's house at Maitland. One evening Lachlan Larkin came to the table after hearing confessions in the cathedral for two hours. 'Something weird happened to me this afternoon. A Protestant came to confession and wanted me to hear his sins and give him absolution.' Toohey began to show some interest. 'What did you do?' 'I didn't know what to do. We talked for a bit while I tried to make up my mind.' 'Yes. Yes. But what did you do?' he asked again, impatiently. 'It was really hard. I couldn't decide. Then I thought I'd do what Jesus would have done.' Toohey swallowed hard, one gulp, before blurting, 'You didn't, did you!'

There was also Guilford Young, the coadjutor bishop of Canberra and Goulburn diocese, later to be Archbishop of Hobart. He looked too immature for a bishop, unnaturally thin for such an episcopal heavyweight. He had been guaranteed episcopal rank before he turned forty because of his impeccable Roman connections. At thirty-two, he had been the youngest bishop in Christendom. He was aware of this, and pleased in the knowledge that women loved to kiss his episcopal ring and gaze admiringly at him from a distance. Their knees trembled. He was an uncommonly handsome man, with such poise, such good manners, so smooth, and yet at the same time, so artificial. Who was this plastic man behind the confident smile, the pompoms, the lace and ample cape?

I used to smile at the photograph of Archbishop Eris O'Brien as I processed slowly down the passage to chapel. In the photograph, he appeared educated, with a heavy book open in front of him. He looked so urbane, sophisticated and very handsome. Eris had been my parish priest

Bishop John Toohey

at Neutral Bay from my earliest memories. I had served at his mass often in the parish church, on occasions reminding him when he lost concentration and omitted the words of consecration, or began all over again when he was supposed to be rattling through the last gospel. He was always late for the second weekday parish mass, at 7.15 a.m. officially, but no one complained. We knew he used to stay up late, reading, preparing lectures in Australian History for students at Sydney University, poring over historical source material from the days of Father Therry and the establishment of the Catholic Church in Australia. All Neutral Bay loved this man who later became bishop, then archbishop. He was not typical of the Sydney clergy who in general were muscular, practical, tougher, working-class men. He had no faults we could see. From primary school, my life was influenced by and modelled on him. As I sauntered by, I would glance with respect, sometimes feeling homesick just looking at his portrait.

Archbishop Eris O'Brien

There was Algernon Thomas too, glorying in his red finery and his first-class trips and five-star hotels. He was very important, with contacts in Rome and all over the world. And Jimmy Carroll, the grey eminence of the Labor movement in Sydney, looking somewhat embarrassed in his lace surplice and poncy episcopal gear.

Archbishop Guidford Young

> *a canonist,*
> *well practised in dissembling double thought*
> *In double speech; skilful to wind and twist*
> *All meanings till they cancel in pure naught.*

Captain Quiros, James McAuley

I passed a youthful, grinning Norman Thomas Gilroy, the Cardinal Archbishop, a man of rigid routine and a mouthful of inanities.

> *A cold mean creature with placarded smile*
> *who God to try the faithful had bereft of magnanimity and honour.*
> *He made baseness seem a mode of piety;*
> *His right hand blessed the victims of his left.*

Captain Quiros, James McAuley

But I did not know such things. Had I heard such scurrilous allegations, I would not have believed them. He was my ordinary archbishop before whom I knelt in awe. I was his adopted son. I remembered our interview in the sacristy of St. Mary's Cathedral, me in my school uniform with long, grey socks, him in his plumage and pearls.

In the centre of the shadowy corridor, just off the door which led to the library on the left, across the corridor from the professors' downstairs common room, hung a portrait of the reigning Roman pontiff, enjoying a position pre-eminent in the college corridor. Several times each day, as I processed to and from the chapel and refectory, to the library or the classrooms, my gaze would be attracted to the portrait of Pius XII. He looked rather thin and severe, his penetrating black eyes framed by circular, granny spectacles. As I remember it, the portrait of the pope in our Springwood corridor was the same as had appeared in the small, green catechism from which, guided by the sing-song, rhythmic voices of the nuns and their hard-edged rulers, I had learnt in primary school the basic answers to essential questions of life. The chapter on the papacy and infallibility was accompanied by a full-page portrait of this supreme, exceptionally powerful representative of the gentle, suffering Jesus. The

Pope Pius XII

large, framed picture of his Holiness was a reminder of the prelate who mediated God to us, and a sacred icon inviting obedience, loyalty, reverence and respect.

Mine was a simple faith. I knew that the Catholic Church had been founded by Christ, that the pope had been appointed his visible successor on earth, and that the institution of which he was head was the *societas perfecta*. It had its own language (Latin), its own legislation (the Code of Canon Law), its own system of philosophy to explain the world, and its own traditions of bureaucracy, education, health, social security, international relief and global diplomacy. We were taught, and I believed in all seriousness, that outside the Church there was no salvation.

I had no doubt that the pope's form of governance was the best of all possible systems. There was someone in charge at the top who wielded absolute power, power which came from God, and who was infallible. He was appointed (really by God) through the secret votes in conclave of elderly, holy, celibate men who had themselves been appointed in turn by the pope's predecessor. What could be neater? What better way to guarantee unbroken continuity of tradition, belief and practice? The pope appointed bishops throughout the world from the ranks of obedient clerics, most of whom had been specially trained in Rome, in the heart of Christianity.

The pope was at the centre of a monarchical and hierarchical system of government in which his people, the believers themselves, the little people, and the priests and even the bishops did not need to bother themselves with responsibility. We could bypass the agony of decision, the confusion of searching, and the efforts of discovery. There was no need for discussion, dispute, compromise or conflicting 'yes' and 'no' votes. Our system had come to us from God and was therefore 'perfect'.

Walking the corridor, I knew nothing of nationalism or fascism, of dictatorships, of natural justice, the rights of man, international diplomacy or anti-semitism. I had much to learn. My world had been the parish of Neutral Bay where I had gone to school, served on the altar and processed as a pageboy spreading frangipani petals.

I did not know that Eugenio Pacelli, who was to become Pius XII, had never walked up and down the corridor in disciplined ranks, or prayed in columns in the seminary chapel, or eaten institutional rations in the company of other hungry teenagers. I later learnt that because of his family's position in the Vatican, he had lived at home with his parents, his two sisters and a brother, while studying for the priesthood. His training had not included any rough and tumble struggle for survival, or a grab for food in the refectory, pushing and shouldering for personal space, jockeying for a position of advantage. He had continued in the cocoon of the family, cared for by his attentive, proud mother, reading his *Imitation of Christ* (in Latin) in the privacy of his room, where he had begun the labour of learning the text by heart. He used to move around his parents' confined, bourgeois apartment in the heart of Rome, in Via Monte Giordano, on the third floor, close by the Chiesa Nuova, always in his cassock, even as a teenager with his raging hormones and pimples.

Eugenio had been an altar boy at the local church where he used to serve his cousin's masses. In his spare time, and for recreation, he used to dress up in fancy clothes, and act out the ritual of the mass in his bedroom, mumbling mock prayers like the priests rattling off Latin texts, imitating rapid, compulsive crosses and circles with the right hand, multiple genuflections. His mother had encouraged him, helping him to set up the baby altar complete with candles, providing some frilly material to serve as vestments. Then, ordained as a promising two-year-old at the age of twenty-three, he had been immediately seconded into the Vatican bureaucracy and the fluffy, surreal world of international diplomacy. As a diplomat and as Secretary of State, as well as pope during the war, Pacelli had followed the Roman agenda of completing the Vaticanisation of the known world.

On one occasion Pius XI had sent Pacelli to Argentina as his representative, where he was treated like royalty. He had been taken on a tour of Buenos Aires in an official aircraft and in his regal cassock (never laid aside for street clothes, whether in England, America, Argentina or Germany) and he had passed the entire flight reciting his breviary, without so much as a glance over the city. He was so totally other-worldly, perhaps to the point of rudeness – but I did not know. As far as I was concerned the man on the wall was a saint, setting for me and my confrères an impossibly high standard of priestly holiness. With his beautiful, tapering, feminine hands, his large black eyes, his overmeticulous enunciation of pious thoughts through a thin, high-pitched voice, Pius XII was at the centre of religious power and authority. Pacelli was the pope par excellence, the ultimate pope, destined without doubt for canonisation.

I knew nothing of this man as I walked the Springwood corridor in silence, as I glanced at his cold, aloof, steely figure, his pale, ash-grey face, and absorbed the subliminal message that holiness consisted in studied control, angelic chastity and a sexless demeanour. Jesus might have been surprised to learn that his vicar on earth had negotiated a tragic concordat with Herr Hitler.

My Roman Church had been showing signs itself of a fascist orientation, with its centralisation of power, its oppression and persecution of dissenters and minorities. During the very years I was passing his portrait in the hall, his Holiness was himself responsible for the persecution of theologians who would later become famous and who would influence my life - Congar, du Lubac, Chenu. There were harsh, often eternal penalties for dissent. A developed system of devout spies, dobbers, secret enquires and kangaroo courts maintained order. Emphasis was placed on secrecy, and on public demonstrations of loyalty through medals, knighthoods and token rewards for service. As the first multinational organisation, propaganda was a convenient substitute for thinking. At the end of the war, Pius XII had told Cardinal Tardini, 'I don't want colleagues, but people who will obey!' Orders came from on high. Truth was delivered to us in packages from above. The Supreme Pontiff made all decisions, and he was always right, because he was under divine inspiration and enjoyed the gift of infallibility.

Jesus would have been horrified. The attitudes and trappings of fascism had been so foreign to him. He had rejected the offer of power. He had come to set prisoners free, to give sight to the blind. No honours, no badges, no vestments, no epaulettes. The Code of Canon Law might have been a source of amusement to him. How far they had travelled in his name!

When I was marching in line as a young neophyte through the seminary corridor beneath the framed portrait, I accepted his Holiness and his Church as a gift from God. This was the way it had always been. This imperial figure was a central character in the eternal, divine plan, playing an unchanging and unchangeable role as the centre piece in the best of all possible worlds. This man was God's representative in 'this vale of tears', displaying all the ideal virtues of the priestly life – aloofness, other-worldliness, severe purity, cold virginity. I never questioned. I entertained not the least doubt. I had been immunised from childhood.

The framed image of Pacelli with St Peter's thunderous basilica in the background, the square crowded with worshippers, did not display the reality, only the distorted myth of the modern papacy. This was the image of a man who insisted on a daily walk alone in the Vatican garden. Some might have thought it strange that any luckless gardener who had delayed his departure and had been caught unawares, was obliged to hide behind shrubs for the hour during which the Supreme Pontiff chose to wander in complete isolation, but I did not. Jesus might have thought it peculiar that his bishops and cardinals only spoke to his vicar on the telephone while on their knees. We accepted it without question, without the least criticism. It seemed normal in those strange days when Jesus was hidden behind the figure of the pope.

The portrait on the wall was finally taken down in October 1958, the year following my departure from Springwood, and replaced for too brief a time with the picture of a happy, jovial, warm-hearted man. The earlier powerful symbol of imperial, autocratic control was toppled from his lofty pedestal and obediently returned to the earth. His naked humanity, so studiously hidden in life, revealed itself in death. The opening words of his last testament would read:

> *Have pity on me, Lord, according to thy mercy; my knowledge of the deficiencies, failures, sins committed during so long a pontificate and in so grave an epoch has made clearer to me my inadequacies and unworthiness. I humbly ask pardon of all I have offended, harmed and scandalised.*

I now know what he meant, and my heart can go out to him as a fellow human being. His humanity was revealed in death, not during his life. I wish someone had had the grace, the courage, the wisdom to have spoken honestly of him to me, and to my fellow searchers for perfection. My life would almost certainly have been different.

Walking and Sporting

After a brief, pop-in visit to the chapel, rapid exit genuflections and a charge for the chapel exit, through which we passed like sheep crushing through a gate, we were free for half an hour before classes commenced. The head prefect for the year, whether Jack Shanahan in 1951, Tubby Hayes in 1956, or Kevin Manning in my senior year, would pass the half-hour after breakfast receiving special messages, directions and orders from the rector or dean. Around examination time, the swatters among us would study their notes, conjugate a Greek verb or two, learn by heart the dictated definition of some otherwise incomprehensible philosophical concepts.

This period after breakfast was our first opportunity of the day to converse with someone human. Gerry, who was later ordained in Canberra-Goulburn diocese, had his own way of passing these precious moments of free time. He earned the nickname of 'Gerry the Jet'. Every morning after breakfast, he would rush from chapel and race everyone else to the smelly sandstone toilet block at the end of the gravel path which passed by the large, college belltower. He would throw himself into one of the private cubicles, slam the door and blast away. Then he would burst out, at urgent pace, religiously cleanse his hands and disappear into the college routine as he buttoned up his cassock. Many of us were very amused by the Jet's daily routine. Someone would time him. Some would compete, but no one could match him for speed. Like an Olympic hundred-metre sprinter, he had carved off every available fraction of a second from the performance. The ritual was gradually reduced to twenty seconds. Gerry provided some scatological amusement for us and is remembered now, whenever Springwood boys gather, for his daily feat.

Juniors used to walk in a special area, on the driveway in the front of the college. When it rained, as it often did in the mountains, we were permitted to walk slowly around the quadrangle, on a covered, red cement pathway outside the classrooms. Only three sides of the quadrangle were available to us – the fourth section passed by the windows of the brothers' study, the spiritual director's room and the priests' downstairs common room and was therefore out of bounds.

For five years I walked the front driveway, guarded and supervised by the more respected trustworthy senior prefects, and I was pleased, even relieved, on the occasions when I was accepted into a walking party of three or four other boys. On other occasions I was relegated to the ranks of those who dwelt on the fringe of the common groups. I was sometimes brutally informed I was not welcome even to hover on the edge of the fun crowd. My alienation or acceptance would depend on the whim of some other more popular junior.

The winter winds blew fiercely at Springwood. Woollen jumpers were worn even in full, midday sunshine. For two years my legs in short pants froze and a grey lumber-jacket kept me protected against the mountain chill. I soon became accustomed to walking up and down, listening to others, participating in the conversation when and as permitted. Juniors in general were not highly respected and carried no weight, but there was a pecking order even among us, an order which depended on your years of service, your particular group and your place within it, your ability at sport and your smoothness factor. For those first five years, I had no idea what the seniors were doing on the other side of the college. When one is young, one's mind does not focus on those who are out of sight. The front drive was where my world was concentrated.

After five years of service, I graduated to spending the half-hour before class on the other side of the college grounds where, in groups of three or four, and dressed in cassocks, we would take a lengthy walk around the perimeter of the cultivated portion of the college grounds. The ghost track wound its way down past the football field, round the back of the handball courts, past the shuttlecock area and the parallel bars. It skirted the edge of a makeshift boxing ring where Slim Pendergast, Bubber Blanchfield and others used to work out in the afternoon in boxing gloves and headgear. It continued on near the basketball court, and made a left turn to join the other side of the football field. This rough, dirt, stony track was about half a mile from start to finish at the chapel exit.

I used to haunt the college ghost track. I walked it many times while on retreat. I made my way round after breakfast, and again warily late at night, before night prayers, when the stars shone brightly and shadowy figures seemed to peer out of the bushes. In the afternoons I often made my way on the run to the basketball court along one section of the ghost track, in my smelly sports gear, sometimes with holes worn in the rubber soles of cheap sandshoes. More frequently I went to the handball courts where I began to shine, but only after five or six years of dedicated practice. For many years, the old boys at the college, the senior juniors, knew how to dominate the handball court, where they played a game called shark, which occupied ten, twenty or thirty students for hours. The fewer the better, as only four players could be on the court at any one time. The rest of us waited in line for our turn to compete. Two players dominated the serving squares in the front, while the two in the rear squares competed for a position in the front.

The experienced players, those who had been at the college for some years, were practised and merciless. Two of them together could occupy the court for half an hour or more, belting low fast serves to inexperienced players like me at the back. They lobbed the little black handball over the side wall, making the ball impossible to be retrieved by anyone but the highly skilled, smashing the ball with open palm or closed fist into one of the front corners, low down, sometimes so low the ball would roll back flat along the cement surface. Dead butt! Join the queue.

No one taught his opponents how to play handball. The technique was picked up slowly over time by bitter experience. No quarter was asked, or given. The senior juniors such as Gordy Dick, Dudley Lennox, Pud Sweeney dispatched us with a bullet-like service, a huge lob to the back of the court, or preferably a dead butt. It was Darwinian survival of the fittest. Most of us endured by waiting in line for long periods, impatient for our turn to come round again, socialising with one another, thumping, teasing, laughing, pushing, until another turn arrived to occupy a back square on the court, to be removed immediately again. The professionals asserted their superiority.

Slowly, over the years, the art of handball came to me until I was the one to show no mercy. I asserted my superiority by dispatching all opponents without ceremony, as rapidly as possible. I too taught no one, and took no prisoners. As the supremos ahead of me left for Manly or to reclaim their secular lives, I studied and practised to replace them. For the last two years of my life at Springwood I was the champion of the handball court, though my position was seriously challenged by Donk or Billy Allport (now a medical practitioner on the central coast north of Sydney), sometimes by Kevin English. Major challenges came from Billy

Rohan, who could extend me to five sets during championship competitions. Victory ensured status, and status was sweet after so many years.

Later in my service at Springwood, I learnt to play tennis. I would compete for a place on one of the four cracked and uneven asphalt courts at every available opportunity. I began my tennis career with an old, warped, second-hand racquet which had several gut strings broken. I had recovered it from a throw-out pile of junk at the college where I had also scavenged a pair of football boots. But I had set my sights on a new racquet and, saving my money from holiday work at the post office, I ordered a new racquet through my cousin, John Maclean. I remember catching the tram from Neutral Bay to Wynyard to take delivery of it. I had chosen a heavyweight Maxply, with an extra thick handle as I somehow believed that large and thick were masculine characteristics, thin and light, feminine. I was conscious of my increasing strength, my budding manhood. Maybe I was thickheaded too!

I used to play tennis several times each week – when the wind blew, when the hot sun shimmered off the asphalt, even when it rained. Sometimes I was able to persuade a classmate, Kevin English, to play with me, though he often had better offers. While I enjoyed beating him, I was not often successful. He was tall and lanky, and a relaxed, natural player. He only agreed to play tennis with me when the charity-bug was biting him.

I played often with other classmates – Joe Giles, Michael Bach, on occasions with George Turley. I also played with Terry, who had come to Springwood at the same time as me in 1951 and who used to mince around the court in a rather feminine manner, without a respectable first serve. I felt annoyed about the way the others mocked him, and hurt when they ridiculed me. I thought of myself as a macho tennis player and modelled my game on Lew Hoad, the current tennis idol. I had no finesse, and would serve the first ball as hard as possible, seldom hitting the target, pop the second in softly, and then hit as hard as one would expect from any young man. The nuances of the game escaped me. Many years passed before I realised one could win with soft, well-placed shots. Sport occupied a great deal of my waking hours, dreaming, planning, even in the chapel. I was only young.

Driving at full throttle

During morning walks with others, chosen at random to avoid the forbidden particular friendships, I would skirt the tennis courts and sometimes wander off as far as the handball courts. But in my youthful fervour, walking and talking seemed such a waste of time. I was anxious to achieve success rapidly, at sport, study, and also at public speaking and reading, which, after all, would be central to my future success. To that end, no opportunity should be wasted.

Every morning, even in my fifth year of secondary schooling, but especially in my two senior years, I spent the leisure half-hour before class, reading aloud to the trees in the bush. I shouted out pages of serious social history (not anything as ordinary or entertaining as a novel), at full voice, in a manner liable to cause damage to a boy's vocal chords. Bryce Fraser also used to position himself somewhere in Jakes Gully, declaiming across the valley. Michael Bach would occasionally perform. Joe Giles used to wander past with smart remarks to mock our enthusiasm. On any one day there would be perhaps twenty other students orating to the wilderness, though not of course as loudly or as intensely as myself. I was over the top. Some of my confrères knew this, but not me. They tried to tell me, but I was not listening. They were giving me the treatment, and I was responding in my usual manner. I was in a vicious circle.

Once or twice a week, I would vary my usual routine by delivering a ten or fifteen minute speech to a tree or to an empty space across the valley. I was impatient to learn the art of speaking fluently, to be able to develop my ideas out loud, out there. While those who were rostered for refectory reading were practising their public reading, others were aspiring to be performers from pulpits throughout the land. Jakes Gully being the location of the college sewerage outlet, we were troubled in summer by flies and unpleasant odours, as we fought to make ourselves heard across the vacant valley.

Blinkers and shutters

I was a keen competitor in the annual oratory competitions, in the junior years as well as in the later senior classes. Sometimes I won the prize, and when Ray Weaver or Bryce Fraser topped me, I could not understand why

I had come second. I was an intense boy, without humour, with a superior mask and a combative air. Unbeknown to me, I was unable to establish contact with an audience who thought they knew me well and were not happy to be victims of my energetic speeches.

One year, I delivered a diatribe about Metternich, lifted straight out of Robert's potted *History of Europe*. On another occasion, I spoke in praise of Garibaldi. I also shouted a crass piece on the White Australia Policy, and another against the twentieth century presenting itself as the greatest period of development. It is sobering, and embarrassing, to review my early speeches from a distance, and to compare them with the ideas of my son Patrice at the age of sixteen, or of Pascal at fourteen.

I can retrieve some of my early attempts at speech writing. I was a recorder. I kept my class notes in Philosophy, for example. When I attended the three formal chapel lectures during the annual three-day retreats, I would take note of what the retreat master was saying, his gems on clerical obedience, on prudence or purity, on the joys of the celibate life, or the life of Jesus, or when priests should shave, before or after mass, as Monsignor Harrington once discussed with us before I had touched my face with a razor. Later I would write out the notes in a retreat book marked 'private'. I used to keep notes so that I could revisit ideas later, so that I would not forget, so that I could savour the insights of the moment. I wanted somehow to preserve the past, to hang on to the ephemeral second and prevent its disappearance. In most cases, I never read my notes again, but they were there just in case.

It was with this same innocent compulsion that I kept a copy of my early Springwood orations. Reluctantly, but wishing the full story to be told, I turn the pages of the texts. The handwriting is surprisingly raw and unseasoned. I had not as yet developed an adult style of running writing.

In my first attempt I praised Prince von Metternich for holding back 'the flood of nationalism and liberalism' for thirty-three years, and compared him to another man, Pius IX, who 'ruled the world by his good example for thirty-three years and ended his life in apparent failure.' Pius IX and Pius XII would both have been pleased to learn of my condemnation of liberalism. I am proud to be able to claim, however, that, before I knew anything of the standards of the academic world, I formulated a blunt plea for judging everything in its historical context.

> *Are we going to judge Metternich on our modern standards?...Do you consider Napoleon less a man than Churchill because he used scented lace handkerchiefs? Do you consider the women of today are less ladylike because they wear their dresses above their knees?... Metternich was a reactionary when judged by present day standards.*

I was overindulgent on oratorical questions, and even then, a little cynical. In another performance I offered a simple, mythological, naive image of Guiseppe Garibaldi who was 'a simple, lion-hearted man who lived, fought, and killed for his country and its unity.' Even in those times, I was prone to simplicity and overstatement.

> *People flung themselves in the river merely to bid him farewell... widows for his sake sacrificed their sons and offered them to die on the battlefield.... Boys clad in their red shirts, ragged, starving, bleeding, homeless, at Mentana, at Masala, at the Volturas, would rush on the blistering bayonets of Austria, or charge against the murderous chassepots of France and, tortured in vain to reveal their hiding-place, they would die with a smile on their lips.*

I was in full flight. Even at seventeen, I exaggerated. I invited tears, anger, heroics, vivid colours, blood, death. I was at least having a go.

These old speeches help to explain my vocation, and my personality – passionate, extravagant, energetic, confronting. In praise of Garibaldi, I naively contrasted the power of his charismatic character, the magnetic hold he had over his followers, with our weary existence at Springwood. 'How many would get up ten minutes earlier in the morning, how many would put their hand into the bursting and overflowing purse of their boundless superfluity...for you or for me?' I was on the trail of the classical Redemptorist preacher, preparing myself for the pulpit, for hellfire and brimstone, and perhaps to extract money from the mass attenders. The polarising, critical, oratorical questions would flow out, though I showed no signs of the other, more mature rhetorical techniques of humour, wit, mocking fun. My speeches were deadpan serious. This was not fun, but work in preparation for a vocation. I quoted Garibaldi, though I may have only constructed the words (falsely) for effect:

> *I have passed my life – in what? In money getting? In small self-*

seeking? In an aimless round of frivolities? No, but — in the hope of seeing populations ennobled, and to the extent of my power, have championed always and everywhere their rights. But sadly, I confess that I have partly lived in a false hope.

I compared Garibaldi, approvingly, to the Saviour. I can see my fascination for the eccentric rebel, my quixotic idealism, my anarchy already in the making. My Irish passions were on display.

The only excuse I can muster for my crass views on the White Australia Policy in the fifties is that I was young, unsophisticated, and immature, and that I was speaking in a college debate in support of the policy. However, these excuses fail to justify the crude, blind bigotry of my words. I feel chastened now to remember my youthful writing, and a little amused. 'Aren't Chinese constantly trying to avoid the Customs and landing in Australia in small bays around the coastland?' It was more than another oratorical device. It was not true then, but perhaps prophetic.

My sentiments were a crude reflection of the Menzies scare tactics and the old Australian fears of the yellow peril. And top this for brainwashed propaganda:

The Asiatics, as you all know, are a very ductile (sic) race. Communism has spread very rapidly through China and Japan and has obtained a very firm footing in India. If these people are permitted to settle in Australia the communistic doctrines shall spread even more rapidly than they are today. Not only shall we get more communists but also more people who are easily influenced.... If these peoples from Asia came to our country, surely employers could not hesitate to employ men who would work harder, longer and more contentedly than the Australian worker.... Australians would lose their jobs. It's all very well to speak of charity among nations — self-preservation comes first. Australian families must be fed before Asiatics.

I must stop. This was pure rednecked, Pauline Hanson bigotry from an innocent, idealistic young man from a Christian family, training for the priesthood. The authorities at Springwood must have been excessively permissive to tolerate such extreme views. They would surely not have condoned these shocking prejudices? Perhaps they knew I would eventually grow out of them.

Such were the raw thoughts developed by a young, impressionable aspirant for the priesthood. I was not censured, or even booed. The world should have been horrified by the narrow bigotry, the crudity of the argument, the selfishness, the crass stereotyping. Perhaps my speeches are a true reflection of what the world was like back then. I should have been sent home as unsuitable for public office, or at the very least, submitted to an even harder labour camp for radical re-education. I was growing up in a different world. Education was mainly a process of rote learning. We did as we were told. History, English appreciation and faith were simply ways of learning what was handed down to us, like mathematics, or the study of Physics.

Times have changed, radically. My sons have participated in a completely different educational process. They have been encouraged to examine and assess primary sources, to study different points of view and interpretations, to discuss, reflect and respond. They have developed their own ideas on religion, on historical events, on literature. I have had the pleasure of discussing with them the poetry of John Donne, the writings of Cicero, the poems of Catullus, the plays of Shakespeare, the Church, family structures and the novels of Patrick White. I have been amazed by their insight, by their ability to converse on topics in a way which would have been completely beyond my powers. Their education has enriched their lives, and mine.

Gradually, I did acquire some proficiency in the art of speaking in public. It came to me slowly, techniques to begin with. I began to use oratorical questions more sparingly. Later, when I was almost thirty and more comfortable and accepting of myself, I was able to develop more friendly contact with my audience, to banter, to share, to smile a little.

The system at work

THE BASIC ORGANISATION

I soon discovered that the junior seminary in the Blue Mountains had a divided regime, a type of apartheid. The senior section included students in first and second year Philosophy who were studying such exotic subjects as Latin, Greek, Ancient History, Logic, Metaphysics, and Epistemology, plus a second group of more mature students who were spending a full year in a Specials category, struggling mainly with the intricacies of Latin before they began to tackle the other subjects. Mass was celebrated in Latin, the breviary recited in Latin. Official Church documents were published in Latin. The theological textbooks at Manly and the two-volume philosophical textbook at Springwood by Carolus Boyer SJ were all in Latin.

Those in the Specials class were struggling to acquire a semblance of the lingua nostra so they could function in the Roman clerical system – say mass, recite the breviary, administer the sacraments, even if most of them would never understand what they were saying.

The juniors were much younger students, still involved in secondary schooling, preparing for the public Leaving Certificate examination. I was to be a member of this group for five years. Some juniors wore long, black cassocks, even at the age of thirteen and fourteen. I did not.

We were taught by a small team of dedicated Marist brothers (Brothers Gerard, Valerius, Geoffrey, Kevin, Gerald, Gregory), and regimented by an iniquitous system of prefects. We were also supervised, guarded and sometimes entertained by a group of trusted seniors from the other side of the track. Hos Dryden, Happy Byron, Colin Rice, George Connolly, Brian Larkey used to take turns in supervising our study halls. They also accompanied us on our regular walks along the front drive near the twin gum trees at regular intervals throughout the day, acting as a type of older, responsible brother. They were our scoutmasters when we hurled ourselves down the dangerous bush track to the weir for a swim or suffered scratches to exposed hairless legs and arms as we ploughed through the prickly bush on exciting paperchase excursions. These senior prefects travelled in pairs, just as policemen working their beat, not merely to support one another at a time of anarchy, but also to protect each other from suspicion or accusation.

Brian Larkey was known to us as Bicky because his father used to work for Arnott's biscuits company when it was Australian owned. I cannot remember whether Happy Byron was uncommonly cheerful. Maybe his nickname was meant to be ironic and in truth he had been a bit of a moaner. In any event, in later life he proved to be a rather jovial, nonconformist character who grew comfortably into his name. Colin Rice was always a neat, meticulously perfect seminarian, born for routine and ritual, though in later years he could not maintain the sprung tensions of the seminary system.

Guts and doggedness

Springwood seminary in the early fifties was not for the faint-hearted. There were months of cold days and nights, freezing mountain winds and biting rains. Not a heater anywhere, at least not one at which any student could warm himself. There was not much food. Despite our religious vocation and our ideal to be *omnia omnibus* (all things to all men) we were sometimes exceedingly, mysteriously cruel.

Clem was a boy from the north coast of New South Wales, who suffered in those days from an uncontrollable and embarrassing stammer. His brother, Gordon, whom we knew as Gordy, was also an intern at

Springwood. He was a type of tribal leader like Van Damme. A mountainous, muscly man, he took no bullshit from anyone, even the staff, and was unashamedly interested in birdwatching and in the delicate flora on the Blue Mountains. Gordon was an independent bushie in an institution built on obedience and conformity. Over the years, he had become friendly with a wily old rouseabout. Jimmy Lawrence was employed by the college to hunt and trap foxes, stoke the boilers, do odd jobs, and talk commonsense to the innocent students out of the side of his sunburnt face. He and Gordy were mates.

Clem's brother used to be constantly hassled by the institutional powers. Monsignor Dunne could hardly stand the sight of him, and as the vice-rector, Noel Carroll simply echoed his boss. Gordy left our priestly training programme at Springwood when he could stand it no more. Mythology records that he became a student at St John's University College in Sydney. When the seniors attempted to humiliate his mate in some barbaric initiation ritual, he smashed one know-all's jaw, and permanently damaged an eye of a second. Gordy later lived with his family as an Australian ex-pat in New Guinea where he became the principal of the nation's most prestigious agricultural college, and introduced exciting innovative programmes. He later became an adviser to the agricultural arm of the United Nations, travelling the world, attending conferences, working in Central Africa, Burma and other parts of the Third World. I heard tell that he had also skippered a fishing trawler and continued his adult life with his family, doing the sorts of things which as a boy he had enjoyed at Springwood.

Bill was another chronic stammerer. Despite their obvious disability, neither Clem nor Bill were exempted from the ritual duty of reading publicly to us in the refectory. Gripping firmly *Across the Nullarbor*, a biography of John Henry Newman or a Victorian novel by Robert Hugh Benson, they were expected to declaim slowly and loudly, to a large refectory of eighteen or twenty tables. They had to cast their voices from one wall to the other, perhaps forty metres in all, against a background of a hundred and more distracted students stacking plates, shuffling cutlery, dishing out meagre dobs of food.

Neither had a hope in hell. I have no idea what made the holy powers at Springwood stand them in public and belittle them so cruelly. When their turn came to read, neither could utter one sentence, not a phrase, without long stammering and agonising pauses. Inevitable failure did not excuse them. No, their obligation had to be met and the challenge answered. And so they were goaded on, remorselessly, not for five minutes only, but throughout the long, painful meal. At first we were shocked. Then embarrassed. Later, the tittering began, and the giggling. A burst of laughter would be followed by an embarrassed silence. Bill or Clem were struggling to utter just one sentence. We waited and waited. The normal din had abated. Like the Suffering Servant, they were being held up to public ridicule.

At one fateful breakfast, Con Keogh, who was the dean of discipline at the time, hit the bell angrily to stop the reading and eating, to command an early end to the meal. He paced up and down the refectory aisle, white with anger, castigating the students for their insulting, childish behaviour. But this well-deserved remonstration was not delivered in the absence of the humiliated public reader who had to stand and listen to every embarrassing word. This experience would put steel into his soul, perfect him in the fire of adversity, or ruin his ego forever.

Keogh was a man of learning and compassion. He was just a young tyro at that time, only recently returned to Australia, triumphant from studies in Rome and Louvain. I wonder how he felt, surrounded by his personal library of existential philosophers, suddenly isolated at Springwood? I wonder what he thought of that awful, public degradation of a struggling human being before a crowd of cruel students.

Yes, life was harsh at Springwood. But Clem's seminary life had its successes too, its sweet moments of joy, as well as times of crushing embarrassment. In 1955 (my Leaving Certificate year), Clem was twelve months ahead of me, in first Philosophy. We were playing Rugby League and Clem was the hooker in the opposing team. Though I was underweight, I was an enthusiastic, crash-tackling lock-forward. No one showed the other side much gentleness or beatitudinal peacemaking on the football field.

One day, I was playing the ball with my left foot, in front of Clem. Just as I was leaning over to place the ball on the turf, his illegal knee came up sharply into my face, crushing my beautiful top front teeth back into my mouth. Blood began to gush freely. Trouble. The roots of both front teeth had pierced my gums. Within a few minutes my face, particularly my upper lip, was swollen and bruised. As much as I loved my football, I had to leave the field and take an early shower.

As usual, Monsignor Charlie Dunne was wandering in the vicinity in his red-piped cassock. Instead of hiding behind one-way glass or spying through binoculars, Charlie often roamed the corridors and grounds of the institution, feigning prayer. While mouthing the obligatory Latin formulae in his breviary, he was observing his students closely. When I showed him my bleeding teeth, Charlie gave them only a casual glance. Even though it was not the scheduled time, I asked whether I could go to the dormitory. I wanted to change out of my muddy football gear. He agreed the rules could be varied in exceptional cases. I asked if I could go into the village to consult a dentist, although I did not think who would pay for treatment and did not have the ready cash. He said, 'Go if you like, but I wouldn't be bothered if I were you. You'll lose them anyway. You'll only be wasting your time going into Springwood to the dentist.' I went anyway. I changed into my good clothes and walked down the long drive of St Columba's to the front gate, approximately one mile. I turned right, passed the golf course, and trudged the three miles further into Springwood, my bloody handkerchief to my mouth.

The village dentist was not encouraging. He wanted to remove my teeth. I was sitting in an antiquated chair with him leaning over me, peering into my mouth. He was operating the drill by pumping bicycle pedals frantically with his old, flaccid legs. I realised I was not receiving up-to-the-minute treatment. I thanked the old gentleman and left. Instinctively pressing my teeth back into place with my tongue, I walked back to the college. No one ever enquired how I had fared. The subject was never raised again. It was as if nothing of any importance had occurred. Fifty years on, I still have my front teeth despite the loss of others not affected by the injury.

The next year, while I was working among the pigs at the seminary pigsty, I injured my left ankle when I sprang over a barbed wire fence. I limped to the infirmary where Kevin Barry-Cotter was attending the sick and lame and had the foot bandaged. I was hopping about on crutches for a week or so with my ankle swelling and throbbing before circumstances intervened. It happened while I was sitting in class listening to John Burnheim philosophise, with my left leg propped up on a fruit box. I had no mind for abstract ideas, for anything except my left ankle. Pain dominated my cerebral landscape. It was impossible to focus on Hume or Descartes, or to grasp the definition of truth or beauty. I was taking some scattered notes, when Charlie Dunne wandered into the classroom, spoke quietly to Burnheim and made his way down the narrow corridor of desks to me. He asked how my ankle was. I was puzzled. He had shown no interest before. I did not know he had even noticed I had sustained an injury:

'The doctor has come out from Springwood to examine another student', he groaned, breathing his tobacco smell over me. 'You had better see him while he is here.' I picked up my crutches and made my way out of the classroom, down the polished corridor, to the visitors' parlour. I sat there for sometime alone, waiting for the doctor. He burst in, obviously in a tearing hurry. He wrapped his fingers around my ankle and said. 'It's broken. You will have to go to the hospital at Penrith and have it set in plaster.' My ankle had been fractured for more than a week. Now it was to be fixed, again by accident. We were all on our own, well away from our mothers.

Suspect friendship

> *The Rector shall appoint over the several classes Prefects chosen from the most prudent of the students. These shall diligently see to the exact observance of the Rule. They shall also take care that the students converse in a gentlemanly, polite and serious manner as becomes ecclesiastics. All excessive familiarity and particular friendships are dangerous and contrary to charity. [Rule 22 (a)]*

Later I came to understand why the juniors and seniors were so strictly separated at Springwood, why senior prefects appeared only in pairs when mixing with us juniors. The system was structured for the mutual protection of the young and of those sexually maturing. Juices and fluids were circulating in bodies of boys in their late teens and on the edge of rebellion. Pubescent boys found themselves sealed off, starved of the sight and company of females, with all the powerful drives and impulses of youth conspiring to overflow. A few were delighted to be living among males, while others were content to be living with mates. Most of us suffered from the ache and harshness of a defeminised world.

It was not until I was an adult that I understood why one of the senior larrikins whom I did not know would steal a few furtive moments to converse with me, or wink at me in chapel, or smile a private greeting when our paths accidentally crossed. I was flattered at the time and began to believe that I was accepted by some of the more senior men. Those who played in the senior football team or were stylish tennis or handball players belonged to an exclusive, high profile team. Blue McNamara, John Ford, Jimmy Timbs, Dennis Davis (Foghorn), Billy Meacham, John Conway, all hung round together, having fun, challenging the regime.

In such a lonely, isolated setting, young pubescent boys can seem feminine and attractive. The seniors were not permitted to speak to us, or play sport with us, eat at our table, or kneel beside us in the chapel. In particular the seniors were not permitted to sleep in the same dormitory as us. St Columba's dormitory at the top of the stairs was the exclusive domain of the juniors. The big boys changed and slept elsewhere. Their dormitories were also identified by names of saints – St Charles Borromeo, St Francis Xavier, St John Vianney (who was the pious though strange Curé of Ars) and St John Bosco. The very senior men who were specially trusted to behave themselves and to preserve the silences, enjoyed the privacy of a small dormitory, known as Paradise, immediately under the belltower.

We were in protective custody. Apart from separating the big ones from us littlies, the supervising powers had other means of controlling, if not subduing, the natural, impulsive urges of young males starved of normal stimulation. The students were all strongly discouraged from becoming friendly with each other. What was known in the seminary as 'particular friendships' were prohibited by the little green rule book, and regulated by the prefect system, teachers and the general student body.

We were being trained to live a life of loneliness, like desert wanderers, a type of spiritual tramp. We were to be ready to move from place to place at the bishop's whim, self-reliant, without roots, without family or friends. It would be a serious weakness to grow close to anyone, even someone journeying in the same direction. We had not left mothers and fathers, sisters and brothers, to fall into the trap of drawing human warmth from fellow seminarians.

But the danger was more subtle. The priesthood, with its vestments and ritual, the incense and piety, seemed to attract a certain minority of effeminate types, young men who tended to behave in a mincing, slightly camp manner. Just as in the prisons, in the army or the navy, monasteries and seminaries were no different. When men of 'normal' impulses are thrown together, without female company, and without the opportunity of expressing their sexuality in a 'normal', heterosexual context, without strict regulations, behaviour can begin to distort, young men can begin to focus on boys, pretty boys can become strangely attractive, one man may find himself suffering a crush on another.

If two students were seen walking too frequently together, sitting with one another in the recreation hall on Saturday nights, regularly playing tennis or handball together, working in the same chain gang, bookbinding in the hut, or generally spending what was considered by others to be too much time in one another's company, they were teased by some, criticised by others, gossiped about, reported by prefects to the eager authorities, and counselled.

An established protocol was established in the seminary to avoid 'p-fing' [forming personal friendships]. For example, as we left the classrooms or the chapel to go walking on the ghost track or around the college, each of us was expected to walk in the company of the boy within reach, whether we liked him or not. In principle there should have been no selection of one's companion. There should be no preferences. Each of us had to be free and willing to walk and talk, to share with and relate with anyone at random.

But life is always a compromise. Even highly motivated clerics do not always perform to a standard. I remember some boys who were awkward, uncool and unpopular, those whom others loved to tease and ostracise, who hovered without belonging. Some fellow students seemed unmanly. They would mince around the paths, walking in short steps, knees suspiciously together, talking perhaps about lace vestments, or organ practice, maybe Gregorian chants. Michael could be an annoying urger, so he was not popular with some of the boys. Donk was too sanctimonious with his rosary beads, John too theatrical. One harmless, angelic waif had developed an odd fetish for German military discipline and uniforms. He was untouchable behind his permanent smile. So even in such a faceless, amorphous mass of males, there were boys who stood out from the crowd through pimples, bad body odour, rumbling stomachs and annoying habits, or by being too sanctimonious or pompous. It could be very difficult, day after day, to take the next student on the rack and walk with him. Friendships were not easy in such a regime, but not impossible.

But the anti-friendship protocol was generally observed and, in the circumstances, it was a good and noble policy. In theory at least no one was made to feel rejected. We all had to cope with one another, learn to adapt, to be sociable, to make conversation with people to whom we were not naturally attracted. To be 'all things to all men' would be our lot, and particular friendships were contrary to charity.

So as we crowded towards the exit of the chapel or classroom, each would jockey for a position near someone with whom he could be comfortable. This human crush was often an unpleasant experience. As a teenager, I was not comfortable with many of the students. Some would refuse to walk with me as they considered me a dork. But while this cruel rejection was humiliating at the time, and impossible for me to comprehend, I eventually survived to find a place in the crowd.

Some 'pfs' blossomed. We all knew who was friendly with whom, who walked regularly with one another, who made their preferences obvious. Kevin and Michael were good mates, and others like Steve could be drawn in on the periphery of that relationship. Terry, who was a devout little person with a girlish manner, and George, who also seemed somewhat effeminate, struck up a warm, innocent friendship with him.

Tony was the type of boy who was fascinated with long, lace surplices and playing the organ, and was constantly doodling with religious symbols. To execute his extravagant, profound double genuflections in the chapel, he would lower himself onto both knees, bow slowly forward until his forehead touched the floor, and remain prostrate for ages. On leaving Springwood, he gravitated naturally to Christ Church St Lawrence in the city, the reputed sanctuary for men fascinated by the trappings of worship such as vestments and incense.

Tony was close to a coterie of like-minded seminarians who dwelt on the fringes of the student body and mixed in their own crowd. He was friendly with a lanky, thin, pale student, famous for his collection of Vatican stamps. Another member of the group experienced the excitement of a vision of the Blessed Virgin which had occurred one dark night as he was sitting on the toilet in St Columba's shower block. George Joiner had not been impressed!

At one stage in my later years, I became friendly with a rather sulky, curly-haired student from the Glebe. He had worked as a bank clerk in various country districts before Bishop John Norton of Bathurst broke his golden rule of accepting only Irish priests for his diocese, and agreed to send him to the seminary. For a while we were close friends, though I cannot think what we had in common, apart from our divine vocation. He was older than myself, worldly-wise, sophisticated in his modern taste for Coca-Cola and clothing, and a constant inhaler of Craven 'A's. Perhaps it was these last characteristics which I found attractive. He was always his own man, and had survived on his own as a city boy in lonely country towns. He was not interested in projecting a sporting image, or in popularity. He was rather too ill-tempered, too petulant, too self-sufficient to be popular, and in maintaining a cool aloofness, he radiated a certain hauteur among the ranks. But we were friends, even 'pfs' – until a blunt, artless student, loudmouthed his accusations of being particular friends. This bulldozer was no prefect, not being one of the most docile of students. But he was a direct communicator, and the disease of friendship was a matter of public importance.

For some reason which I did not then understand, a reason more disturbing and threatening than breaking the college rules, I took fright. Despite my innocence and ignorance, I must have felt unconsciously that in the circumstances, friendships were dangerous and best avoided. No more walking together. No more talk about our families. I withdrew into a cold, formal, clerical world. In hindsight, I must have wounded him by my sudden response to those cruel, confronting remarks. Though later we sometimes travelled together, even overseas with others, we were never close friends again.

Yet it was difficult to survive without friendship, even in the heady, ethereal atmosphere of the seminary. Just to know you were a little out of the ordinary for one or two others, seemed important. It was not possible to be the same angelic person to everyone. When God is meant to fill someone's life to the exclusion of close human contacts, to the exclusion of books, music, dancing, laughter, fun, and family, the God who appears is steely cold, distant, unsiphoned through a human face.

There was not much opportunity in our excessively regulated life for boys to become entangled in one another's company. Every moment of the day was dedicated to some activity. Our time was programmed, moment by moment, around prayer, study, manual work, bushwalks, meetings and regular short, brisk walks. By the end of the day, exhausted young men snuggled up alone in narrow single beds and slept until reawakened at 6.00 a.m. in the morning. At least this is my memory of my time at Springwood. We were active for almost every minute of the day. No devil's work for idle hands.

Sport and work were compulsory, and no excuse was tolerated. Every student, whether asthmatic, frail or centrefold, was obliged to swing an axe, root up trees, clear arid land or play sport, whether it be tennis, football, handball, rugby, Australian Rules, cricket, or hockey. Every afternoon, after the main midday meal, groups of students would rush from the dormitory in their sports clobber (known as BO clothes) covered with a tatty, torn cassock (a BO soutane), to make their way to the different sporting locations spread through the vast college grounds. Some of the more effeminate might pretend to play sport, or perhaps spend the afternoon in the bookbinding hut gossiping, but pity help them if the powers should find them out.

A safe distance between students could also be achieved not only with rules and prohibitions, but by isolating each student in a cocoon of silence for long periods throughout the day. When the periods of silence were added one to the other, the solemn silence from night prayers until after breakfast each morning, the meals taken in silence when public readings covered the noise of cutlery and plates, the afternoon and evening study periods, innumerable brief or prolonged visits to the chapel, the five or six hours spent in lectures each day, there remained a remnant of less than three hours for us to speak one to another. Even this period was broken up into more than one hour of sport when little creative human contact could occur, though there were short, rapid bursts of five or ten minutes here and there while students made their way from one silent activity to another. Love and faith were paramount, but friendship was suspect.

An outsider at an early age

I passed my first five years in the Springwood seminary preparing for my final secondary examination, the Leaving Certificate which was the forerunner of Higher School Certificate. I had become a minor cog in an ecclesiastical system. I was young, and keen to succeed, to become a priest, a holy priest.

I did not often join in the spontaneous and somewhat rebellious fun of many of the other boys. In my rather extreme seriousness and anxiety to please, I was not willing to fracture the solemn silence. I would not smuggle lollies or other contraband into my locker, whisper in the library during the silence of retreats, twist the rules, or nudge the clear boundaries of acceptable behaviour. I slotted naturally, almost immediately, into the disciplined, regulated life of a priestly aspirant and seemed to annoy others by my competitive spirit and by my over-zealous behaviour. I tended to be somewhat priggish, being too contained in chapel, too committed to running, to handball or tennis, and too intent on doing well in examinations. The seniors did not appreciate younger ones who could run in ahead of them in the cross-country, and older boys did not easily accept being beaten in examinations. They made me pay for my keenness but I did not understand the dynamics of what was happening.

Springwood was a silent, lonely place, at least for me. Some seemed to have fun, but not all. Many students endured teasing and a lonely isolation, or were foreigners in a crowd of young males. I was one of them. I was too serious to go with the flow and enjoy myself. The institution had collected different and differing young men from around New South Wales: slow, awkward, country boys, tough, athletic, muscly boys, scholarly boys (though not many) and dainty types who sat with their knees together. There were also larrikins, boys from poor families, sly, secretive, cheeky young men, neurotics, the super scrupulous and more complex characters. Everyone was welcomed at the feast, from byways, from under hedges.

My peers punished me for my immaturity and my over-eager anxiety to be included. For some years, I would be the last one selected in any pick-up team. Twenty or thirty boys might stand around in a group while two leaders, selected by popular acclaim, chose their soccer teams, or football teams, perhaps a cricket eleven. I remember the hurt of being the last chosen, of being 'deputised in' as goalie for the soccer, the last to bat late in the afternoon at the cricket, never bowling, fielding in the outfield in the hot paspalum grass on warm, summer afternoons amid the buzz of the bush flies and with the leg itch of long grass. Perhaps I expected too much of myself, and of others. Maybe I had no appreciation of my abilities. From being very important in my family and at school, I was now an odd number at the bottom of the pecking chain. I certainly had no experience in living in a large community – and no one to ease the burden of initiation.

I was chuffed when I ran in seventh in the annual six mile cross-country race. There had been a hundred or more competitors grinding round the course, and at the age of thirteen, I was the youngest. Many were over twenty, some more than thirty. We ran over the top field, across the cricket pitch, down to the Grotto of Our Lady, up hills, along the drive, round the ghost track, and around again. My slender frame passed lumbering groups of seniors. Few were as determined as I was.

I was the youngest seminarian at Springwood for several years. As I finished my first year and was automatically promoted to the next senior class, looking forward to the luxury of juniors below me, the next first year class did not make an appearance. The powers had mysteriously decided not to invite young boys to commit themselves to the celibate life at such a tender age. Perhaps the decision was forced by dwindling finances. The same happened the following year. As I completed a year, that class was cancelled, forever. The authorities obviously knew something I did not. The recommendations of the Council of Trent were finally under revision. Centuries of policy were being secretly jettisoned. The world was changing beneath me.

I was in my fourth year, before I was to enjoy a class of boys behind me and to peer down on them as my juniors. In the meantime, senior students of fourteen and fifteen, even members of my own class who were only a year or so older than myself, would keep me in my distant place. They would tease me or talk about me to others when I was present, as though I was absent, or refuse to walk or sit with me when I tagged along. I was determined not to let them know how I felt. There would be no display of weakness. They were hard days, and my responses were as staggering as a fresh born foal.

Five other boys began their first year of secondary studies with me. It was 1951. Bob Spackman, Tony Starr, Terry Hynes and myself were in short pants. Kevin English was a year or so older than me, taller, more worldly-wise with an older brother and sisters. Dennis was repeating his first year. He was considerably older than any of us, and maybe a little slow. He used to throw frequent, uncontrollable temper tantrums and seemed incapable of passing the simple subjects we were studying. Dennis was privileged to dress in a cassock even though he was just in his second year at Springwood. Over the Christmas holidays the all wise powers had decided that the new aspirants would start their training in civvies and advance to wearing clerical cassocks only when they had started in first year Philosophy. The authorities must have had their reasons. They knew more than us, but their reasons remained secret. Those in authority did not have to explain. Advancement to the black ecclesiastical cassock which covered a multitude of sins was something to look forward to, and in the meantime, one must show respect for those senior enough to be clothed in the sacred cloth.

The school

The brothers at Springwood were commissioned to teach Christian boys who were inspired to give their lives to God and his own, holy, Catholic Church. They were the pride of the order – disciplined, educated, talented teachers. And they had the blessing of small classes. I had come from a class of forty-six under the cane of Brother Baldy at Mosman, to a class of six boys. Those men, especially Brothers Gerard and Valerius gave me a love of books, a respect for learning and a thirst for knowledge.

The secondary education programme at Springwood was simple, and rather rudimentary when compared to today's standards. Every subject was compulsory, or almost. There were no electives, and no frills. I studied English, French, Latin, General Mathematics, History and Physics. A small, ill-equipped science laboratory was situated near our recreation hall, within smelling distance of the college septic system. The masonite shed contained a few sinks, three or four Bunsen burners, a set of precision scales which had never been adjusted for accuracy, and a shelf of flasks of varying sizes. This equipment was never used with any enthusiasm as none of us had plans to become scientists. We were on a different trajectory.

As students moved through the secondary course, the results showed that some could not cope with the French (though no exceptions were made for Latin), or Physics. These slower learners were reluctantly permitted to take up the study of Ancient History as a soft option in their last two years of school. I turned out to be sharp and quick in both mathematics and science and I was able to score in the high nineties in both subjects when I sat for the trial Leaving Certificate. Though I was not gifted in language, hard work paid some dividends.

Student numbers in our junior school were small. There were three teaching brothers, at times four, and our facilities too were limited. Those were the days before television, when tape recorders were a novelty. On the odd special occasion one of the brothers would organise the use of a tape recording device – a bulky square, heavy machine with large spools of tape to assist in our practice of French comprehension. Those like me who were gifted in mathematics, for example, were not able to follow the more advanced courses in mathematics I and II. Chemistry was not available, or biology or physiology. Our education was basic, but thorough.

1951 – Spackman, Geraghty, Hynes, Starr
Sherry, Bro. Gerald, English

School is school in whatever language or country, wherever one is. It lasts for years and is a painful, turgid process for nearly everyone. The muscly Brother Gerald was in charge of the small composite class of first and second years. He continued my earlier education in mathematics and English, and the other subjects, including religion, as if there wasn't already enough of it in the chapel. It was under his supervision that I continued to count, and learn to spell. Six first year boys turned up each morning for his classes. I was the keenest. I had been infected with the need to excel.

I am not sure where this powerful urge had come from. My father had always been anxious for his children to succeed, and was so proud when I did. I wanted to be first, and this was a taxing burden as my fellow students were all older than me, more canny, more knowing. Though perhaps not Terry, who seemed even younger in his head than me. He was still collecting holy cards and swapping them as boys later came to swap baseball, football or telephone cards. All six of us in first year followed the same subjects. There was no choice for us in the fifties. My whole education, through to my doctorate studies, was over before elective subjects became available. I did not need the soft option of Ancient History in my final Leaving Certificate year. I was competent in French and Latin, in Physics and mathematics. While I was not an exceptional or gifted student, I knew I was above average and I had faith that hard work would bring its rewards.

Brother Gerald began drilling me in Latin declensions and conjugations, like I had been drilled in primary school with the Maths tables. With the aid of Kelly's Latin grammar, I worked my way slowly through the four verb conjugations, and the five noun declensions, translating simple passages at first, about Caesar's Gallic wars, gradually gaining both confidence and expertise as the years passed. There were Livy's stories about Hannibal leading elephants across the Alps to invade Italy. Later I deciphered Virgil's interminable poem on bees (*the Georgic IV*). I worked hard, and strove to impress. French was also compulsory. I mastered the grammar and texts, but I never really managed to converse well. I was too shy to reproduce the awkward, funny sounds. I was too controlled, too deliberate, and there comes a stage in learning a language, or playing tennis, or making friends, when over-striving destroys the rhythm, tenses the muscles, erects barriers and produces mediocre results.

Besides our many daily chapel activities, we also followed a compulsory religion course, reading our way studiously through Michael Sheenan's *Apologetics and Christian Doctrine* and studying a Reader's Digest-type book which presented a potted history of the Catholic Church, though not of the whole Catholic Church, only of the Roman Catholic Church in a revised, establishment modern version, rather than the true history, warts and all. At least I had left behind the rote learning of questions and answers from the green catechism.

As a schoolboy, I was over-serious and self-conscious, and dreaded making a fool of myself even in front of such an intimate class. Try as I might, I sometimes set myself up for a mocking outburst of laughter. As for example, when I asked Brother Gerald to show me on the map where Christendom was. While the others knew the word was a noun to describe the collective body of Christians throughout the world, I did not. And there was much else I did not know. I remember informing Michael Kelly, who was one of the glorious seniors and a trusty prefect, that my father worked as a stevedore on the waterfront. He laughed at what I had told him, and laughed again at my embarrassment. He realised Dad was a waterside worker, a wharfie who worked in a gang with other wharfies for our daily bread. I had been caught trying to pretend that my father had a more important position than he did, trying to impress. Stevedoring was grander than labouring for a living, or so I thought then.

Mathematics gave me a chance to excel. Because I was quick and gifted, my teacher encouraged me to make my own pace. I ploughed my way through chapter after chapter of the textbook, glorying in being weeks ahead of the field. Brother Geoffrey used to take a special class of mathematics in the library in the year when I was preparing for my intermediate examination. I was fifteen years old. We would sit facing one another, books open, with scribble paper at the ready, while I worked out the answers in my head, a hundred at a sitting. Later, in fourth and fifth years, I used to amuse myself poring over geometrical or algebraic problems, searching for the solutions. Mathematics allowed me to show my colours and my teacher took a special interest, for reasons which I later learnt might not have been purely academic, though he never gave me any reason to be suspicious.

Brother Gerard, the brother superior, was one of the 'ancient of days', and a crack Latin teacher. He came packaged with peculiar mannerisms developed over years and was well into his seventies. He used to press his tongue into the side of his swollen cheek, beat his foot rhythmically on the wooden floor and his arthritic index finger in the palm of his other hand, while he recited Ovid, Horace or Virgil, teaching us to scan hexameter-pentameter verse, though never really succeeding.

Old Brother Gerard adopted the same stance while he recited Shakespeare to us. *Julius Caesar* and *Wuthering Heights* were set texts for the English course in my final year. The books were compulsory. We could make no selection from a wide range of authors as there was only one English course which everyone in New South Wales had to study. Brother Gerard (known as 'Bopper') would hitch the frayed black cord of his religious habit higher around his paunchy waist, gather chalk dust on the shoulders of his black habit, and occasionally lose his cool in his attempt to introduce dull afternoon students to the language and flow of a Shakespearean play. The intimate, smouldering relationships in *Wuthering Heights* involved passions and juices that I could hardly imagine. It is strange to think of my compact world at Springwood, full of prayer and pure spiritual longings, being invaded each afternoon by Heathcliffe and Catherine, with people tormented with jealousy, uncontrollable lust, with anger and violent outbursts of passion.

But my first steps in Latin, French, English, mathematics and history were guided by Brother Gerald, a young, nuggety, athletic religious, who was responsible for launching six aspirants to the priesthood on their educational journey. Later, at St Joseph's College, Hunter's Hill, he earned the nickname of 'God' because of his inflexibility, his authority and punishing power. He was also called 'Greaser' because of his olive complexion. He was tough and exceptionally disciplined, and eventually became coach of St Joseph's top first-grade rugby team, and of the senior eights in rowing. In those early days at Springwood, Brother Gerald seemed so old and capable, but I now realise that ours was his first class. He was not much older than twenty-one, just out of training, inexperienced, and not someone really to be feared.

Gerald found me difficult as he ploughed his way through Latin grammar, or explained the intricacies of *The Merchant of Venice*. I was too bold and pushy for my age. He found me bumptious, and somewhat discourteous. I presented a challenge to his authority and, though in the fifties the cane was used frequently in religious schools throughout the state, no caning was tolerated at Springwood. We were good boys, training for a noble, heavenly vocation and the cane seemed somehow inappropriate.

How then to punish an insolent young aspirant and bring him to heel? Though I sometimes spent wasted hours facing the back corner of the classroom, public humiliation was better avoided. He would also glare, and mock, even threaten. His method of control was successful in the end as I acquired some interest in learning. I bless a couple of my religious teachers for my continuing enthusiasm for books and ideas. Old Brother Gerard stands out as one who had a lasting influence on my life. He was a true scholar, and it was clear even then that he loved teaching and valued learning. As a young boy, I understood that he took pride in his work. His eyes would shine with delight as he read to us the poems of Horace or Virgil. He was excited by the language of Shakespeare, keen to unravel the plot and explore the complex characters. Sharing his knowledge and his joy for discovery was his life, and I was privileged to sit at his feet.

Some of the brothers used to like to referee our violent Rugby League contests, which were held on Thursday mornings, although there were shorter games in the afternoons on other weekdays, before the study period. When I was in my fourth and fifth years, one of the brothers who used to referee games and train our college team, began to take a flattering interest in me. He advised me how to train, how to build muscle bulk, increase my strength and endurance. Even though my class was small, he supervised my study programme in European history – the causes of the First World War, the Treaty of Versailles, the unification of Germany and Italy, Cavour, Garibaldi, Metternich, Bismarck. He was so warmly encouraging that I was honoured, and the others began to imagine I was the teacher's pet. My energy and youthful enthusiasm for sport and study might have been uncommon in the professional life of a teacher. But he was always proper, always appropriately distant, always the one in charge, my teacher, always the religious brother.

Some few years after he had left St Columba's and the Marist community, the ex-brother wrote me a long letter and sent a tape (one of those bulky, brown tapes on a plastic spool) filling me in on his wanderings around Australia. To my amazement he confessed that he had been attracted to me. It was a surprise, though I did not fully comprehend at first what he meant, or what his intentions were in writing to me. I read the letter and put the tape away after I had played it. I never discussed their contents with anyone – not with friends (except perhaps Lex Levey) or my family, or with my spiritual director. I was puzzled, flattered, and a little amused. I was somehow aware that he must have travelled through difficult times, that he was sentenced to endure a lonely, painful, secret journey. Wherever we are, danger surround us. Our journey, our future, our hopes, our lives are fragile, and always in peril. But at least on this occasion I was basically unmoved. I was on my own lonely path.

The brothers used to attend our crowded chapel each morning for mass. Brothers Gerard, Gerald, Geoffrey, Gregory, Valerius, Kevin (in groups of three and four throughout my five years of secondary training) would sit or kneel at the back of the chapel, in stalls on the left-hand side, wrapped up warmly in their serge habits, entering and leaving noiselessly, like phantoms in their black capes. Brothers Valerius and Kevin took turns as the resident choir master. From time to time, one or other would pace up and down the chapel aisle, conducting the Gregorian chant, inspiring us to heights of angelic delight as we practised, over and over, a *Kyrie*, a *Sanctus*, the special rhythms of an *Introit* or Communion verses, the *Dies Irae* or the special Pentecost *Veni Sancte Spiritus*. As the senior brother, Brother Gerard occupied the front stall at the back of the chapel. All of a sudden, my whole world seemed to be arranged in seniority. He sat or knelt in his fraternal cassock, his shoulders covered with an ample black cape. I too occupied the front bench for many years, but at the top of the chapel, just off the marble sanctuary, where all the juniors were herded and isolated from the senior pray-ers. There was no logic in where we were sitting, merely the tyranny of rules.

Though I was a gun barrel length of the chapel away from Brother Gerard, I knew that he followed the daily mass devotedly with the aid of his precious *Missale Romanum*. A few of the more senior students also buried their noses in a Latin missal, while the others, including myself, handled a missal with English on one side of the page and Latin on the other. We followed the Latin mass, mostly at a racing pace, from the English text. Brother Gerard needed no such linguistic assistance. It was incomprehensible that someone would be able to follow and understand the Latin texts in the missal.

I was content with my fat bilingual missal with its imitation black leather cover and red edges, which my parents had purchased at some expense from Pellegrini's, years before I went to Springwood. I had buried myself in it at the 6.45 a.m. weekday masses at Neutral Bay, always hurrying to keep up, but rarely succeeding. But as the years passed, I hankered after a genuine *Missale Romanum* of my own. They were imported from Vatican publishers in Italy and, at about one pound fifteen shillings (the modern equivalent of perhaps one hundred dollars) they were too dear for my shallow pocket. Although my parents had agreed with Norman Cardinal Gilroy to pay a modest fee for my board, it was a burden on a working-class family of six. I was miserly in buying writing paper, toothpaste, even soap. The *Missale Romanum* was a luxury which was well out of my reach.

Some years later, while I was still at Springwood, I purchased a Latin missal, one with bright red edging rather than the more expensive, gold-leafed edition. I was aware, perhaps too conscious of the need to be frugal. As a wharf labourer, my father earned a modest, varying weekly pay packet, accepting all available morning, afternoon, even midnight shifts and as much overtime as was on offer. In his spare time, he marked lawn tennis courts during the weekend and tidied gardens for extra family income. He was also well known to the flamboyant Bishop Muldoon at Mosman where he did the episcopal gardening each week.

My mother continued to slave as a waitress and cleaner at Hazelhurst, the private hotel which was just a short walk each evening down the hill from home. She used to cook our evening meal which we ate together, early and rapidly, and then, while my father tidied up and washed the dishes, my mother would race to the scullery at Hazelhurst for two hours. Some nights I would go down to meet her and walk her home. Mum also had a limited clientele of wealthy women who engaged her and her friend Edna Hilton, to visit their homes, prepare a party or a formal meal, and serve the family and their guests. She was energetic, and keen to contribute to our limited family finances.

So my father and mother both scratched and scrubbed to support us. They paid Fred Patten a rent of thirty shillings each week. It was not much. The house was blest with a protected tenancy, so silly old Fred could not raise his rent without the agreement of the Rental Board, which was known to be on the side of the worker, not the landowner. Over the years in Florence Street, our reasonable rent slowly became more and more attractive, which must have been the reason my father could not bring himself to buy a house – at least until he had retired and moved to Manyana, where he paid cash for his new home.

So I began to chase the daily celebrant through my Latin missal, turning pages, flipping coloured ribbons, understanding a little of what I was skimming, struggling to keep up as he raced through the readings and prayers.

The ogre

Our seminary timetable was arranged on the European model. Saturday was an ordinary, working day, full of lectures and study. Sunday was a day of rest and prayer, of longer periods of meditation. We woke half an hour later. There was a quick mass at seven thirty, a solemn high mass with Gregorian chant and organ music at nine thirty, and vespers sung at the melancholy hour of five thirty in the evening.

Thursdays were dedicated to bush picnics and sport. These included the annual athletics carnival and regular football matches. One could also spend a full, tedious day of cricket on the top field if one was not careful, or if one was too agreeable to refuse. In summer, when the bush flies groaned and the cicadas sang, crowds of seniors and juniors passed Thursday mornings and afternoons swimming in the chilled waters of the weir, down in the valley, sunbaking on mountain rocks to the sound of bush birds and the silent movement of snakes and geckoes. But as juniors, we were not supposed to fraternise with the seniors, even at the weir. Trusted senior prefects were commissioned to remain vigilant to supervise our recreation. There were prayers at the beginning of the Thursday routine, and prayers and study at the end. But in between, pushing, running, hitting, much puffing and sweat.

In 1955, I passed sleepy Sunday and Thursday afternoons in August, September, October, practising my mathematics, and revisiting the underlined pages of Robert's *Modern History*, going over Virgil and Livy one more time. I was too keen for my own good. As the band of Marist brothers prepared me and others for the Leaving Certificate, we all grew tense. Days grew longer, and hotter. The constant buzz of bush flies could be heard in the study. Even those who had been slow to study before, began to bury their faces in books. My results were four As and two Bs. Not bad. Enough for a Commonwealth scholarship to the university.

But before I presented myself for my Leaving Certificate examination, I had visited Monsignor Dunne on the first floor. One windy evening, somewhat nervously, I made my way up the stairs to his lair. I reminded him I was sitting for my public examination in a month or so, and announced that I wanted to apply for a Commonwealth scholarship. Those were the days when tertiary education in Australia was not free for all. While most students were required to pay fees, the Commonwealth Government used to finance the education of those students whose parents could pass a restricted income test and who scored a certain level of pass in the examination. The level was not too high, and I expected to surpass it.

I do not now remember what was on my mind. It could not have been anything very cunning or secretive. I was not plotting to leave the seminary. Perhaps I wanted all my options to remain open, other choices to be available. At least that was what Charlie thought. Maybe I wanted to reconsider my future if I scored results which entitled me to a scholarship. At least I could keep other possibilities on ice for some years, just in case Springwood, Manly and my ecclesiastical aspirations did not work out.

The monsignor was standing behind his desk in his red-piped soutane, breathing rather heavily, slowly smoking a cigarette which he had rolled in a Zig-Zag rice paper from Ready-Rubbed tobacco. His room was shadowy and pungent with tobacco smoke, his chubby fingers stained with nicotine. He was a large, powerful figure of a man, with a ruddy complexion, and red, unruly hair. He was overweight, silent, and threatening, a figure of absolute authority who needed no advice, no second opinion. He expected every muttered, whispered command to be obeyed without question. He listened to me attentively and said, 'No.' He gave no explanation. No questions were asked. He did not enquire what was on my mind, and I did not ask for any reason for his refusal. There was simply no discussion. I can only assume God's representative did not want me to have an alternative to seminary education up my sleeve. There would be no escape hatch, no temptation to lure me away from my goal. He had assessed that I was well-suited to my chosen path. There were to be no distractions. I accepted, without question, this decision of my superior and proved myself the docile student.

Charlie Dunne liked me. He also liked my father, and my little sister, Colleen. Perhaps he appreciated my naive directness. It was clear he expected me to be honest, not duplicitous, with him. I was always in awe of him, but unlike many of the other boys, I did not stand in trembling fear of him. Even as a young boy, I would look him clear in the eye while accepting his correction if I had breached a college rule. This monsignor was a dictator (most of them were). He used to play on the fears and neuroses of vulnerable students, and seemed to enjoy his little games. He was capricious and threatening like Matthew Arnold's nineteenth-century headmaster at Rugby. He was omnipotent, and likely to appear anywhere, anytime, without warning. But he did not frighten me, and never treated me unfairly. The other members of staff did not seem to like me, but Charlie did not share their opinion.

On one occasion, after playing tennis in the rain with Michael Bach and Joe Giles (an activity expressly forbidden by rule), Charlie carpeted the three of us. We were in deep trouble. Charlie welcomed every opportunity to press his seminarians into subjection. I informed him the rain had in fact stopped before we had left the college building and that it had started again only when we were some way through the first set. We were in trouble anyway, and we were all punished. However, the monsignor paid me a compliment which I now remember. He said he believed what I told him and accepted I would not deceive him. I was flattered. He may also have been wrong.

Nevertheless, he was a fearful character. On one occasion, in his monsignorial regalia, he met Kevin English in the corridor. He closed his breviary slowly and breathed at him. 'Did you get my message?' 'What message, Father?' Kevin replied. 'Did you get my message?' The monsignor breathed more heavily, through his red, hairy nostrils. 'What message, Father?' 'Mr English, did you get my message?' Charlie heaved at this fifteen-year-old student. 'Yes Father', Kevin eventually replied. Of course, he had never received any message. He did not know what on earth the rector was speaking about, yet he was too nervous and too overawed to say 'No' to the man.

I did not realise then that the monsignor was strange, that he was (to be blunt about this) a little mad. I was almost sixty before a flash of insight struck and I began to peer into the soul of the monster. He was able to engender fear in the breast of any seminarian, and also in the staff, though they were adults and ordained. He seemed to derive satisfaction, even glee in his power to elicit dread. When he was away in Sydney, a dancing, laughing mood of joy would come over students and staff. But when he was among us, his presence overshadowed all. Students were terrorised by the lazy wave of his fat, freckled hand, by his silent stare, his impatient grunt and by the whiff of tobacco which preceded his appearance. They shuddered at his slow, deliberate drawing in and expulsion of breath. He was the avenging, fearful god-figure in the mountains.

Our daily life was governed by a crawl of prefects. They were the routine eyes and ears of our monsignor. They mingled with their fellow students, eating, praying, and playing with them, observing, recording,

Monsignor Charles Dunne

judging, and controlling. Having once identified a student or clique of students who were offending the rule, whispering in the corridor, giggling in chapel, walking with hands in their pockets, arriving late for class, neglecting to answer the bell immediately, failing to rise at the first sound of the bell or talking after night prayers, they would order the offenders to report to the dean of discipline. If the offence was major, to the grand monsignor himself.

The authorities appointed serious, responsible young men to these positions of power. It was a privilege to be chosen – God's work was advanced by their wonderful service. The divine institution of the Church depended on how they performed. They were God's thought-police in our midst. Charlie Dunne and his cohort of prefects paid special attention to the control of food within the college. Food could be accessed only in the food hall or refectory, and was restricted by harsh prohibition elsewhere in the college.

Like any prison or boarding school, food was a valuable commodity at Springwood and in short supply. The giant refrigerators and freezers containing carcasses of hard beef, crates of oranges, hooks heavy with fat sausages, and the institutional pantry of stale bread and plain biscuits, flour, rice, salt, sugar, were double-padlocked, against thieving students. The head nun carried keys jangling from her leather belt, fighting for attention alongside her black rosary beads. Occasionally, when Mother Therese would forget to secure the food, some courageous and unscrupulous priestly aspirant would raid the supplies and escape with half a chicken or some arrowroot biscuits, or a pocketful of green apples. The rector would then appear in the chapel, rumble to the marble sanctuary, within striking range of where I was sitting. He would attempt to intimidate the student body into giving up the thief and to force the guilty one into confessing. We all shook in our pews. 'Privileges' would be forfeited, perhaps the next film evening might be jeopardised, or silence might be imposed during meals, on a major feast day, or a bush picnic would be cancelled. Of course, no one ever owned up.

There were at least three other ways of acquiring a cache of food apart from swift raids under cover of darkness: one could stock up illegal supplies of lollies and chocolates when on the annual bus picnic to Katoomba or when one went on the monthly bush picnic in parties of ten students and a prefect, and walked towards the lookout, past the corner store at North Springwood. Some adventurous boys would even escape on Thursday afternoons from the pigsty area. They would crawl under the barbed wire fence through the bush out onto the road and visit the shop for supplies, aware that if sprung, they would be on the train home. They would never fulfil their spiritual potential and reach the pinnacle of supernatural success. It was a terrible price to pay for a packet of Minties or twenty Ardath cork-tipped cigarettes.

Twice each semester, we were permitted to welcome visitors and to entertain them on the top field, or in the classrooms if it happened to be raining on that particular Sunday.

> *Students shall be allowed to receive visitors from their immediate relations at the appointed times and in the public reception rooms. [Rule 17 (a)]*

My parents used to travel to Springwood by train and then to the college by bus, unless Dad could persuade Donald Grassick's father, or Mr Pidcock from Reid Street to drive the family into the mountains for the day. They would arrive laden with cakes and lollies, baked chicken, homemade biscuits and fizzy drinks. The feast would be spread out on one of the rough bush tables around the field of sticky paspalum and we would fill in a few family hours until 3.30 p.m. eating, talking, walking to the grotto or through the bush to the lookout, lying on tartan rugs and brushing flies away from food and face. This was a small concession by the ecclesiastical institution to the demands of familial piety.

Though I was too nervous or conscientious to offend, many boys would take the opportunity to stock up. They would return to the dormitory laden heavily with sweets, chocolate bars, Life Savers, a fruitcake – whatever could be hidden under cassocks and secreted at the bottom of boot-boxes or under the bottoms of chests of drawers.

But the annual Manly football day was the best time to replenish supplies. Clergy, young and very old, turned up at St Columba's from around the state. Tall and thin, fat, cranky, extremely pious, larrikins, loafers, weary ex-footballers who knew everything, and those stricken with infallibility, all came. They rolled in from Wilcannia, or Hay, Glen Innes, Bathurst, Burke, or Wagga Wagga. All descended on Springwood in their clerical gear to watch the Manly men in red play and sometimes even pulverise the opposition. Occasionally the reds would be beaten by the Springwood boys in blue, but only very occasionally. We seminarians were mostly dressed in long cassocks, though for my first two years, I was out of place in my short pants, and for a further two years, I was in grey long pants and lumber-jacket. The men from Manly came in buses, in black suits, black ties over white shirts, and black hats. We would mingle, and gaze at an ugly game of brutal Rugby League, the workingman's game, refereed by a senior grey clergyman with white, hairless, spindly legs in shorts. We observed students for the priesthood pushing, puffing, heaving, bullying, and wrestling others to the ground. While I watched in amazement, the experienced clergy and the worldly Manly men, led by the deep-throated Bull Muldoon, would shout and barrack.

After the annual conflict had been resolved, we shouldered into the refectory, squeezed into a seat somewhere, and feasted together. It was an occasion for lolly water and roast – no sausages or mince meat! We were spared the daily reading of the martyrology. I sat quietly and observed. The clergy were away from their parishes, off the leash, unscrutinised for the day, able to drink, shout and generally misbehave, but not so as to scandalise the young.

The day concluded with solemn benediction in a crowded, overflowing chapel sweetened with incense and brightened with an array of many flickering candles. The Manly choir performed. We had heard of its fame and they never disappointed. They could sing polyphony without stutter or quaver. Manly Day was an occasion for old friends, jokes, laughter, memories and mateship. But not all of us had been sufficiently initiated into the clerical club to participate, except on the fringes. Some of us knew no one except those in our junior class and the seminary priests who mixed around and played host.

Before the great day, a list of the names of the Manly men circulated from classroom to classroom, passed on from one student to the next, in strict seniority, as each of us chose his companion for the day. Of course the senior boys at Springwood knew at least the junior men at Manly and so had a basis for choice. They would know whom to select, and perhaps even more importantly, whom to pass over. But for some years I knew no one at Manly, though even if I had, there would have been no point. I was so low down on the list, I had no choice by the time the names reached me. Most students were already paired for the day and I scored some unknown, faceless senior, a deacon from Western Australia, appropriately named John Challis. This was in my first year at Springwood when I was a raw foal.

So the Reverend Challis was doomed to be entertained by an unknown twelve-year-old seminarian. He stepped out of the bus wearing his black gear and a Roman collar. He had a shy, angelic expression below a head of blond hair. He was the dux of Manly, a gifted budding scholar. But I was only concerned with the extent of the booty he had brought. Challis came loaded with Cadbury chocolates, Fantails, Jaffas and Minties for his anonymous companion. The day would be a success, though we did not spend much time in useless conversation. I was more like a baby altar boy, a cub scout, a ball boy following him about, chewing sweets, while he exchanged serious talk with grown-ups.

Against my angelic instincts, I smuggled some leftover Challis goodies into the bottom drawer of my dormitory lowboy, and hoped I would not be caught. Some days later, at the Sunday morning rector's conference, Monsignor Dunne turned on us in the chapel, blood pressure on the boil, hot air filtering through ginger nostril hair, and demanded the surrender of all contraband:

> *Students have been seen chewing. You all know, and have been told often enough, that food is forbidden except as provided in the refectory. Many of you have been disobedient. You are flouting the college rules. Some have abused the special privilege of Manly Day and kept food for themselves. They are selfish, mean-spirited, unworthy and rebellious* (these words were each uttered with a heavy breath as Charlie pulled on the corner of his crimson cape). *If they persist, they should not be here in the seminary. I have been persuaded to give these greedy boys one last chance. A washing basket will be placed outside the door of my room. I expect anyone who has unlawfully kept any foodstuffs, to deposit all of it in the basket within the next twenty-four hours and no further action will be taken. If any student is found with food or sweets after next Tuesday, he will be expelled immediately. I hope that is clear.*

I was shocked. Offenders like me rushed to the basket outside the rector's office. The official threat and ultimatum filled the container to overflowing – tins, packets, loose lollies, chocolate bars, a few fruitcakes. It was an impressive haul, surely beyond the expectations of the rector. For some mysterious reason, the basket contained twelve or more tins which were unlabelled – just shiny, silver containers which were unidentifiable. I learnt later that one of the guilty students, in delivering up his booty, had soaked the labels off the tins so that the authorities who would undoubtedly enjoy the benefit of the confiscated contraband, would not know when opening a tin, whether they were going to enjoy peaches or pears, spaghetti or sausages, sauerkraut or perhaps strawberry jam. I also found out later that some free-enterprising seminarians had taken the unprecedented opportunity of visiting the basket in the dead of night and replenishing their private supplies. Instead of depositing their own illegals, they relieved the basket of whatever they found too tempting. Despite their vocations being on the line, they would undoubtedly make good religious leaders.

Something else was surprising. The trustworthy Michael Bach and our mutual friend Joe Giles had not surrendered their cache of goodies. They had not sought the benefit of the amnesty. Instead they moved their contraband to a safer place. Joe and Michael had shown some interest in bee keeping, and were often seen down near the orchard where there was a suburb of beehives, with working bees landing and taking off throughout the day. None of us was sufficiently observant to notice that one hive was unoccupied. No bees laden with Hawkesbury honey were landing on its threshold, or disappearing inside to flatter and pay homage to the queen bee. One dwelling in the suburb remained vacant. Every day, many times, groups of students would walk up and down, within metres of the Bach and Giles treasure. They had secreted their valuable goodies in a beehive, away from the suspicion of the proletariat and the powers.

At the end of term, before we rushed from the college for our summer holidays, Charlie summoned Bob Lawler to his den and, without comments, returned all the tins from which he had removed the labels. Bob picked them up from the floor and withdrew in confusion.

No one ever found out how Charlie had traced the label-less tins to Bob. His spy network must have been outstanding.

Classes and more prayers

THE COLLEGE LAYOUT

Our classrooms were located along two parallel sides of the college quadrangle. Visitors used to enter the imposing two-storey, sandstone building, go up a few stone steps, and pass through an arch beneath the belltower into a vestibule which was in the shape of a hexagon and which contained four heavy stone urns perched on four opposing recesses cut into the fresh, smooth stone walls. The urns were empty. From there our visitors could enter the central quadrangle. The building was constructed of heavy blocks of clean, golden sandstone which had been quarried on the property. Offices, clergy sleeping quarters, an ample priests' common room from which I sometimes heard muffled conversations and laughter as I waited nervously to report some misdemeanour to the dean of discipline, were all situated on the upper level. All the dormitories were also on that same floor, except Paradise which was an isolated area for twelve or so trusted students, on a third level, up a narrow, wooden stairway and immediately under the belltower.

The was no bell in the college tower. It was simply a lookout, high up over the entrance to the building, with a view on all sides out over the ridges and valleys. The tower was forbidden territory. Those who pushed up through the covered entrance, who penetrated the enclosure of

Paradise, out into the vast space beyond, were probably committing a mortal sin. Charlie was always impressively displeased whenever he caught one of his subjects in *flagante delicto*. On an odd occasion, only once or twice, I flouted temptation, ignored the voice of reason, and climbed into the copper-covered space on high where I could see my world spread out below the lush, ordered quadrangle, straight down; the boiler room, the laundry, the chook yards over at the back; the beehives, the rose gardens, the Twin gums and rust-coloured drive down the slope to the college gates in the distance. The settlement was plum in the middle of a grey, green carpet of trees as far as the eye could see. Space to the north as far as the Grose River, to the west up to Katoomba, and Sydney to the east as far as the bridge on a clear day. The tower dominated the landscape. It would act as a beacon to guide us home through the scrub, along the ridges on bush picnic days. It would be a strategic lookout to spot fires in the distance.

Down below, flowing out from the back of the building, winding through the gum trees and undergrowth was a rough, native path we knew as 'the ghost-track'. It was sometimes ill-treated by hot, dusty winds, or frosted over in the morning mists. At night it was crowded with praeternatural figures, by shadowy, threatening ghosts, or illuminated by a full moon, or silent like a dark brown snake under a twinkling array of bright stars.

On the ground level of the main building was located a large refectory for eating, a crowded chapel for praying, several classrooms for learning, and an extended assembly hall which was for most of the year divided into several other classrooms. But the partitions could be removed to open up a splendid hall with Gothic leadlight windows. The end of year prize-giving, marked by solemn speeches from the rector and the cardinal, and polyphony from the choir, all took place in this hall. Occasional dignitaries were also welcomed there.

The interior quadrangle was bordered by a cloister which was enclosed by a series of sandstone arches and columns, on both levels. On the upper floor there was a protective railing, whereas the columns and arches on the ground floor were open. The cloister echoed with the clatter of leather shoes on a smooth, red, polished cement paving. The grassed space inside the quadrangle was set a metre or so below the level of the

Aerial view of St Columbas College

Front view of College

The interior quadrangle

cloister and was divided by intersecting pathways. In the centre a white statue of Our Lady Help of Christians stood high on a pedestal. It was eventually surrounded by four leafy, green, rotund port wine magnolias. These were planted on the nearest corner of each of the four, grassed squares, and grew strong during my period of internship. When I arrived in 1951 they were just slender, delicate seedlings, but over the years I noticed them producing flowers and heavy perfume, nectar for the bees, grow into thick bushes, then sturdy trees where blue wrens and willy wagtails used to play.

One side of the quadrangle (the one which looked down across the bushland to the city) was open to the weather and the red pathway along that side was often soaked after rain. There was no second storey on that fourth side, only trestle beams through which thick vines of wisteria twined, bloomed purple in spring, and hung down overhead like bunches of grapes, heavy with wine. The college building, set in its mountain isolation, amid the buzz of bees and blowflies, was sandstone solid and stable, removed from the world, self-sufficient and a symbol of lasting authority.

A SPECIAL KIND OF TERTIARY EDUCATION

After five years under the brothers' tuition, armed with my results in the Leaving Certificate, I entered first Philosophy where we were joined by the Specials Latin class. This included old fellows like Lex Levey, Pat Martin, Brian Pearce, John Tinkler, Laurie O'Neill and others, and a herd of new, innocent teenagers who had arrived from country towns and city parishes of New South Wales. I was on my way. I was one of the old, established boys in a class of fifty-four aspirants.

We were a virgin corps of newcomers and old hands. Some of us were prissy and pious, some lost and friendless, some untrained in the niceties of community living, some self-centred and spoilt, some rough, uncouth lads. Most were simply rawboned, awkward young Aussie men from loyal Catholic parents, anxious to play football or cricket, to avoid thinking, loving to muck up, ready, like the Anzacs, to toe the party line, to sacrifice their manhood for a noble cause.

I purchased some new exercise books and a ream of white paper from the college store. It was run by one of the students (the econome) who was allowed to go into the village every Thursday to purchase soap, ink, toothpaste and other goodies – all ordered by us and itemised in our personal accounts. I bought a brand new fountain pen, second-hand textbooks, including a two-volume work on scholastic philosophy in Latin, written by the Jesuit, Carolus Boyer, and published in Rome, and an elementary grammar for Greek New Testament. With these I launched myself enthusiastically on a new phase of my career – two years study of Philosophy and other ecclesiastical subjects, at Springwood, with the third and final year of Philosophy to be completed at St Patrick's Seminary, Manly.

In retrospect, the Springwood Philosophy course was a serious waste of time. Two years spent learning little of any lasting significance. As I reflect on those critical years in my education, I feel waves of anger and loss arising in me. Father Noel Carroll, who for a time also doubled as bursar of the college, tried half-heartedly to teach us some titbits of the history of Ancient Egypt, Rome and Greece, but it was difficult as he hardly knew anything about the subject. He invariably arrived late for our class with his mind preoccupied with other problems – the sewerage system, the proportion of stale to fresh bread for the next meal, the meat order which had failed to arrive, the dairy, the golf club.

As soon as Noel arrived in the classroom, he would let loose a river of words, slavishly based on some out-of-date Ancient History textbook. His lectures were pockmarked with inaccuracies and exaggerations and interwoven with stories of Ireland and the priestly life modelled on Bing Crosby. We heard about clergy golf days, or eccentric, clerical characters like Monsignor Tom Wallace of Darlinghurst, the super-clerical Tosi brothers, or the mountainous Bill Clarke from Earlwood who could organise Marian processions or Holy Year pilgrimages like Alan Bond could arrange the America's Cup challenge or a subversive raid on his shareholders. He was so large that we had to open the double doors for him to enter the refectory. He couldn't climb out of his Buick without blowing the horn. Noel also tried to teach us a little Italian. It was only a little because he only knew a little. After we breezed past *'Come sta?'*, 'What is your name?', and *'Roma non fu fatta in un giorno'*, we moved on to the practical matter of hearing confessions in Italian, mainly because there were many Italian migrants in Australia in the fifties who were Catholics and obviously needed to go to confession. Many of them were Easter and Christmas believers.

Bryce Fraser remembers these Italian classes with appreciation. Pat Martin was also attentive and keen, as later events proved. After he had ceased as chaplain to the Australian airforce, married Margaret, begot two lovely girls and had retired from his cushy job with a pharmaceutical company, Pat began to sell furniture for his mate John Cootes, who had also left the priesthood and made his way in the world. His huge furniture warehouse was located in Western Sydney. It was patronised by a multicultural mix of Australians, including Italians, on whom Pat could try his limited Italian, although they spoke English infinitely better than he spoke Italian. But Pat was one of those happy, resourceful people who could create opportunities to exploit every skerrick of his education. Though he could not converse with his clients in their own language, he could hear their confessions! *Ultima confessione fu?* When was your last confession? Have you been blaspheming? How many times?' At Springwood, we had obviously been trained to think that the Italians had a scandalous habit of blaspheming. One would have to say this was an original way for a furniture salesman to entice someone to purchase a bed or filing cabinet, but it was very successful. He was always primed and ready to draw on his life-experiences.

Pat was always a mad football fan. For example, when he was employed as a bank johnny in the bush, before his conversion to Springwood, he sometimes had to work on Saturday mornings. If Clive Churchill was playing for South Sydney that weekend, he would charter a light plane, fly to Bankstown after work, listen to the first half of the match on the taxi radio on his way to the oval, and arrive at the match to watch in awe as his hero played the second half. But when South Sydney descended into the doldrums, Pat transferred his fanatical patronage to the Sea Eagles at Manly and would attend their matches every week, no matter what. Storms would certainly not stop him, or even weddings. He was committed and his devotion knew no limits.

On one occasion, accompanied by his wife Margaret and some of their friends, he was watching Cliff Lyons play for the Eagles, when he heard a groan and saw a disturbance a few rows in front. A group of worried onlookers gathered round an elderly man who had collapsed. At half-time Pat wandered down the steps for a stickybeak and found the old gentleman lying on the ground, two daughters with him, waiting for a doctor. He did not look well. Pat enquired discreetly of one of the girls whether her father might be a Catholic, and when she told him he was, Pat half moaned under his breath, 'He bloody well would be', and began to burrow his way through the crowd. He announced that he was a priest, and without revealing that his wife was sitting a few rows back, he proceeded to minister to the dying. He moved straight back into his old role, dispensed a rapid, unsolicited absolution of sins, and climbed the few steps back to his wife and friends to continue abusing the referee. Pat had learnt his Italian well enough to use what he knew to his advantage. He had also absorbed a good deal of the other formation on offer in the seminary.

Dr George Joiner, a Jimmy Cagney-style cleric, doubled as the dean of discipline and our lecturer in Greek, Latin, and Psychology. He had grown up in the working-class suburb of Newtown, spent some years at Springwood as a humble student and because he was considered bright, had completed his education to doctoral level in Rome. George had a sharp, one-dimensional mind, showing no regard for scholarship, no love of books, no empathy with students. His attitude to learning seemed equivalent to any book-burning barbarian. Strange for a teacher!

A few of my class were skilled enough in Latin to participate in a special course in Cicero, so under George's supervision, we painstakingly translated *De Amicitia*. The class was conducted in the Physics laboratory which was near Jakes Gully. It was freezing in winter, a sauna bath in summer. George also taught Greek to all fifty-odd of us, but it was not a subject with which he was familiar, or one which attracted our attention. We slavishly followed the grammar, learning the alphabet, the tenses, the vocabulary, the declensions and conjugations, while George thundered about filling in the time. He was simply not interested in us. We realised, as teenagers so often do, that he was suffering the fifty minutes each day, longing to light up his Craven 'A' as soon as the bell rang. He wasted a golden opportunity.

George was a big, jowly man who used to pound up and down in front of the class in his serge cassock with heavy lumbering steps, unhappy to answer questions, pushing students to learn material which he did not like and they could not appreciate. We did not understand why we had to learn such an obscure and useless subject. Unlike Latin, Greek did not seem relevant to those whose principal aim in life was to be holy, practical parish priests. We had not been in contact with any scholarly, educated clergy, and we were so far removed from any centre of learning. Things were not explained, just imposed.

Frs John Burnheim, G. Joiner, Bede Heather, Ted Shepherd, Charlie Dunne (Rector), Noel Carroll

George also taught a disgraceful course in Psychology. Not only did he lack interest but he seemed to regard the subject with contempt and managed to make the subject extremely tedious. He did not recommend any reading material and there were no set textbooks. George stood in front of the class with his own handwritten notes, slowly, painstakingly dictating, phrase by phrase, as we recorded his definitions. He described various parts of the brain, different physical human functions (including a rather restricted, summary version of the purely physical and chemical aspects of the origins of life) and other useless material. His attempts to deal with the mechanics of sexual engagement only left me more bewildered. Addressing a room full of teenage boys dressed in cassocks. Dr Joiner began:

> *Anyway, anyway, this class is not to be, anyway, a source of amusement. Anyway, there's to be no giggling. This is serious, anyway, and must be treated so. Now, anyway, copy this down. Anyway, a rigid penis ... a rigid penis, anyway ... penetrates ... penetrates anyway ... a receptive vessel anyway ... receptive vessel (spitting out the 'ive' like 'receptiffe') ... called a vagina, anyway, v-a-g-i-n-a, anyway.*

Crass, blunt passages followed, describing sperms, ova, their secret encounters, their passage together through tubes. I was eighteen, and this was what all the fuss what about! I scribbled notes industriously in case this topic would be on the examination paper. George was dealing with the sexual function of the human animal, totally removed from considerations of love and intimacy. These were aspects of the human condition which were never mentioned. Let's not talk about that! When the bell rang to conclude the lesson, George would pause in mid-sentence, light a cigarette, breathe a sigh of relief and resume his dictation in the exact place he left off, on the next occasion.

Full marks were awarded in the examination by regurgitating the notes, word for word. Marks were lost for any deviation. There was no discussion, no reading on or around the subject, and no questions, because 'Everything is clear. What's the problem, anyway.' George was known to us as 'anyway, anyway' because he often prefaced his remarks with these nervous few words. His Psychology course was a complete waste of time, an insult to our youthful intelligence, and to our conscientious efforts to improve ourselves for the sake of the Gospel.

George was also our only contact with the outside world. He would carry the Sydney Morning Herald into class each day and summarise the headlines for us, to let us know, in telegrammatic form, what was making news in the outside world. Occasionally one of us would ask a question, invariably about sport. We did not know really what questions to ask, except perhaps who had won the weekend league matches. Peter Delaney always asked for the yachting results on Port Hacking. George would generally oblige with this information.

Dr John Burnheim who had come to Springwood fresh from Louvain, with a doctorate in Philosophy, was different. He used to lecture us in Logic, and in another subject which we knew as major Logic but which was referred to elsewhere as Epistemology, and is the study of the processes by which man comes to know, and the various theories to explain these processes. We all knew Burnheim was an intellectual, because he showed all the signs – a multitude of books, a certain awkwardness, a distracted vagueness. He seemed preoccupied in a world of ideas, and while we admired and respected him, he was not a role model.

But we Springwood boys were not convinced that as priests we would be called upon to discuss philosophical matters. The priests we knew were robust good blokes, more interested in sport, building churches, collecting money, organising housie, and performing public, pious functions. Burnheim tried to teach us the history of philosophical thought, some syllogistic reasoning, as well as the complicated system of logical positivism. He stuttered and stammered his way through class, often struck dumb for minutes as he searched for the accurate word or phrase, dictating a passage, then cancelling it, to dictate a further note. Few of us understood what he was talking about, though we realised he was teaching us real philosophy, even if it was a potted version, whereas some of the other clerical teachers were not seriously engaged in any real educational pursuit.

In his Logic and Epistemology classes, Burnheim was seriously shackled by the curriculum requirement of guiding us painstakingly through our Latin, Vatican, two-volume text on Philosophy. The Vatican had an official line on philosophy, one initiated by Pope Leo XIII, one which was closely linked to St Thomas Aquinas and Aristotle. While Burnheim spoke to us about leading philosophical personalities down through the centuries, while he tried, in simple form, to present their insights and line of thinking, we were not required, or encouraged to open any philosophical book. In those days of frozen isolation, I did not read a page of Descartes, Pascal, Bertrand Russell, Jean-Paul Sartre, Thomas Aquinas, or any thinker. But I was anxious to learn, and I followed John Burnheim's classes keenly, dreaming that one day I would be scholarly and learned. This was the ego-image I had chosen for myself and which I sought in some naive fashion to project. The memory of those dreams and of my Springwood education has left me to reflect in anger, to suspect that gifted, enthusiastic teachers elsewhere might have drawn up a map for my education and might have initiated me into a life enriched by searching.

None of the other staff members were of such a calibre. Only Burnheim fired up the mind. He was a man of ideas, interested in learning, but with little rapport with us young students, and no obvious interest in training clerics. Time showed that he had his own personal problems which eventually led him away from Springwood to St John's University College, out of the Church, to a rejection of his Christian beliefs and traditions. Later he turned his back on rationalism, and eventually retired as an associate professor of Philosophy at Sydney University.

Burnheim was a young man in my Springwood days, at the beginning of his twisting, contorted career. He was awkward and uncoordinated in his movements, and surprisingly inarticulate, even to the point of embarrassing silences. But there was a refreshing depth to him, an uncommon dimension of thoughtfulness, a seriousness. However much he found communicating difficult, and though we were young and isolated seminarians, many of us sensed we had a scholar, but no educationalist in our midst.

The others, all except our gentle Scripture lecturer, Bede Heather, simply wasted our time, and their own. They were precious years of lost opportunities. Instead of exploiting our keenness, our education consisted of pedestrian style fifty-minute lectures during which we were fed fat with definitions and official teaching. All this was topped off with end-of-term written examinations. It was an outmoded system of education even for the fifties. I cannot help but think that our youthful time was occupied, day by day, in the expectation that by supervised discipline, constant exercises in obedience, many of us would be judged worthy to assume the immense and eternal responsibilities of a celibate priesthood.

Bede Heather was a product of the same minor seminary where I had started my clerical career. He had been sent on to Rome where he had studied scriptural literature at the Biblicum and, though he was never successfully Vaticanised, he eventually became the bishop of Parramatta-

but that is another story of bastardry.

Bede used to teach us Biblical studies and supervised a six month novitiate-style training in my first year of Philosophy. The new boys were given six months to settle in, to fit into their cassocks, to learn the rules and to get comfortable in the chapel, without blowing their noses or banging the kneelers. They were supposed to be experiencing an intensive period of extra prayer, more silences, more isolation. Bede was in charge. He was our leader. He had only recently returned from Rome and was finding his bearings back in Australia. Father Heather used to deliver classes on spirituality, about priesthood, virginity, purity and the other virtues, cardinal, theological and moral, on devotion to Our Lady or to the Sacred Heart, and on the sacraments. During this time, we worked more in the scrub, clearing stumps, stacking rocks and tending rose gardens. We endured longer periods of silence and meditated twice each day instead of the regulation half-hour before mass.

Bede took his job seriously. Everything was well prepared and tightly scripted. He was a man who was restrained, unworldly, ready to listen, accepting of others, reluctant to judge. He seemed to believe in the Gospel maxims, even the one which required us to forgive again and again, seventy times seven times. He seemed genuinely prayerful, puzzled by any form of brazen behaviour, a little slow on the uptake, but without guile. He was alive to the message and values of the Gospel. As students, we came to admire Bede. Later, in adversity, he and I became friends.

In my later years at Springwood I began to develop a deliberate interest in Art and Philosophy, in History, and particularly in historical theory in Catholic literature. I was also intrigued by that form of Roman Catholic philosophy which had revived under Pope Leo XIII into a form of neo-Thomistic neo-scholasticism and which was well out of the mainstream of philosophy in Australia. Despite my shallow pockets, I purchased heavy books by French Catholic philosophers, Etienne Gilson and Jacques Maritain, in English of course. I laboured through some of the chapters, but could not find the iron-fisted discipline to persist to the end. They were too dense, too arid for a young buck without the help and advice of a real teacher. These same two French scholars also wrote works on the philosophy of art which had been published in paperback translations and which were not beyond my financial means. I tried to read their obscure material on art and the creative process. I tried hard, but my mind was not up to the task.

I puzzled over a few of books by the enigmatic G K Chesterton – the life of Francis of Assisi, and, if my memory serves me correctly, of St Thomas Aquinas. During one of my annual retreats, while on silence, I read *The Everlasting Man*. I also purchased some dry, neo-scholastic, philosophical tomes. One of them was by a Belgian scholar from Louvain, Canon Ferdinand van Steenbergen. Heavens knows why. In retrospect, I was not able to understand this material, though I tried. I kept reading, and reading, doggedly. I shared my father's admiration of the educated man.

One cold evening at Springwood, Monsignor Charlie Dunne crept silently into the classroom where I was studying with fifty other restless teenagers. We were all supposedly engaged in a private reading session. This did not happen often, maybe once a week. Some were reading Charles Dickens, others enjoying a story by Robert Hugh Benson who was quite old-fashioned but strongly recommended. I was labouring over a tome of Christopher Dawson which purported to analyse at length the mysterious dynamics of world history. A mammoth task, for him and for me. But I was determined to achieve an education. Charlie floated round the room, leaning over the shoulder of each student, spreading his tobacco incense, whispering slowly, gently, menacingly. Like an old eagle, he peered over my shoulder, observed what I was reading and slid in beside me on the seat. He perceived more than I had imagined. He offered me the only piece of good, friendly advice which I can remember receiving at Springwood. He said, 'If you don't understand what you are reading, my boy, just put it aside and choose something more interesting.' I was somewhat overawed by the monsignor, but managed to reply, 'Oh no, Father. I can understand it all right.' Perhaps I did not know it at the time, but I was not facing the bleeding obvious. Maybe I did believe the material was within my grasp. At least I was trying to educate myself. I only wish that someone had guided my steps more energetically in those precious years.

By the time I had reached the first philosophy year, the rhythm of the college life had become part of my body and mind. Eating, sleeping, thinking, praying, studying, all in unison, on the dot, whenever the bell rang. Every day was more or less the same. The even ebb and flow of clerical life had entered my soul. Imperceptibly, over the years, what had seemed so foreign in the beginning, had become the natural rhythm of my life, as natural to me as the world was to others. The regular rebuffs, the struggles for acceptance, for recognition were part of my daily existence. I was not questioning my vocation or reviewing my presence in the seminary. I was committed, determined, perhaps stubborn, holding on tight. I did not entertain the possibility of failure, of letting people down, disappointing Archbishop Eris O'Brien and Father Lander, the nuns, my parents, my sister, the parish and even the priests who were teaching me. I was someone important, even if only one face among many, and I was destined to be more important yet.

Forbidden intercourse with pagans

The Springwood scene was an educator's nightmare. We had no access to any of the morning or evening newspapers from Sydney. In those days, both the Sun and the Mirror were published every afternoon, although on Saturdays they only offered a few pages of race results. Newspapers were forbidden in the college, as well as secular magazines and journals. No student was free to tune a radio dial. I spent seven years in Springwood without seeing a radio set, a telephone, a record player.

> *It is strictly forbidden to introduce into the College newspapers, periodicals or novels without the permission of the Superiors.*

The novels which circulated throughout the college were generally of a religious genre, though a few rebellious students, like Eddy Campion, Brian Johns and Milky Clifford, had smuggled in copies of Graham Greene and Evelyn Waugh. Their books were on the college index. If discovered, they would have been confiscated and the offending student dealt with.

From time to time, perhaps once every two months, we were privileged to enjoy a full length American film screened in the recreation hall. The college possessed a sixteen millimetre projector and at the beginning of term, from a vetted list, we would all vote on two or three films to be ordered from Sydney. The authorities would solemnly deliver to the president of the students' society a list of acceptable, censored movies. In the hothouse of the Blue Mountains, care had to be taken to ensure that the films we were to see did not display cleavage or too much female leg, or beach scenes with voluptuous, two-piece swimming costumes. There was no fear of naked bed scenes, even under sheets, because in the fifties people who kissed on screen had to be dressed, and married couples only slept in twin beds. Anyway, films based on love stories were vetoed. Strapless evening gowns and plunging necklines forbidden. Consequently, we watched such films as *The Cruel Sea, The Robe, Quo Vadis, The Dambusters,* and *The Lavender Hill Mob.* It is not hard to understand how I came to grow up without a working knowledge of American films, actors or singers of the fifties and sixties. I knew little about contemporary music, or even of political, social, or sporting events which occurred in my home town during the years of my youth. The Menzies era, the Korean war, Johnny O'Keefe, The Suez Crisis, Lolita and the Melbourne Cup pretty much passed me by.

My contact with the world beyond Springwood was nourished by my mother's letters which would arrive every week, almost without fail. Any delay of a day or two would throw me into an attack of anxiety. And occasionally I would receive a letter from one of my siblings. Opportunities for personal development were also limited. Apart from my two sisters, my mother and several nuns, I had sparse contact with persons of the other, more attractive, better-built sex. Throughout the whole period of my teenage years, I had no contact with girls of my own age. There was no meeting in milkbars, no dancing or listening to music, no Saturday afternoon movies, parties, tennis, or picnics and no lazy days in the sun on the beach.

The world of fashion and style went unnoticed at Springwood. I was never invited to be aware of the colour or texture of the shirt I was wearing, the matching colour of my tie, or the general cut of my jib. But I do not blame Springwood entirely for my ignorance. I belonged to a working-class, Irish family which could not afford the luxury of style. I had not been born into a family whose members were accustomed to shop for fashion, to dress up as a statement, to assert their individuality. My father treated such pretensions with sarcastic contempt. And Springwood was a world nude of art, devoid of style and fashion, without colour, music or poetry, with basic food supplies about which no one thought to reflect whether the taste was subtle enough, or the presentation attractive. Such values were not part of my upbringing, but foreign, even hostile to my world. They belonged to the realm of the devil, as they were considered by our clergy and their traditions (wrongly) as lacking a spiritual, Christian dimension. They were considered as pagan, and we were rather puritan.

The challenges at Springwood were not intellectual or social, but exclusively spiritual. I was challenged to struggle to overcome my Self, to purify my spirit in the fire of denial, to learn obedience, docility and acceptance. The ideals with which we were confronted were the passive virtues of sanctity, humility, service for others, and self-denial. The heroes on which we were encouraged to model our lives were people, past and present, like Don Bosco, Thérèse of Lisieux, The Curé of Ars, Monsignor Harrington, or Lou Tosi of Kensington. These characters were all obedient. Some were excessively pious or obsessional, and were largely anti-intellectual. Most were suspicious of genuine learning as a result of Pius IX's cruel condemnation of the exponents of the Modernist movement. They were unworldly, even aggressively hostile to earthly realities and values – celestial and angelic in their spirituality. Some now appear neurotic, or paranoid. Thomas Aquinas, for example, was not presented to us as an exemplar for our intellectual pursuits, or Thomas More as an ideal of the dominion and freedom of individual conscience, or St Francis of Assisi for his simple love of creation. Of course, we had no secular heroes like Gandhi or Mandela.

I survived in a world on the edge of the vast Blue Mountains which was dominated by silence, in a college where an army of students of similar ages and aspirations received their formation, but in isolation. My movements were ordered, my daily programme regimented. Most of my days passed in enforced silence, studying, praying, listening, and sleeping. The official advice not to maintain friendships with old school friends, was not a problem to me. I had left the local school at such a young age that I had not thought to maintain contact with boys from my class at Mosman school, except John O'Brien who lived close by in Cremorne. John's father had been a wharf labourer, like my father. He and I had served as altar boys together at Neutral Bay, and we had often played and fought after school, in the local bush around Mosman foreshores. John and I have always kept friendly contact, but apart from him, and in accordance with the dictates of the college, I isolated myself from almost all lay contacts. Later at Manly, Dr Murphy, then dean of student discipline and later bishop of Broken Bay, counselled me when I requested leave to attend my sister's confirmation ceremony in my home parish. Apparently he had observed that I was too close to the members of my family, that I should be more distant, more aloof. Proximity to people, affection, fraternal love would only lead to problems. I did not go.

At Springwood when a disoriented tradesman happened to knock on the double door at the end of the polished corridor near the statue of St Joseph, a fellow student who had grown mad with scrupulosity, answered the call and recited to the visitor the college rule as set out in the tiny, green book.

> *The unauthorised intercourse of students with externs, inside or outside the College, is forbidden. [Rule 16 (a)]*

He told the bewildered man: 'Students are not permitted any intercourse with externs.' I am amused now to imagine the man's reaction. The student seemed to have said more than he could have imagined.

I accepted without question that I should not maintain any, even a harmless, innocent relationship with a female person of the opposite sex. The stringent demands of clerical celibacy restricted our young lives and we were aware what was demanded, though completely innocent of the long-term effects. I was anxious not to lose my vocation, not to be waylaid and distracted by losing my heart. I had set my sights on an eternal goal, and I knew that I had to be single-minded, though I cannot say the task was difficult for me. By living in a thoroughly protected environment, I was seldom in a position of temptation. There were some matters I would not and could not allow my mind to dwell on. I observed what was known to us as custody of the eyes. I kept strict control over the body. Picture books to incite the imagination and pump up the bodily fluids were unavailable. It sometimes required determination to avoid the display of magazines in the newsagents, though this material was discreet and harmless compared to what is now on show. I cooperated energetically in my training and sought, with gritted teeth, to impose some control over my senses, over my powerful drives, and I succeeded, for the most part. My partial victory was achieved by living in isolation, on limited rations in a world without alcohol, radio, film or magazines. It was a world without dresses, stockings, perfumes or facial creams, without any sensual stimulation.

A MEDIEVAL SYSTEM

> *The philosophical course shall comprise: Logic, Metaphysics, Ethics and the History of Philosophy: at least the principles and elements of the physical sciences shall also be studied, so that the future clerics will be prepared to detect the pernicious errors that are commonly mixed with these sciences. [Rule 26 (b)]*

> *Studies in rational philosophy and theology and the student's formation therein shall follow the method, doctrine and principles of the Angelic Doctor, to which the Professors must religiously adhere. [Rule 28 (a)]*

My learning during the philosophy years was programmed on a kind of catechetical model. Ask a simple question, listen to the simple answer provided by the Church, then learn it by heart. What is truth? Learn this definition of truth. What is beauty? Learn this brief Aristotelian description of beauty. Record the following definition. Whether in our philosophy or theology course, our teacher presumed that complex areas of knowledge, moral principles, dogmas about the Trinity and incarnation, grace, hell, purgatory, theories of knowledge and reality, all complex matters that have mystified mankind, could be neatly summarised in a short, pithy statement. The summary was called the thesis and was expressed in simple Latin.

In the learning process, the thesis was always prefaced by a potted summary of the thoughts of wise men and thinkers from various periods who had opposed, even if only by implication, and often without their knowing, the truth expressed in the thesis. We believed this pretence, though it was ridiculous. Many of them would not have heard of the subject raised in the thesis, much less addressed their minds to the nuances of the topic. They were of a different age, land and culture.

These thinkers were identified as the 'adversarii'. Their ideas and systems of thought were contorted, pressed into a short, unsympathetic paragraph which might refer to Harnack, Kant, Plato or Luther, and looked like a fifteen-second grab by a modern politician.

After the thesis was crystallised into a brief statement, the sacred author of the textbook would expose, in a few short sentences, the patent errors in the thinking processes of the 'adversarii'. The author then proceeded to develop the different proofs to establish the truth of the stated thesis. The process was ordered and rational. The simple statement of truth, chiselled to a purity, was proved from one or more passages from the Scriptures, excerpts from the Old or the New Testaments. These isolated passages were set out in Latin. They did not appear in their original language, and certainly not in their context. There was no attempt to interpret or develop an understanding of the scriptural passages. They were just there, as a proof of a formula statement. The encapsulated truth was further proved from simple excerpts from the writings of the Fathers of the Church – again often quoted outside their contexts and applied to the thesis only by pulling, pushing, shoving, and closing one's eyes to any historical or textual considerations. The third layer of proof was an appeal to reason. Recourse was made to considerations of appropriateness, harmony, order, balance, in an attempt to seal eternally the truth captured in the thesis.

This regime, especially in our theology years, was the unalterable format of our Latin textbooks, and to pass our examinations, we were required to learn by rote the formula of the thesis, and the proof from the three great fonts of Scripture, Tradition and Reason. The institutional Church supplied the answers because she was the infallible source of all revelation. We students learnt the answers, not so much for our personal enrichment, or for our enlightenment, but because, as our Church was militant, the answers would be available to persuade people who might be interested in the Church, or crush those who might be hostile and who challenged the established and reasonable truths of God.

The process in which we were engaged was thought to be modelled on the ecclesiastical schools of Europe in the Middle Ages, the so-called golden age of the Church, when all was in perfect order and harmony, when everyone knew their proper place in the world. It was the age when the grand Gothic cathedrals of Europe had sprung out of the ground, to glorify God. It was the age of the calm sounds of Gregorian chant and of the flourishing of religious orders. The pope was imagined as supreme lord of earth as well as heaven, bishops as true lords who could re-enforce their authority with interdicts and excommunications. The Church was the ideal society, with its own laws, its own authority-structures, its property, culture, heavy-handed bureaucracy, religious calendar and esoteric language.

In the seminary the authorities were drawing on the intellectual system of the medieval Church, a system established by Peter Lombard, St Bonaventure, St Thomas Aquinas. Our textbook, written in the language of the Church, followed the structure of the writings of St Thomas in his *Summa Theologica*. Had we thought about it, we would have assumed our regime of learning faithfully reflected the teaching methods of St Thomas. We would have thought we were doing what he had done so successfully at the University of Paris, but without the inconvenience of reflection.

But this assumption would not have been true. Ours was a closed, frozen system which admitted no free discussion. We did not join in debates, or disputes, or disagreements, or any meeting of minds, as they had done in the Middle Ages. That period had been on fire with vigorous discussions and disputes. Tensions existed between regular clergy and the seculars, between bishops and the lords, the emperor and the pope. There was conflict between the proponents of orthodoxy (such as it was) and various supposed 'heretical' sects. Bonaventure disputed with St Thomas. The Dominicans and Franciscans were intellectual opponents. The political, religious and theological spheres were intermingled and forever in ferment, so that the intellectual life of the Church was in constant flux.

My education was not flavoured with the same belief. Some people may have wanted to imagine the formation at Springwood was based on methods tested in the Middle Ages, and found efficacious, but if they believed that, they were mistaken. There was no need for discussion, or argument, or search. Truth had already been revealed and was clearly codified. We were expected to accept the formulae and to hand them on uncorrupted.

Except on Thursdays and Sundays, our mornings were filled with a string of fifty-minute lectures. Our system of education had developed before the discovery of electricity and the light bulb, and before the Gutenberg printing press had been invented. We did not seem to need to read books, or at least not many. The system was built not on reading, discussion, analysis and reflection but on forced-feeding. Truths were handed down in formulae from one class to another, one generation to the next. Even the teacher did not need to be educated – he only needed to have a passing familiarity with the material handed down to him and which he was repeating for our benefit.

This system of seminary education was simple. Teachers taught and students learnt. The man with the knowledge of the truths to be revealed, lectured for fifty minutes each day, slowly so that we could record his words in note form. If an idea was not explained clearly, someone might ask a question, though few were really interested. The keen seminarians studied their notes assiduously, during study periods, but the battlers and stragglers were happy to cram the contents of someone else's notes before the examinations. Pat Martin used to seek access to my notes, but when he returned them, he would remark that they were beautiful, neat, but incomprehensible.

We were expected to regurgitate the contents of our notes in answer to examination questions which were based solely on the material explained in class. One could write short answers to questions about Descartes, Pascal, Aristotle, Socrates, St Thomas Aquinas, Husserl or Sartre, without having read a paragraph of the author's works. Printed material was superfluous, except that we did consult a Greek grammar, a copy of the Bible (in English) for Scripture studies, a book of Cicero (in Latin), and a two-volume work, also in Latin, which presumed to deal with every important question raised by systematic philosophy – Logic, Metaphysics, Cosmology, Epistemology.

Most of our teachers used to consider Philosophy merely as the handmaid to the study of theology. The subject was not pursued seriously for its own sake by teachers or students. A summary version of neo-scholasticism was taught. Burnheim did attempt to present a summary history of philosophical thought, but again without any need to read even one of the philosophers. Their principal ideas, their train of thought was summarised by the teacher while the keen boys scribbled sketchy notes, and the others doodled as they waited impatiently for the bell to sound the end of class. Burnheim's classes were not generally applauded. He was written off as an intellectual, which in our world was someone akin to a wife-basher or a drunken driver.

We received a summary version of the philosophical world of Aquinas, with all its nuances, categories and sub-categories, distinctions and further distinctions. This was done not in order to understand the intellectual world of St Thomas, or to come to terms with his highly developed philosophical system. Much less was it done for the purpose of developing a critique or an analysis of his system of thought, either within its medieval setting or against the backdrop of the mid-twentieth century. The main purpose of investing three years, hour after hour, in an antiquated system of thought, was to establish categories, and to define terms, to refine distinctions in which theological truths could be developed and presented. This philosophy was the antechamber to an acceptance, to an understanding of the theology of moral principles, sacraments, God, Trinity, to grace, redemption, to everything.

We would need to be able to explore and understand such concepts as 'transubstantiation', or the difference between 'person' and 'nature', between 'essence' and 'existence', or the relationship between 'body' and 'soul'. Ahead lay four years and more of systematic theology during which our professors would expound, from a rostrum high above the assembled students, the eternal truths, for example, about three persons in one God, two natures in one person, the Eucharistic change in the substance of bread and wine, the nature of grace, the salvation of eternal souls, immortality. Each of these and other truths would be explained not as mysteries of faith, but as truths which were self-evident, explainable by a system of philosophical thought developed by scholastics such as Bonaventure, Aquinas and Duns Scotus.

There were no heretics at Springwood as no one was challenged to think or reflect. The eternal truths were simply propounded, and remained unchallenged. Like blotting paper, we absorbed what was handed on and handed down. The deposit of truth must remain intact, its integrity preserved, to be handed on again, preferably, though not necessarily, after it had made an impression on the spirit of the individual student. This was my understanding of tradition and the teaching authority of the Church, in other words, of the Vaticanised pope.

Obedience was an essential part of the system. An accepting faith was demanded – not an inquiring mind. It was not considered essential that the eternal truths become part of the fabric of an aspirant's spirituality. Every doctrine seemed of equal importance. There did not appear to be any hierarchy of importance between one eternal truth and another. No truth or doctrine seemed central. The Assumption of Our Lady, the Immaculate Conception, Purgatory and the salvation of unbaptised children were all presented, examined, defended, proved, explored in the same way as the mystery of an enfleshed God, the trinitarian life of the divinity, or the redemption of a stained creation. I had to wait until Manly for the truths to be explained. Springwood was only the beginning.

When everything is important, nothing seems important. When one is force-fed fat on a multitude of truths, without distinction, no profound, personal spirituality can be easily developed. Nothing is truly absorbed – no richness oozes out. The end result is not personal faith, but a faith-box like a treasure chest.

Back to Chapel

The longed-for midday meal was approaching all too slowly, and only after a further restless stint in the chapel. A short walk close to the sandstone building after morning classes provided a rare few minutes to talk. We assembled in the cramped chapel at twenty to one for what proved to be an elongated, tedious five minutes – a period of pump and grind which was demanded by the spiritual exercises of St Ignatius Loyola. Some years passed before I grasped what I was required to do to fill up these gnawing minutes before lunch, and even after my illumination, I was still not able, successfully, to occupy the time. My body ached with hunger. My mind floated off towards the pending three-course meal.

After only a few months of the seminary routine, I had learnt what lay ahead. I knew whether the imminent meal would consist of a greasy shoulder of lamb, or an aluminium dish of twenty-two sausages in gravy.

The same silver container might also be filled with watery mincemeat, bulked out with boiled vegetables – potato, turnip, pumpkin or swede, and tapioca to follow, or watery rice or a sinker as pudding. My starved brain could not focus on serious chapel work while my stomach rattled for food. I was at the age when a man's world centred on fodder. Jim Salway's stomach could be heard rumbling from the other side of the chapel. We had christened him 'Dr Rumbles', in memory of the priest who used to provide acerbic answers to hostile, Protestant, anti-Catholic questions on our Catholic radio station every Sunday night.

The five minute particular examination in the chapel was a mystery to a young teenager and it continued to be a mystery through my later teens. At the age of seven I had been taught by the nuns to examine my conscience before I made my first and subsequent confessions. I had learnt to recognise when I was naughty, or bad, or mean, jealous, distracted at prayer. The uncharitable tag covered a multitude of sins. I had heard frequently about impure thoughts but, as far as I can remember, I had yet to learn what they were exactly. That trauma lay ahead.

This particular examination was an Ignatian exercise. Over time I came to realise that I was required to select a particular area of my life which I considered to be deficient and which I sincerely wished to transform – excessive gambling, or unrestrained consumption of alcohol, perhaps a fascination with pornography, maybe an undisciplined curiosity, an inordinate passion for money, selfishness, a tendency to distort the truth, to peddle rumours, particular friendships, turning up late for chapel, free-floating during mental prayer. I had to identify, carefully, conscientiously, some aspect of my life which was a source of personal dissatisfaction, to examine it thoroughly, each day, to observe myself closely, and to fashion new, more satisfactory behaviour on a day-by-day basis. These five minutes were to be spent examining the past twenty-four hours under the microscope of my chosen focus, seeking divine guidance, requesting supernatural assistance, making detailed resolutions which would guide the next twenty-four hours and against which I could judge my behaviour at the next day's examination.

Now that I am much older, the particular examination appears quite reasonable, and helpful. I can see the attraction of such a practice. Towards this end of my life, I can readily accept that a regular survey of my behaviour and attitudes might nudge me slowly towards perfection, whatever that might be, or at least might help me become a better person. But at the Springwood end of my life, the method was imposed before I had experienced the need, and the exercise had become oppressive years before the penny had dropped.

Though the routine and format of this daily spiritual exercise were presented to us on a number of occasions, no one took time out to explain to me, personally, privately, how I should proceed, gently explaining, over a period of time, and revealing to me what could be achieved. We were being treated like battery hens. Those five minutes, day in and day out, year over year, were wasted. I suffered them in anticipation of being fed at last.

The prayerman knocked loudly on his wooden kneeler. We recited a ritual prayer in Latin, exited the chapel in seniority from the back to the front, processing two abreast down the chequerboard corridor, past the portraits of our heroes, the pope and his bishops. On entering the refectory, we took our places at table.

FOOD AGAIN

Like all other occasions throughout the day, our main meal was framed between a blessed beginning and a concluding prayer of thanksgiving. In Latin we asked the Lord to bless our food – in Latin, we thanked him for what we had received. Once the noise of scraping, moving, dragging chairs had quietened, the daily list of martyrs and saints was read out in English. Most of the saints seemed to be Italians. Many came from a region called 'Too Dirty' in Umbria, to which we responded with constant amusement, only later discovering the town's name was Tuderti. And there seemed to be an inordinate supply of saints, obscure, foreign and faceless.

> *At the principal meal the reading will frequently be limited to a portion of the Sacred Scriptures and the Martyrology of the following day. [Rule 13b]*

When I had progressed to the major seminary at Manly, the martyrology was announced in Latin at the beginning of the main meal, rather than in English. In this way aspirants to the priesthood received training in reading publicly a Latin text, as they would be required to do each day in the celebration of the Eucharist, or in the administration of the sacraments of penance, extreme unction (later known as the anointing of the sick), and baptism. It was unimaginable, perhaps even treacherous, to think that the sacred ceremonies could be celebrated in any other language other than the Church's own tongue. Although within a few years the entire Church liturgy would be celebrated in the vernacular, praying publicly in our own native tongue never entered my mind.

Except during our monthly and annual retreats, when we were on perpetual silence, and on the solemn days of Holy Week, we were permitted to talk during this main meal, in a gentlemanly, restrained manner. I say 'permitted', since nothing was taken for granted. Though conversation was routine, bell power was still exercised. After the reading of the martyrology, the rector with red nostril hairs, in his red-piped cassock, would lean over the silver service and press the bell to indicate his gracious permission to the assembled crowd to burst into relieved conversation. On retreat days, however, the public reading at our midday meal was devotional in order to provide fodder for reflection.

Once the reader had completed the daily martyrology, trolleys began to move around the refectory. The head prefect, full of importance, would slowly process down the corridor of tables, pushing a special trolley to the top table, where the professors sat waiting for service. The trolley was laden with a soup tureen for the first course, a tray of carved lamb, or thick, juicy cuts of beef, bowls of hot vegetables, a boat of gravy, and a plate or crystal bowl of delicate sweets. The head prefect solemnly placed each item on the white table cloth in front of the rector, or whoever was presiding. Duty done, he would return to his place in the refectory.

Among the seminarians, soup was guzzled, mutton hacked, and runny mincemeat spooned onto plates which were passed around the table. A crowd of young men in cassocks chomped and chewed, until the tiny golden bell was sounded again, to reduce the assembly hall to silence. A thunder of chairs, a loud *'Deo gratias'* at the end of a mumbled Latin formula, and the crowd disappeared down the corridor to the chapel, again in a two-by-two procession, again past the portraits of those before us who had been eminently successful.

Our Springwood fare was plain and frugal. I recall meals of pale spaghetti lying limply on the plate, without sauce or butter, just pasta. The food was bland but filling, though some days, especially in winter, the bulk was not sufficient to suppress the hunger pangs.

The bursar's job must have been impossible as it was governed by severe budgetary restrictions imposed from afar, from the cathedral. Many of us were benefiting from bursaries or pensions and were supported by our dioceses, in my case by the Sydney diocese. Our parents were not paying anything near our full fare, mainly because most families were working class and could not afford to support a boy at boarding school. In the ordinary course of events, had we not been called to higher things, many of us would have been working, at least after school, and contributing to the family coffers. Presumably the bursar was doing the best he could as there was no financial advantage for him to keep us on the breadline. This was not a privatised gaol. The dioceses, however, were not overly generous in the grants made to the seminary for the keep of their students.

After lunch, there was a brief visit to the chapel, lasting only moments. A token gesture, then we were free, at least for an hour or two. I was being trained by a rigid routine to frequent a sacred space, whether chapel, parish church or cathedral, at regular intervals throughout the day, sometimes for extended periods, but often only for a brief moment to recite a ritual formula of prayers, ostensibly to contact the transcendent, in reality to maintain a rhythm of clerical life.

St. Joseph's Presbytery,
Lindsay St.
Neutral Bay.
22. 12. 1950.

Very Reverend Monsignor Dunne,
St. Columba's College,
Springwood.

Dear Monsignor Dunne,

    This letter is being sent to you as a recommendation concerning CHRISTOPHER GERAGHTY living at 16 Florence St., Cremorne, who has applied for admission to the Minor Seminary, St. Columba's College, Springwood.

    I have known Christopher Geraghty for the past three years and during that time I have had the opportunity of observing him closely.

    I have always found him a splendid type of catholic boy. He has a strong manly demeanour; he is honest and truthful, respectful to parents and elders, and particularly respectful to ecclesiastical superiors and religious teachers. For more than three years he has served as altar-boy at St. Joseph's Church Neutral Bay, and has always discharged the duties connected with that office with marked piety, promptness and regularity.

    Finally, Christopher belongs to a splendid catholic family which is well known in the district and highly respected.

    With every good wish,

    I remain,

    Yours sincerely in J.C.,

J. E. Lander
Administrator.

Life in the afternoon

Mail from home

The students herded out of the chapel. Most were in long, black cassocks, buttoned down the front from neck to toe. As one would expect, some of these garments were in better repair than others. Some were faded and tatty, with remnants of soup and gravy decorating the front. These cassocks, of whatever age or condition, often covered ragged underclothing, kneeless long pants, throwaway, collarless shirts. In my early days, the ordinary, secular dress we juniors used to wear, the shirt and tie, the grey lumber-jacket, made me feel somewhat underprivileged, as though I had some further obstacle to negotiate before being accepted as a real seminarian, a few years to wait before being permitted to wear the identifying and convenient coverall of clerical dress.

Like cows wandering along, one behind another, to a routine milking session, we made our way to the corner of the recreation hall where the head prefect and his assistant would distribute the mail. This event was staged Monday to Friday with Jack Shanahan, Tubby Hayes, Allan McPherson or Kevin Manning (depending on the year) standing on the corner of the red verandah path which surrounded the recreation hall. The assembled students would stand crowded on the unpaved, gravel area, a metre or more below. Some students would hitch up their cassocks and perch on the wooden fence, while others would drape themselves over the wire gate. There were those among us who received letters every day, and others who never seemed to be blessed.

The head prefect would call out the name on the envelope of each letter – up would go a hand to claim the prize and the distributor would flick the envelope like a missile in the direction of the claimant. This was a tense moment of the day when each of us waited in the expectation of some fleeting contact with someone on the other side, someone who lived outside the perimeter of our mountain retreat. This was the time when a student momentarily became an individual, separated from the mass, with his own brothers and sisters, his friends, a faithful mother. We could enter our own world, contact our roots, escape for a moment from the routine of the system to become someone's friend, a brother or son again.

The letters which were spun out to the addressees had been examined by a member of staff who had had the opportunity of vetting the incoming mail. Not many of the letters were delivered opened, though the power to check always rested with someone in authority. Parcels, however, were regularly checked for contraband food. Heavy fruitcakes to supplement our diet were sometimes detected in the mail and confiscated. Unacceptable, disturbing, religiously incorrect books or journals seldom reached their target.

I waited expectantly for my regular letter from my mother. She was my only reliable correspondent. Each week I could be assured of two pages set out in my mother's clear, flowing, well-formed handwriting, full of family news, of my brother Sean, of my sisters and my father. My mother's reports were always good. While life went on at 16 Florence Street with all the ups and downs of any normal household, the usual struggles, explosions of temper, unresolved power plays, the uncontrollable brother and sister running off the rails, no item of bad news was passed on to me. At home, years went by as my parents struggled to make ends meet and worried out loud, constantly and inordinately, about Colleen and Sean, while my life was cocooned at Springwood. My mother wrote to me faithfully, revealing nothing of herself, not a word which could be judged as personal, never mentioning a hope, a wish, a disappointment, a cause of anger or worry, always to reassure me that elsewhere life passed without problem, always graced by peace. I had only to worry about myself.

Apart from my annual holidays when I played the role of a candidate for the priesthood at home, this regular page or two from my constant mother was my principal contact with the world outside the gates of Saint Columba's. My sister Maureen wrote from the convent, but irregularly. She needed her superior's permission before a letter could be forwarded to her brother – a letter which was read and censored before it left the convent, and theoretically, as it entered the seminary. From time to time, my mother would dragoon Colleen or Sean into writing a page or two of the usual, newsless formula. They would enquire about my health and inform me about the weather, perhaps even about some sporting fixture, or school event, but nothing more.

During the seven years I spent at Springwood I received two letters, perhaps three, from my father. Each was several lines long, maybe half a page at most. The writing was scratchy, the spelling unconventional, somewhat like the letters written home by Irish convicts from Sydney or Van Diemen's Land. Also like such letters, there was no news, only the unspoken assurance of his concern for me and his abiding, unexpressed love.

I was touched by his letter when it arrived, but hardly conscious of the effort and concentration which had given birth to it. The hours of preparation in the kitchen, the toing and froing, the cursing, the resolution to begin, the opening and closing of cupboards in the kitchen when people were trying to sleep, the challenge of the empty page. It was difficult, almost impossible for a father who could hardly read or write, to communicate with his son by letter. My father would much rather have worked a week, marked a tennis court, repaired shoes or cemented the backyard than face the challenge of a pen and empty page. But very rarely, he was shamed, perhaps by my mother, maybe by himself, to struggle to produce a few simple sentences on a page: 'How are you son? Your mother and I are well. We think of you often. Come home when you like.'

I cannot now remember receiving any letter at Springwood apart from those written by my mother and occasionally by other members of my immediate family. Our family was small and close knit. We were six altogether. I was the second eldest child and very protected. As I had left home and school for Springwood at such a young age, I had not had the opportunity of making friends, at least not friendships rich enough, deep enough to give rise to correspondence. Letter writing is built on commitment, on a depth of relationship, on an expectation of continuity. Roots like these had not been laid down for me before I was interviewed by the cardinal and accepted as a candidate for the celibate life. Such bonds do not normally exist between children of twelve or thirteen. The ecclesiastical training system seemed to have been developed to preclude contact with others, to prevent the flowering of friendships. I was a cleric from my youth.

SPORT AND MANUAL LABOUR

After the distribution of parcels and letters, some students would wander off, absorbed in their fresh mail. Others were content to continue waiting for the letter they were expecting, while others, who attended this daily ceremony, were doomed to be daily disappointed. They may have had no one interested in their isolated life, or perhaps able to put pen to paper. Most of us simply headed off to the dormitories, to change into shorts, football jumper, boots or sandshoes and BO cassock to cover our smelly gear, collect a tennis racquet, perhaps a tiny black handball, or to select a pick and shovel from the toolshed, and disappear to some corner of the college grounds. I know the timetable at the front of this book reports that on normal days we would attend classes in the early afternoon and recreation later on, about four o'clock. But memory plays funny tricks after fifty years. My memory is that we rushed out to the tennis courts, the hockey field, the labour camps immediately after the main meal and the mail distribution. On reflection, perhaps when the junior school was in full swing, we all had to return to the classrooms, after the heavy, midday meal and the physical exercise which would keep the mind healthy in a sweaty body was scheduled later in the cool of the afternoon. But then juniors gradually disappeared from the system. The fresh, unopened rose buds were left at home on the bush until they began to spread and ripen. My memory chimes in when the age make-up of the student body was more homogeneous, when we were all pimply teenagers with rebellious hormones, when the senior secondary school was on the decline and we could safely disperse into the fields after our main meal without dragging ourselves back to the weary, sleepy classrooms.

Up to a point, we were free to choose how we wanted to spend the recreational time after lunch – playing sport, or doing some manual work. Work was encouraged, but generally not compulsory. Students of all shapes and sizes, mostly young, some approaching middle age, drifted into the vegetable garden, the rose beds, or to feed the chooks and clean out their yard. Some went down to the dairy or pigsty, near the old Federation home where the nuns lived at the bottom of the drive, or out into the bush where land was being brainlessly cleared, for no good purpose.

Cassocked chain gangs carried mattocks, picks or shovels to some isolated location in the bush – the usual, harsh, prickly Hawkesbury territory coloured in various shades of dirty greens and browns. The ground was of sandstone, clay mixed with pebbles and rocks of all sizes. No grassy areas, only sharp Australian natives, black boys, an occasional waratah plant, scrawny ironbark trees and eucalypts.

Days and weeks passed as a clerical gang, its members now divested of their cassocks, manhandled large stumps out of unyielding earth under

A work party 1956 – Barry Nobbs, Chris Geraghty, M Harfield, Kevin O'Brien

the sun. We were covered in perspiration, amid tormenting flies. We were not blessed with the necessary equipment like blocks and tackles – no four-wheel drive to prise the stump free. Our training was in the hard, physical labour of chopping away at earth and roots with nothing but a mattock. An area of hard ground was cleared slowly, but the space would never raise a crop or be transformed into parkland. The work was like the drudgery of convicts breaking rocks in prison. There was no plan or purpose, except to provide an opportunity for aspirants to raise a sweat, exercise the body, exorcise the vapours and purify the mind.

Some of the seminarians were workers by nature. They loved to frequent the vegetable garden near the convent, the rose plots near the college, or to obtain satisfaction by tending the chooks, delivering slops to the pigs, and increasing the porcine population by rotating litters from sows. I was not a worker, that is, not by nature. I much preferred to spend my time playing sports. I would pass many an afternoon, in the cold wind or blazing heat, on one or other of the handball courts, or at least on the line, waiting for a brief turn on the court.

I spent many hot summer afternoons, many windy, wintry hours, waiting in this way. But slowly I mastered the trade. Learning also had its advantages as I was part of a line of other students, pushing, shoving, teasing, relating to one another as normal competitive boys. It was easier to be accepted in the queue.

In winter I was also an enthusiastic member of a Rugby League team, relegated for the first few years to play on the wing on account of my size and age. I gradually learnt to tackle ferociously and, though I was never big and bulky, I put on some weight and muscle despite the diet, and was brought in from the cold wing position, to play in the second row, sometimes at lock. To my great disappointment, at Springwood I was never selected to play in the prestigious college representative team for the grudge match against the Manly men. I did not grow big enough, quickly enough, for selection in the sky-blue-and-white team which was invariably made up of boys less developed, less brutal than their Manly opponents.

I had to wait, impatiently, until my transfer to Manly to wear the red-and-white of the senior college football team, and in the four years I played in the Manly team, we lost every annual grudge match we played against Springwood. The students on the mountains were bigger then, bulkier and faster. Playing in the lock position, I exhausted myself in my attempts to control the marauding runs of players such as John Cootes who later played for Australia against England and France, or Dick Laffen who was a cruel man of steel.

At Springwood we also played hockey throughout the year on a rough, dangerous surface, and in winter, soccer – in summer, the dreaded, hated cricket in the long paspalum grass on the top field, persecuted by flies, and sometimes scorched by hot westerly winds. For a time I was also interested in the art of boxing, in body building and running. I proved to be a good runner – all distances from sprints to marathons. In bursts of boundless energy, I could run without stopping for an hour or more, round and round the ghost track, mile on mile, or through thick bushland, wasting body fluids and pouring out superfluous energy. When I had the opportunity, I would run with other keen distance runners, with Toots Toohey or Gerry Iverson, along fire trail tracks on the ridge of mountains, pushing through thick, valley bush on the way to Saint Joseph's Bowers or across the valley to Carmel. In those days I had energy to burn, and much to prove. The expending of physical energy was a central feature of our training. It was important to balance study, prayer and work, and to flop into bed at night, exhausted.

Skills to Last a Lifetime

Brian Larkey used to pass his afternoons down in the bookbinding hut near the handball courts, where, assisted by his young apprentices, he made leather sleeves for missals, sewed quires of Latin texts together, glued the binding and masked cardboard covers with mock leather of black or red. Brian was a true craftsman who enjoyed passing on his skills so that our tiny library might be well serviced, books given new life, periodicals bound into years. The primitive hut was of corrugated iron and therefore seething with heat in summertime. Entirely open on one side, it sheltered a few crude cupboards, a rough wooden bench and was permeated with the smell of glue. Brian's freckled, puffy hands and thickened fingernails were stained with the cloudy, brown tint of dried glue. Bookbinding was too fussy and inert for my tastes. I needed to go mad with activity to drive the demons from my body.

At the other end of the college grounds, another group of working students occupied another hut, a confined fibro construction joined onto the back of the prefabricated Physics laboratory. They were the college barbers who volunteered to shear their fellow seminarians on request, gratis. In addition to attending the establishment, each month on average, for a haircut, for some years I went there irregularly to learn the trade. The hut was always pretty messy, with hair clippings everywhere. They covered the floor, sprinkled over the dirty linen drapes used to keep the hair off shoulders (black hair, and blond, brown, straight and curly, auburn, but never grey). There were two broken mirrors, and one ancient, collapsed barber's chair with the silver fittings but which was unusable and only added atmosphere, as well as several rickety kitchen chairs. I learnt to work the electric clippers, to run the thin comb up against the grain of hair and to snip the scissors busily, officiously, stepping my way up in ridges. There was only a few days difference between a good job and a bad one, and we were not going anywhere to look our best. At an early age I became used to not paying for barbering services. Even though I have heard tell of attractive salons where pretty girls with boobs bare style gentlemen's hair, or where pretty men with firm bottoms and soft hands provide facial massages and hot towels in addition to a basic haircut, I have not consulted a professional barber since I first arrived in the seminary.

I have often blessed the days I spent at Springwood learning to cut hair. Over all the years, as a teenage seminarian, a young priest, a doctor of theology, a married man, a father myself of two boys, I used to cut my father's curly hair, first in the family kitchen at Cremorne, and later on the back lawn, under a blue sky, overlooking the beach at Manyana. Dad would have his silver locks cut by no one else. I was his barber by appointment. Even though he looked bushy and unkempt, badly in need of a trim, he would stubbornly wait for my irregular visit from Sydney. He would then get out the scissors and comb, the towel to go round his scaly neck and the chair, and we would set ourselves up in full view of the beach and go to work.

Those were precious moments. Barbering was something special, and personal, an intimate act of service I could perform for my father. I could delicately cut the hair in his nostrils, clip and fuss, brush and comb, trim the back, and talk casually to him about everything – politics, friends, and life in general. I could touch him, and look at him, listen to him, converse with him without strain for half an hour. They were joyful, magic moments. The barbering skill brought me closer to someone I loved. Seminary learning and training tended to sideline me from the world and has erected an almost impenetrable barrier between me and those I have encountered throughout my life.

The barber's hut was also the assembly point for budding mouth organists. Michael Kelly was the head barber, and the owner of a flash harmonica. He could play a medley of folk tunes, and often entertained us on Saturday nights at the students' debating society. Kelly organised a choir of mouth organists which sounded something akin to an ensemble of cicadas. He would train the beginners, select the repertoire, arrange the music, and conduct the performance on the stage in the recreation hall. It was always great fun for the participants. For the others, anything was better than the grind of study.

I began my musical career, such as it was, with a simple ten-note Boomerang mouth organ on which only simple tunes could be tortured – *Silent Night, The Seine, Irene Good Night, Swanee*. I practised and practised without much improvement, driving the family insane during the holidays, feeling for the right notes, searching like a blind man, vamping heavily to hide my incompetence. I tried hard at everything I undertook but without a good ear or any musical training, I was doomed to failure at worst, mediocrity at best. While many of the students could play their mouth organs by ear, I had to be more painstaking in my tortured renditions. I had to follow the numbers, like following a bouncing ball. I finally bought the harmonica on which I had set my heart, a fat one, with a press gadget to change from sharps to flats and back again, but I never really mastered the tricky instrument. The only complicated tune I came near to dominating was *The Donkey Serenade* which I played a million times, if only to show I could use the slide mechanism on which I had invested money, status and prestige.

A MOMENT OF PUBLIC SHAME

I look back with some amusement now, and a residue of shame, on one particularly dark day at Springwood. Every year the college-elected sports committee arranged a sporting carnival during which, for this one occasion, the seniors and the juniors were permitted to fraternise. We grouped ourselves into four competing teams, each with a distinctive colour so that the members could dye their T-shirts. Each team designed a large banner for the march-past which came as the high point to the day. Thirty-five or so of us in each team practised marching in unison, turning left, right, stepping high on the mark, round and round the football field for the march-past on carnival day.

The day itself was crowded with events – the 100 and 220-yard sprints, the 440-yard cruises, the graded half-miles and miles, long jumps, high jumps, hop-step-and-leaps, cricket ball throwing, which Dave Perrett always won because he was as strong as a bull. The marathon or cross-country race had been completed some days before the carnival. The all-in handicap mile race involving the whole college crammed around the football field was the final event after the colourful march-past.

I was fifteen, perhaps sixteen years old, and excessively competitive. It had been a long hot day. All four teams had performed splendidly in the march-past and were separated by only a few points. The day's events had been suspended for an hour in the middle of the day while each team cooked sausages and boiled a billy for its competitors. Wave on wave of races had been run with the aid of a starter's gun and a team of officials. Fat and thin, tall and small, fast and slow seminarians had thrown themselves into the sandpit, or leapt into the air to clear the crossbar, so that, by the end of the day, we were all sore and weary. The individual points scoring had me one point in the lead, challenged by Gerry Iverson from Wagga, who was several years my senior and a gifted long-distance runner. One event remained to be run.

The organisation of the final race was a major feat. More than a hundred students participated in a handicap race of over one mile, which involved going four times round the narrow, sometimes rocky, perimeter of the football field. A slow student might be allowed a two-hundred-yard start. At the starting line Gerry Iverson and Leon Toohey crouched over the scratch line, poised to spring into action and mow the field down in front of them.

The officials had awarded me a twenty-yard start on the scratch runners. Most of the others were running off marks in front of me. It was going to be a struggle to force myself through the crowded field. I did not have to win this race to win the crown. I had only to finish in front of Gerry Iverson, or ensure he did not fill one of the first four places in the race, thereby scoring points sufficient to pass my overall total.

I was full of nerves and a sense of foreboding. Covered in weariness by the end of that day, I was determined to win. Five yards in front of me a group of students waited for the gun to move off the mark. Paul Coffey, a member of the elite, senior class, was one of them. He was committed to body building programmes which he used to perform with Slim Pendergast before Slim left the establishment. He was also an accomplished, smooth-stroking tennis player. Like myself, Paul did not persevere in the priesthood, and later lived with his wife and family in the Wollongong area, working for the Department of Community Services.

I was tempted, in my anxiety, to crib an extra five yards, to steal a further advantage. I discussed with the runners in front how close I was to winning the day. They knew what was at stake. One of them encouraged me to join his mark, making room for me on the line. I looked round to make sure the officials were not watching me, seized the bait, and stole the extra distance. The gun fired and we all surged forward.

But the race was a shemozzle. With a hundred competitors ahead of me running around a small football field, serious competitors were five or six abreast on the circuit, pushing past groups of slow runners, muscling in for advantage. I need not have bothered. The race was far too crowded for the backmarkers. None of us could fight our way successfully through the mob of dawdlers, many of whom were out for a jog, enjoying the final event of the afternoon. The serious, dedicated thrust was confined to a few runners like myself, none of whom were able to break the tape.

As I scored more points than any other competitor, I was crowned the winner of the individual competition. The trophy came to me. I was to enjoy the glory of the occasion, and the acclamations of my confrères. The handshaking and backslapping gave me a sense of achievement, and more importantly, of acceptance and recognition. There was a bitter taste, however, in victory. Although it had made no difference in the end, I had cheated and the fact that a small group of my fellow students knew it, gave me a sense of doom.

The sporting trophy was to be awarded that Saturday evening while we were assembled in the recreation hall for what we knew as 'society'. After general business, the elected student president was to award the team trophy to the captain of the winning team, and an individual trophy to me as the competitor with the most points. But just at the moment of the presentation, I received a tap on the shoulder and the head prefect invited me outside. He challenged me with a disturbing account that I had cheated. There was no escape. It was true. I confirmed the report and prepared myself for public humiliation. I have never forgotten the brief confrontation with Brian Sheedy that evening outside the recreation hall.

The trophy was awarded instead to Gerry Iverson, compassionate enough never to mention the shameful episode again. We met many times over the years, both at Manly when I was lecturing there, and at Wagga where he spent some time as administrator of the cathedral, as well as later when he was president of Manly seminary. I never saw him without privately recalling with shame our Springwood sporting carnival.

I had come so close to glory. The laurel had been there for the taking, and the hand went out to grab it selfishly, dishonestly. A fatal flaw had appeared publicly in my seminary life, unexpectedly, to keep me humble and within the ranks of humanity.

The episode passed without major repercussions. The authorities never gave any indication that they had heard of my misdeed, apparently dealt with in camera. It is difficult to accept, however, that the head prefect, with his onerous responsibilities to report problems and infractions, did not disclose the details of my offence, especially when the monsignor could find out on the grapevine who had soaked the labels off the contraband tins. It was never mentioned, and as my fellow seminarians, including Gerry Iverson, did not confront me again with my public misdemeanour, shame soon dropped out of my consciousness so that it did not haunt me day by day. While an occasional flashback would cause a shiver and a moment of regret that I had cheated, that I had lowered my guard and exposed myself to ridicule, the routine of my formation continued as before.

I experienced no self-doubt about my vocation. Any sense of weakness and solidarity with a twisted, shadowy humanity would emerge only later. For the moment, I was engaged in a programme to develop moral perfection which, I was assured, was perfectly attainable. All I needed was discipline, energy, self-control and determination. I needed to suppress my basic human and sexual urges in order to cooperate with my ecclesiastical superiors in their God-given vocation of training me for glory.

The world which the seminary of the fifties was creating for its teenage residents was a passive, ancillary world in which the pope or the bishop was father, the Church our holy mother, and we were joining the family to assist our special parents in their work of continuing Christ's mission. Our world was not based on the model of robust, independent heroes such as those who came to life in the epics of Homer or Virgil. They had been powerful, assertive men on a journey of exploration and discovery, who dominated their world without being subject to the whim and fancy of others. The models which peopled our world were of a completely different character – the wan, long-suffering, sexless Sacred Heart, the soft, accepting Virgin Mary and the precocious, dreaming St Thérèse of Lisieux. We were exposed not to St Catherine of Siena, the tough, assertive St Teresa of Avila or the disobedient, aggressive Mary Mackillop, but to the gloominess of Thomas à Kempis and the crazy, devil-obsessed world of John Vianney.

Springwood and the clerical life were constructed on an old-fashioned feminine model of submission, obedience, self-control, temperance and prayer. Instead of our spiritual life being based on the robust dictates of the Gospel, on Jesus the confronter, the friend of sinners, arguer and rebel, we were invited to follow the gentle Jesus, meek and mild, and to base our spirituality on litanies and rosaries, on soft, passive eighteenth-century devotions. We were not heroes on a journey as Jesus was to his death in Jerusalem, living rough, meeting challenges, struggling, exploring. We were boys who would never be men. We were rather children willing to submit ourselves to the ecclesiastical good. Day by day, one year after the other, my seminary life was routine and controlled –

cold showers, bells to answer, kneeling erect in chapel, walking, marching, long periods of silence – a life demanding discipline and control, without crisis, without initiative or excitement.

My youthful goals remained clear, basically as I had bravely recounted them to Cardinal Gilroy when he had interviewed me in that medieval setting at twelve years of age. I wanted to be a priest like our parish priest, like Archbishop O'Brien, friendly, charming, intelligent, to dress up in heavy, colourful vestments with fine lace and gold braid. I wanted to bless people with the radiant, sun-like monstrance, to say Latin masses, hurriedly, mumblingly, with rapid crosses and jerky genuflections, to carry the sacred host in processions, dressed in long, flowing regalia, to wear the black cassock, to recite prayers from a book with gilded edges – in brief, to cover my life with mystery, ritual and status. For this, I delivered myself up for years of training, to participate in a programme based on a well-tried formula, to produce passive, self-effacing, remote controlled clerics.

At the Dairy
Neil Brown, Barry Nobbs, Dave Walker, Noel Sloan, Lyn Holz, Chris Geraghty

Education down on the farm

There was a location at Springwood, well down the drive in the front section of the college, where a dairy had been established. A dairyman had been employed to look after the twenty or so cows that he milked twice a day, to supply the college with cream for the priests and milk for us. This grassy area was situated at the back of the old red brick convent, towards the bottom on the straight drive, before the bends. Some of the more senior students, especially those from the country, would spend their free time each afternoon at the dairy, assisting the dairyman. It was a peaceful, relaxing place apart, where one could escape the intensity of seminary life.

The dairy had been well established before my arrival at Springwood, though the piggery, further down the hill away from the dairy, was founded in my first few years by Paul Simmons, subsequently ordained by the pope in Rome. In those days, Paul was a student who had grown up with his family on an extensive pastoral property near Brewarrina. He had returned from one Christmas holiday on a plane with a small nest of three wild, scrub piglets. This had been the beginning of our piggery.

Industrious students had constructed a rough wooden sty, but as the pigs grew, the sty became smaller and muddier. Gradually, these ugly wild pigs from the back of Bourke were eaten and replaced by noble specimens of more classical breeds like Landraces and Large Whites. In the process, the college established a small business. The powers invested in a lumbering heavy boar to service four or five sows, some of which were bred on the property. The students (or those of us who were handy) built a proper pigsty in which the boar had his own premises. Each sow had her own run, an open yard with a trough and an automatic watering device. There was also an undercover area where she could escape from the rain, drop her litter, look after her tiny piglets and sleep.

The building was like a row of single-storey townhouses. Tin roof, bagged, whitewashed walls, proper taps and hoses, expansive yards, all constructed by volunteer labour. The cumbersome sows gave birth every ten weeks or so to a litter of twelve or thirteen piglets which would fight one another for a place on the swollen milk bar, pummelling their mother to deliver up more milk, pushing the smaller and weaker ones away from the source of all life. Piglets grew into porkers. Porkers were loaded into trucks to be sold at the market, and then transmogrified into pork and bacon.

The dairy and the piggery were out-of-bounds to all but the select few who were permitted into the inner sanctum, supposedly to assist in the care and control of the herd of cows and the sty of pigs. When a privileged student left for higher things at Manly or for another world, his place would be snatched by some lucky, scheming, younger student who had been dreaming of joining the exclusive band down the hill at the dairy. At one stage, I also managed to scheme my way onto the team.

To begin with, I was only a part-time, casual member of the dairy crowd. At various times Allan McPherson, David Coates (both pharmacists by former profession), and Milton Lonard enjoyed the senior positions on the team. David Coates weakened and allowed me to join his team on a one-off basis. After a while, I became a regular. I could slip down the hill with a group in working clothes, almost unnoticed. If he felt benevolent, Coatsie would allow me to take the controls of the rickety truck loaded with pig slops, and drive it down to the dairy. This was pretty brave of him as there was no synchromesh mechanism on the truck and gear changes were done by a double shuffle movement which he taught me.

Members of the dairy team hung off the truck in their putrid clothes as it made its way down the hill. Some stood on the back, others on the running board, three or four crammed into the front cabin. The tray also carried a number of large dairy cans as well as one or two voluminous rubbish bins full of slops for the pigs. Recycling is not altogether a modern discovery. Nothing was wasted in our establishment.

As the piggery settled in, two power bases emerged – one centred on the dairy, with the milking machine, a herd of cows serviced by one lucky bull, and the other concentrated on the newly constructed, whitewashed sties, several large, floppy, grubby sows, and an active boar the size, shape and beauty of a Japanese Sumo wrestler. I joined the piggery push with Milton Lonard, Joe Giles, Neil Brown and others, though Neil was also welcomed to make appearances at the dairy because of his friendship with Peter 'Beau' Ryan, Charlie Mercieca and Barry Nobbs. Another member was Paul Trisley, a country lad who had come to Springwood from a large dairying family in Macksville. He attended Woodlawn College in

Lismore, and spent several years with us in the seminary, the first in the Specials class (for those who had never learnt Latin), advancing then to philosophy studies in the year behind me.

Paul's sister, Mary, later joined the order of nuns whose God-given vocation led them to look after seminarians in Manly and Springwood. These sisters constantly slaved for students and professors, cooking meals, cleaning rooms, working commercial washing machines in between keeping up with their regular routine of prayer. Mary escaped from the dwindling order after a number of years and married. On our trips north in the Christmas holidays of the late fifties, Lex Levey, Michael Bach, John Beaven and myself (and on one occasion, Dick Hazlitt) passed a few enjoyable, carefree days on the Trisley's farm at Macksville. A deep, slow moving river wound through the property. The ninety or so cows which made up the milking herd, delivered gallons of creamy milk from heavy, hanging udders. We moved into the family farmhouse, slept on the floor, ate at their table, swam in the river, and galloped the more exciting ponies around the river flats and up the hill at full speed.

Paul's widowed mother, weather-beaten from dairy farming, and her hard-working son Mick, welcomed us with a smile and treated us like little priests. I accepted the hospitality as though it was my due, without any thought for the extent of the imposition on a family of four or five extra hungry bodies – more food, more noise, more linen, more work, less time to milk, plough, feed cattle, and no privacy. Like many young people, I took everything for granted, as though I was the centre of the world through which I was passing. I knew no better, and everyone, whether at home or in my parish, was trained to see us seminarians as God's chosen ones, as special beings reaching for the stars.

Paul Trisley was a central figure at the seminary dairy and pigsty. He was the source of our know-how. He knew when to mate a cow, when to wean the piglets, how to put a bull across a cow, a boar over a sow, what feed was nourishing, when to summon the vet and how to castrate those calves and piglets which were endowed with onions. Paul passed on to me the delicate art of castration, though my training and expertise were confined to pigs and never extended to cattle, or horses, or chooks.

I served my apprenticeship with Trisley on those afternoons at the pigsty. I watched him operate with consummate skill. To begin with, I held the container of methylated spirits, but as my experience grew, I was able to slurp a generous daub of the painful fluid through the cut skin, into the holes left between the suffering piglet's hind legs. Under his attentive eye, and while a tiny piglet squealed as my attendant held it tight, I practised the delicate technique of surgical incisions (only two) with a used razor blade. If the razor blade was one of those which was sharpened on both edges, I needed to take special care. By far the best instrument for the surgery was the more expensive, old-fashioned blade, even though perhaps a little rusty, with a sharpened edge on one side and a flat metal piece on the other. As I acquired my expertise, many piglets passed under my scalpel. I became the college castrator. Once installed in this position, I enjoyed considerable status.

The pigsty and the dairy at Springwood were an important part of my education. There is some information which every young man requires for survival, but which was not available to me in the cloistered training grounds of Springwood. I had no access to sex education books with explicit pictures. The priests clearly did not see it as their responsibility to inform the young men under their care of the facts of life, to educate them in their bodily functions, to assist in the development of proper responses to the attractive creatures in dresses. For better or worse, the dairy and the pigsty were the picture book and the principal source of my education in sexual matters at a critical stage of my development.

I wonder whether the ever-watchful Springwood staff realised how sexually explicit the behaviour of the animals at the dairy and the pigsty was. While my supervisors ruled over a tight regimen which repressed, discouraged, and forbad any explicit sexual converse, down the drive where we gathered each afternoon, one could watch rigid in awe while a slow, excited bull lumbered onto a gentle, placid cow, searching anxiously for the swollen entrance, and thrust powerfully until he dropped away, exhausted. At first I thought the cattle were playing. But the activity was too brutal, too powerful for play. Then I realised what was happening. That must be how it was done. Here was an example of coupling, before my very eyes. Here was the act of creation, performed with all its ritual, its earthy energy, in my presence. Part of the mystery of life was unfolding.

The same activity was sometimes played out at the pigsty. Tons of heavy flesh lumbered onto a sow while she stood quietly. From nowhere, the boar unwound his long, thin, fleshy, corkscrew penis which probed and searched, as though it had a mind of its own, for the swollen wet opening. With uncharacteristic energy, the fat fellow heaved and thrust. I was fascinated to see how the sow would stand still, ready without complaining to accept such gruff treatment. When their time came to couple, the sow and cow stood passively and quietly while the boar or the bull launched himself with uncontrollable energy and enthusiasm. My education had begun.

HARD LABOUR

There were various work-sites around the seminary grounds. As a member of one of the chain gangs in training, I was dragooned to clear large tracks of harsh, rocky scrubland, earmarked for no one knew what. An endless supply of mattocks, picks and shovels, stood waiting in the toolshed for employment.

George Joiner smoked incessantly as he supervised his almost compulsory work parties. Occasionally, when Noel Carroll pretended to oversee our sweaty labour, he would chatter incessantly, sometimes about his seminary training in Ireland, mostly about clerical heroes from Sydney and the bush – the two snooty Tosi brothers, Tom Wallace the barbarian from Darlinghurst, mad Monsignor McCosker of Ryde, Monsignor Harrington of Chatswood, Bagot and Reeve who both specialised in persecuting their hapless curates.

The unwilling workers like me were also controlled and supervised by prefects who, in turn, were carefully selected and appointed by the powers to ensure good behaviour at all times, punctuality, and a detailed obedience to the rules. Each prefect was responsible directly to the rector and the members of his court. They performed the function of policemen, patrolling the beat, controlling the traffic, mixing with the masses, warning first offenders and implementing policies. They would finally lay charges against anyone who offended seriously or consistently by ordering a student to report to the rector, and ensure he attended by referring a list of names upstairs. The system was watertight.

George Joiner was the architect and chief engineer of all major college projects. He identified the bush area to be cleared and directed what work was to be carried out. Day after routine day, gangs would collect tools of labour and spend an hour or so of scarce recreational time, digging the hard, red, rocky clay from around large tree stumps. Some of the reluctant butts would take weeks of sweat and aching to prize from the earth. Though the college already had a perfectly adequate football field, in addition to a rough cricket pitch and soccer area on the top field in front of the college, the senior clerk of works decided to carve out of Hawkesbury sandstone, a second, larger field for football. This had a majestic viewing area on top of a man-made precipice overlooking an expanse of grass, the result of many thousand unpaid man-hours of labour.

The site selected by George, the dean of discipline, was at the end of a ten-minute walk along a bush track. The seminary was destined to remain at Springwood for only a few more years after I left there in 1957. The many months of hard labour have long since disappeared, rapidly reclaimed to the wild. This was the fate also of other cleared areas never earmarked for any useful purpose other than to be work-sites for celibate aspirants with dangerous levels of energy. No sooner were these stretches of scrub cleared, even as they were being cleared, they were returning to the wild.

Our system did not countenance a moment of idleness in the life of any student. Every moment had to be fully occupied. Constant activity commenced at the moment of waking, and ceased when the last bell rang. A prefect switched off the community lights and weariness, at least in principle, prevented us from becoming too introspective, and robbed each student of the opportunity of tending to himself.

Golf, the clergy game

Like many clerics who used to feel the need to hang out together on their Mondays of freedom, to protect one another from the assaults of the world, like policemen who drink and barbecue together, some of our Springwood professors enjoyed their weekly golf. George Meredith, our spiritual director, was more interested in bowls which he played with his cronies in the Springwood village. Charlie Dunne played no sport, apart from prowling the corridors, scaring students, pretending to read his breviary, bullying, and breathing heavily through his extended nostrils.

He smoked heavily, moved slowly, and breathed loudly. He was also unfit and overweight. Everything seemed a burden to him, and was best performed slowly. His two hobbies were persecuting students to keep them in check, and gambling on the Saturday races.

But Noel Carroll and John Walsh were golfers. So too was little Ted Shepherd, who replaced George Meredith as our spiritual director and tried to inspire us to the heights of scrupulosity. George Joiner did not possess the finesse demanded by golf, or for any sport, or the lungs, which had been ruined by constant, heavy smoking. If he had played golf, it would have been after the style of the proverbial gorilla – woods for smashing, putters for smashing.

The suave, successful cleric was a dedicated golfer, like the president of the United States, or like Bob Hawke. Golf is a gentleman's game, a patrician sport demanding a leisurely lifestyle to develop the skill and pass hours on the course – involving also club membership, mates of a certain social raking, and a certain element of exclusivity, as in *Going My Way*, in which the debonair Bing Crosby plays golf with Barry Fitzgerald, his cranky parish priest.

In the fifties, Noel Carroll and Ted Shepherd were welcome at the Springwood Golf Club any day of the week, and at St Michael's on Mondays, as were Lin Wholohan and Johnny Walsh in the sixties. Monday was clergy day, when the young mixed with the old and seasoned, when accepted attitudes and clerical values were passed down the line. Clerical bonds were strengthened, emotional needs and natural drives satisfied. Often, during retreats or mixing with senior clergy on festive occasions, we would be advised to attend the regular, Monday golf days at St Michael's. Golfing with the fraternity was like a policy of insurance which guaranteed we would persevere in our chosen vocation.

This golfing culture commenced at Springwood, where we heard heroic tales of games at St Michael's. We watched professors disappear at speed on Mondays, to return refreshed, full of clergy stories to pad out what should have been classes in Ancient History or Italian. We sensed from a distance the excitement of midweek golf, or Saturdays at the Springwood course, as a happy group of professors left the main meal early and rushed down the drive, dressed in mufti, golf clubs piled into the boot of their cars.

But our enculturation went even further. Some imaginative, clericalised students had designed their own five-hole golf course around the perimeter of the top field at Springwood. Fairways crisscrossed the cricket pitch. The fourth and fifth holes ran over the dusty, rocky pathway which crossed the field and led down through the bush to the grotto. We would tee off behind the soccer posts near the track out to the lookout, and watch an old, scarred golf ball bounce this way and that as it hit hard surfaces and tufts of paspalum. The greens were not mowed or rolled. They were rough, rickety, uneven spaces around a little ditch.

Dally Messenger, the grandson of the fabulous Rugby League hero, and himself a pennant golfer, dreamt the mad vision of a students' golf course on the top field, gently exploring the idea with Dr Joiner who was the Pharaoh builder of monuments, the clearer of scrub, the smoking clerk of works. 'Just do it, Dally, and see what happens. The rector can only say no. Go to work on it. If he doesn't like it, he will squash the whole project.' So Dally began to appear in the college workshop during the afternoon recreation period. His puzzled fellow seminarians watched him making flags, sewing them onto bush sticks, collecting jam tins from the kitchen. 'What are you doing?' 'I'm making a golf course.' 'Where?' 'On the top field.' 'When did Charlie give you his permission for that?' 'He hasn't. Not yet'. 'You're mad. He'll never agree. You'll be in big trouble.'

Though the boys were sceptical that Dally's project would never get off the ground, he kept working on. The others were convinced that Charlie hated seeing his boys having fun, that he was incurably suspicious of student initiative. Obedience was encouraged, originality suppressed. With some help from Frank Coorey and one or two others, Dally pushed the industrial mower up to the top field. He mowed out nine rough greens according to the design he had been working on in class while the professors were droning on, pressed the jam tins into the hard, crusty, clayey earth, inserted the red flags. Then he stepped up to the first tee and blasted off.

The institution went berserk. This golf course was the talk of the college. Students came from everywhere to claim a place in the line of those waiting to tee off. The handball and tennis courts lay idle. Tools hung around in the shed, unused. No basketball, no football. Four happy golfers were sharing one club. Others played with hockey sticks or shillelaghs – dry, knotted eucalypt branches cut to size. A special committee was established to run the order book (with a group of four hitting off every few minutes) and to organise special match plays.

Charlie was silent – ominously silent. Not a word for weeks. He couldn't be oblivious to the fun we were having. We couldn't believe he was ignoring the craze which Dally had created. Then he struck.

The head prefect approached Dally, just before teatime. 'The rector wants to see you in his office.' 'What about?' 'You'll find out when you see him.' Dally lingered outside Charlie's den, waiting in line. Nervous students, flighty as young racehorses about to enter the windy barriers, went forward one by one. Dally heard muffled sounds, and observed each exiting, head down, suitably disciplined. 'What's this you've done on the top field, Mr Messenger?' 'A golf course, monsignor', stating the bleeding obvious. 'Yes. Yes. I know,' he said impatiently. 'But why did you put a hole there?', pointing to an imaginary map of the top field on his desk. Dally stuttered and stammered, trying to justify its location. Charlie waved his arm in disdain. 'Well, get rid of that one.' Dally began to realise that there was not going to be a total ban imposed. Charlie was discussing the details. Out of his deep cassock pockets, Dally drew a crumpled plan and sought permission to spread it across the rector's desk.

Charlie lent over the design, studying the layout, breathing heavily. As Dally began to point out the features, a sense of elation flooded over him. He had scored a victory against the odds. There were to be only eight holes, but the college had a golf course. 'And that green can't go there. The fairway is in the wrong spot. Get rid of that one too.' Nothing could please the rector. He always had to have the final word. He had to be seen to be in control. OK, only seven holes! 'And this fairway can't cross that path. Someone might get hit, and you would be responsible.' Oh, well. Six holes would have to do. They continued to discuss the details. Golf holes made from jam tins. Golf sticks from dry branches. Dally was helping the rector plan and design a course. Charlie was always in charge. Dally settled for five holes.

The boys were gobstopped and flabbergasted. For once, the old man had agreed to allow his obedient subjects to do something one from among us had suggested. We had not suffered the usual, 'No'. Dally was a hero, and as always, our rector remained unpredictable. In our isolation, this was all we could manage. It was a far cry from the lush greens and scenic fairways of St Michael's, but a source of much innocent amusement and a promising beginning to the clerical life.

PICNICS AND ORIGINAL SIN

One of the few advantages of living in such a silent, isolated place, apart from the fresh mountain air and the Spartan lifestyle, were the regular bushwalks and no-frills picnics to remote destinations. The college was set on twelve-hundred, undeveloped, rough, bush acres. Beyond the unfenced boundaries stretched miles of bush tracks, freezing swimming holes under cliffs, overhung with mossy rocks, delicate native flowers, bursts of wattle, and lonely, haunting bird calls. There were mountain lookouts onto valleys, creeks and moist cliffs with not an electric wire, house, road or fence within view. In the bush, whether high on a mountain or deep in the shadowy valley, we could listen to the great silence of the universe.

As though to add to the strangeness of our world, the European weekly calendar governed our seminary routine so that we attended classes on Saturdays. Apart from our Saturday night gatherings when we enjoyed an occasional film, perhaps a formal debate, Saturday was ruled by a normal weekday routine. The normal Australian weekend disappeared at the gate, to be replaced by a religious programme on Sundays, and a recreational day on Thursdays.

Once every six weeks or so, our published college calendar programmed a day's bushwalk to vary our routine. The controller determined the details of the year's timetable during the Christmas holidays. At the beginning of the year, each of us received our own copy of a printed calendar which set out the principal feast days, identified the rare holidays such as, for example, the college patron saint's day, and nominated the Thursdays throughout the year when the whole student body would disappear into the bush for a picnic. Anzac Day, for example, was not a day of rest for us, though we celebrated mass in memory of the fallen warriors. Labour Day was naturally a workday, as was the Queen's Birthday. We lived apart, preparing to be men apart, constantly touched with a feeling of alienation from the world.

For convenience, the whole seminary contingent was divided evenly into groups of eleven – one prefect and ten Indians. Each group sat together at table in the refectory, morning, noon, afternoon and night, with the prefect supervising the group's behaviour at table, ensuring no one spoke in the refectory during the many silent meals we spent listening to public reading. He was also empowered to carry the breadboard to the back of the refectory and collect extra bread as required, as well as refill the teapot when it ran dry. The bush picnics were arranged on the same basis. Each of us participated with members of our refectory group, supervised by our very own prefect. Each group was allotted a destination from a list of places spread far and wide inside the college boundaries and beyond – a grotto, a swimming hole, a cave or a rock overlooking a precipice.

The Grose Valley was the furthest destination, so far from the college that juniors were excluded from the party because the hikers would need to be able to walk almost all day, stopping only briefly for the ritual picnic. Yellow Rock, overlooking the Nepean flood plains, was also a fair distance from the college. Carmel was tucked away in the corner of a tributary valley, off the main creek, on the side of a steep embankment, between the Grotto of Our Lady and the college weir. There the sides of the valley were so steep that only at noon did the sun penetrate the thick undergrowth to cast dappled light on ferns and native orchids. Or we could disappear off the ridge-track at the back of the handball courts, down into the gully, along a lush, bushy, narrow path to St Joseph's Bowers.

The Bowers was popular with the students (and with other bushwalking groups such as the Catholic Bushwalkers' Club), as the grotto was mossy, cool and shady, and not too far from the college. Trickles of fresh water fell over the main rock beneath which stood a statue of St Joseph, looking prematurely ancient, and a white statue of Our Lady of the Way. At their feet was a natural pool of fresh clear water constantly replenished by the drip off the rock above, or by the rush of water after rain. A tiny creek meandered into the scrub close by. It was overgrown with ferns and rushes, providing shelter for the tiny bush birds in the mountains. A colony of tall, rich, red waratahs flourished in the valleys round this sacred picnic site.

On the scheduled bush picnic Thursdays, it was all go immediately after breakfast. The college was alive. Each party was keen to launch itself on the bush without delay, to escape the normal restrictions of chapel, classroom, refectory. We changed into our tattered bush clothes which had been saturated with sweat many times and left to dry in the damp recesses of a boot-box. While the experienced hikers had bush boots, most of us wore smelly throwaway sandshoes, some without laces, many worn through where the ball of the foot met the ground.

The prefect deputised two members of his party to go to the kitchen to collect the picnic tin which contained the bare necessities – a fat sausage each, dry bread, an apple or orange each, a few matches in a box, a screw-jar of sugar, another of tea, and a blackened billy. Then we were off the leash for the day. Six hours out in the bush, out of sight of the seminary, away from bells, cassocks, and figures of authority, except for one prefect who mostly knew by instinct he was required to relax his guard a little, if only for the day. Most prefects were accommodating, though one of my classmates, Kevin Manning, nicknamed Ming the Merciless, remained as constant as Craven 'A', or Bushells' Green Label Tea. He never varied. As a young man, he was inflexible in any situation.

The lid was off. We could run carefree along bush tracks, swim in mountain pools, scramble up the side of craggy mountains, hide in caves, walk along creek beds, cook over an open fire even in the rain, eat from blackened hands and lie back in the sun. They were idyllic times. I remember these bush picnics without a glimmer of unease or regret, though one particular occasion remained to haunt a number of us for months.

Two picnic parties with their prefects had dragged out along Hawkesbury Road to the lookout over the Nepean River and over the flat plains extending as far as the city centre of Sydney. The major buildings in the centre of town and the bridge could be identified on a clear day. Spring had passed. The days were hot. A few kilometres of bitumen were soon replaced by a reddish, dirt, dusty road. The parallel, rutted tracks and corrugations indicated that the road was regularly used by traffic passing from the Great Western Highway at Springwood, down over the lookout at Hawkesbury, along the Nepean River bank, into Richmond and Windsor.

When the two parties had reached the lookout, the two tins of supplies were dropped under the shade of the water tank (the only source of water in this area of the upper reaches of the mountain). Most of us quickly dropped out of sight over the lip of the cliff. Fifteen or more seminarians scrambled over rocks, skidded down steep embankments, some racing past the slow, careful ones, competing to be the first to the banks of the Nepean River, first raiders into the orchard of some unsuspecting farmer.

We scrambled through the barbed wire fence and threw ourselves without thinking onto the silent, heavily-fruited trees. We filled pockets and jumpers with juicy oranges, more than any of us could eat, as though the fruit had been growing in the wild and was there as *res nullius* for the picking. Some invaders were more discreet than others. Annoyed at the noisy exuberant frolicking, they sought to reduce the numbers of troopers in the orchard and tried to put the mob on silence. But we were away from the seminary routine for a few hours, freed from the tyranny of bells, from the discipline of the solemn silence, and weren't having any of it.

Like an Indian attack on a wagon train, we had come and gone and completed our raid within minutes. Heavy with fruit, each of us made his way back up the mountain, grinding slowly up the steep, rocky face. Our return was different to our approach. There was no easy slipping and sliding, no yahooing, no headlong racing past the dawdlers. The day was hot and sticky, and as leg muscles groaned with each step, the ascent was slowed enough for summer flies to congregate on the back of smelly football jumpers, buzz around the face, worry eyes and occasionally slip like Jonahs down the gullet, gulped suddenly by the uneven intake of breath. The mission had been accomplished – the invasion successful. All had passed undetected. We could pass the day filling stomachs with juicy fruit.

That night the sky fell in on us. An angry telephone call from the fruit farmer to Father Noel Caroll who was acting as rector while Charlie Dunne was away, had blown the raid. This incessant talker now had something to talk about. His thin, affable chit-chat fell away as he worked himself up into paroxysms of anger. He glared at us, spitting out comments about the college's reputation, thieves stealing away from the college to plunder someone else's property. We were pigs on the rampage filling our bellies with forbidden fruit. The dean of discipline, thundering George Joiner, entered the arena, deep red beneath his heavy, five o'clock shadow, uncontrollable. We were in for it.

We were too numerous to be sent home in disgrace. The college would be literally decimated. The controllers worked overtime to devise a suitable regime of punishment for the raiders, one which would persuade other students, present and future, who might be tempted to break out and plunder a neighbour's orchard, to pull back in fear. We were suitably disciplined. The fifteen of us who had gone over the top were banished from films for the rest of the year. While the innocent watched Alec Guinness and Ginger Rogers in a wartime film, or some other harmless movie, we were locked in a classroom, writing an essay on each of the ten commandments in turn. From time to time a threatening, clerical figure would appear in the room to ensure silence was being observed and that all the offenders, heads down, were doing their penance.

But mafia types operate everywhere. Monsignor Giles's nephew, Joe, had of course been involved in the plundering raid, but he refused to come to heel. He wrote all of his ten essays in one rapid sitting, handing them up one by one as required, and then spent most film evenings secretly raiding the fridge in the kitchen while prefects and priests were engrossed in the movie. He even boasted that on more than one evening, after his phantom raids, he had hidden among the shadows of the recreation hall and watched part of the forbidden film.

The proposed essay on the fourth commandment, 'Honour thy father and thy mother', was an invitation to reflect on the virtue of obedience. The topic was appropriate for us offenders, and a proper occasion for the expression of some sincere, self-serving sorrow and repentance. Joe Giles must have been on his way out of the gate, into the world. Respect for authority was not in his repertoire of tricks. He could laugh and mock, scoff and challenge. Obedience was how some people freely chose to respond to others, not a reaction which those in authority could demand. Foolishly, brazenly, Joe challenged the whole seminary ethos by questioning the basis of obedience and authority. At least some of the essays must have been read since George Joiner erupted into anger on reading Joe's work.

Some of the evenings spent scribbling a few pages on one of the commandments, were passed in the sealed classroom, without the supervision of a prefect, in a farting competition. And some of the competitors were true champions. On a diet of bread and bread, the build-up of combustible gases often proved lethal. The odour which floated among the desks, unable to escape, was horrific. Completed commandment pages were fanned furiously to relieve the oppression of the chamber. Marks were awarded for effort. Near riots erupted as the champion contestants were encouraged to greater feats.

On at least two occasions, when a patrolling professor entered the schoolroom to ensure we were taking our medicine, the room was filled with the foulest poison as one person's gases had been mixed in a cocktail with many others. The patrolling officer withdrew, hurriedly, not a smile on his face, without a word or gesture of distaste. It was as though he was either used to such odours, or the room had been miraculously fumigated for him on entry. Even in the heavenly spheres of the seminary, given half a chance, boys would be boys, and original sin would prevail. We were being doubly punished for our theft.

The Catholic Presbytery,
Lindsay Street,
Neutral Bay.
8 · 1 · 1951.

Dear Charles,

The Certificate of Marriage concerning Mr & Mrs Geraghty, which John King sent previously from Coonamble, was not correct in all details, so I procured another which you will find enclosed.

I am very pleased and grateful that you have been able to find room for Christopher this year. He is indeed a splendid boy and should do very well at his studies. My only fear is that the course might seem too long to him and the goal too far away for his is a cleyname disposition. But I suppose that such an aspect would apply to all cases. Wishing you a happy New Year. Yours J. E. Lander

P.S. Since I finished my letter one of our altar boys has indicated that he would like to go to Springwood next year. He is an excellent boy, I would say splendid material for the priesthood. He is about to go into first year at the Marist Brothers at Mosman, has plenty of ability — went for a state Bursary a few days ago — and is a keen student. His name is Christopher Geraghty.

Regarding financial help I think that much assistance would be required, in fact I think that a full bursary would be necessary, his father being but a wharf labourer — incidentally a splendid type of Irishman — with four children in the family, all under 14 yrs old. In fact the boy was vacillating in decision between Springwood and Mittagong, because, he said: "To be a priest costs too much."

I would think it a good plan to communicate with his father immediately so that definite plans might be arranged without delay. Any direction which you might like to give me would be cheerfully attended to without delay. Renewed regards. J. E. Lander.

Address:
Mr. J. Geraghty,
16 Florence Street,
Cremorne. wrote 6.11.'50
J.P.

Chapel again and study

THE BELLS

The massive bell, the one which rang the *Angelus* three times a day, announced the solemn High Mass on Sunday and called us from the fields, hung in the belltower outside the chapel and came to life when the bellman swung on the knotted rope. This giant also rang out the resounding *Alleluia* message at the Easter Saturday Vigil. Most activities were regulated by the harsh sound of a heavy handbell. The miniature table bell was the sign that the student body could burst into conversation. I often waited to hear its sound, but the special privilege was only sparingly awarded. The tinkling, twittering chapel bell, three tiny willy-wagtails on a brass stand, marked the solemn, transcendent moments of the mass as well as the benediction.

These intrusive, steely-sounding objects ruled the college and my life for years on end. A bell woke me from a warm bed, or at the end of the day commanded the pale lights in the dormitories be extinguished, immediately. Some demanded silence even in the middle of a sentence, or alternatively granted permission to speak, at long last. A bell summoned to classes, and marked the end of lessons. They controlled with their relentless rhythm, preparing little men to take their place in an institution of cosmic proportions. The sound was more often demanding and threatening. It was the *vox Dei*, the same voice which had spoken to Samuel in the night, Adam in the garden and Moses on the mountain. We would drop tools as the distant moan rang out over the trees. One last kick, a final smash, a dead-butt into the corner of the handball court, and we were on our way to the showers.

On ordinary working days, halfway through the afternoon tools were put to rest. Balls of all descriptions, handballs, tennis balls, cricket balls, and footballs, regained their breath as the students were warned by the constant tolling that they had only twenty minutes to shower. They needed to dress and be kneeling in chapel before a large, brass handbell was sounded as the clock chimes sounded in the corridor. Sweaty bodies came in from all parts of the college grounds. Smelly working clothes, torn and dirty shorts, and faded football jumpers were modestly cloaked again in tattered BO soutanes. Now the college boilers, stoked to bursting by the boilerman, would pump hard to deliver hot water to various shower blocks for the ablutions of one hundred and fifty bodies.

Groups of students rushed from the fields to the dormitories and draped their shoulders in ample dressing-gowns before stripping off naked. Wrapping one towel around their waist and another over the shoulder, they sprinted to the shower block to wait in line for a turn in a cubicle. We were permitted two minutes each for our daily ablutions. Talking was allowed in the dormitory, but not in the showers, or on the verandahs leading to them. We were expected to fall silent on leaving the dormitory and walk in a gentlemanly fashion to the shower block. Standing on wet tiles or duckboards surrounded by a steamy mist, we awaited a two-minute turn. Prefects enforced the silence and the length of time. Occasionally warnings were issued, especially when the waiting line had grown too long. 'Two minutes, gentlemen, is the maximum, not the minimum.'

Modesty was paramount. Each student wore a towel around his waist to shroud his private parts. Over that he wore a securely tied dressing-gown with a second towel draped across the shoulders. One by one, we entered private shower cubicles, closed the door, removed the modesty towel and performed the basic activity. After two minutes, the shower was turned off. Draped in towels, we dried outside on the duckboards, wrapped ourselves up in our dressing-gowns and returned to the dormitory, in silence.

The forty or fifty students in each dormitory moved about in various states of dress. No one could behave with abandon. We were not like a football team bathing after a match, or like men frequenting a dressing shed in a public swimming pool. Nakedness was not kosher in our world. Each student dressed again, pulling on underpants and pants beneath the cover of a dressing-gown, not a pubic hair in sight – none that is, except John's blossoming crop.

John was a country boy from the west who had boarded for some years with the Marist brothers at Forbes. He knew how men behaved when women and prudes were absent. John would return from the Springwood showers, throw his dressing-gown aside, strip off his body towel and proceed to pass the time drying his bum and balls. After five years in the institution I was unaccustomed to such bravado. I knew how my body would react if I were to strip myself bare and paraded my nakedness. John was the only one in my time to dare challenge the unspoken rule of modesty.

Twenty minutes was not a lot of time to make one's way from the college grounds to the dormitory, change, shower, dress and be in chapel. The ditherers needed much more time, and always left the tennis court or the work gang before the bell began to toll. A few of us were fast and flashy. We could delay on the handball court for an extra ten minutes, or saunter in from far away, arriving in the dormitory when the others were almost dressed. After some years of dedicated practice, I could undress, shower, dress and hurry down the stairs, two at a time (providing Charlie Dunne was not spying from the upper window) to land in my choir stall before the final bell, all within five minutes. Some students were even quicker.

BACK TO THE GRIND

The recreation period over, twenty minutes of public spiritual reading followed. Weary eyelids drooped as one of the prayermen ploughed on about the life of the Curé of Ars, or Charles Borromeo, Pius X, or from a book of devotional thoughts by Abbot Marmion. Although this spiritual reading was extremely tedious, it was better than the community stations of the cross which replaced the reading every Friday and, horror of horrors, every single day during Lent. The Lenten programme involved standing, kneeling, and genuflecting, over and over again. The same prayers, the same weary mixture of up and down activity and excessive repetition, without the opportunity of dropping off to sleep.

While we were also expected to do spiritual reading in our own time, the official college programme wished to reinforce the habit of reading about spiritual matters. It was difficult after tearing around in the open to concentrate without dozing, particularly on summer afternoons. I would often wake abruptly at the end of twenty minutes, startled by the sudden noise made by the transfer of bottoms on seats, to knees on wooden kneelers. Though we were drilled by the rector during his Sunday conference to stand, kneel, sit, and kneel again in unison, all one hundred and fifty of us, the hushed movement of massed bodies in mid-afternoon tended to awaken me from my afternoon nap.

Ten minutes was all that was needed for afternoon tea. Like soldiers, we marched again to the refectory in procession. We sat there in silence, partook of a cup of cocoa, and a slice of bread spread with lemon butter and then dispersed to the study halls. The refectory silence at afternoon tea would be policed as usual by the prefects on each of the fourteen or fifteen tables.

We were on silence now for the rest of the afternoon because study time ran until well after sunset, and then there was chapel again.

Study was a private matter demanding application. We were seated together in wooden desks in the various classrooms. Some were sleeping, some doodling, some secretly reading a novel, or writing a letter home. Others learnt Greek verbs, struggled with a passage or two in Latin from their Metaphysics or Logic textbook, learnt by heart George Joiner's dictated Psychology notes, or just daydreamed. The unheated rooms were chilly in the winter. The work was not intense or demanding, simply routine and compulsory. Silence pervaded the room with greater or lesser success, depending on the prefect who supervised the study hall. Some prefects sought to preserve their ambiguous membership in the student body and seemed anxious not to be too harsh. Adrian Paul Rhineburger, for example, was always reluctant to exercise his authority over us, so each afternoon we would drive him to the limits of benevolent dictatorship. Ming the Merciless, on the other hand, was satisfied with nothing less than total silence, and few among us felt it worth the time and hassle of confronting the dean of discipline or the rector, for the simple pleasure of passing a whispered remark to the student who sat in the desk beside us. Throughout the afternoon, as the bush flies buzzed in the silence, an occasional antiphon would break the silence, 'See the rector', or 'See the dean.' Ming had spoken.

Charlie Dunne himself would occasionally patrol the classrooms and passages during study periods. He would glide unnoticed into a room and stand like a statue holding the corner of the cape on his red-piped soutane, staring beneath his ginger eyebrows until a student misbehaved. Then, with the point of an accusing finger, the offender would be summoned to the front of the classroom and publicly upbraided, or perhaps punished by expulsion for the period. Charlie would embarrass a weary sleeper by advising him, quietly and without criticism, to lift his head from the desk and return to work. Or, he might point silently, accusingly, at another student with his shoes and socks off, picking his feet. The student would know what to do without a word spoken.

Community living was a challenge. Nothing went unnoticed. Everyone's foibles were uncovered and exploited. Breathing problems, rumbling stomachs, the noise of gnawing fingernails, everything could upset fussy fellows in a silent classroom. The law prohibiting nose-blowing in the chapel and refectory was policed with enthusiasm by Charlie Dunne who would identify the culprit, expose him to the ridicule of the mob, and punish him with a penalty. Farting was obnoxious, particularly in sealed spaces like the chapel and classroom. But on a diet of bread, the foul air which built up within human containers, would explode regularly.

A CASE STUDY

Bill's farting feats were legendary. He was a lanky, angular lad, slow at book-learning but doggedly persistent at sport. Later at Manly, he would work more on his swimming than on theology. He would spend long periods each day churning up and down the college pool, rattling off a mile or more in his compulsive way. But we had no swimming pool at Springwood, only a small weir on Springwood Creek which was almost totally silted up. So Bill dedicated his time to handball. He played mostly with his mate when Donk could spare some valuable time from teasing his rosary beads.

Bill was a dedicated and strong athlete. Every chance he had he would spend time on the handball court, perfecting his dead-butts, angling the little black ball off walls, racing backwards to hit the ball on the turn, under his left armpit. Summer or winter, hot or freezing cold, Bill attacked the handball with a devotion which could have been concentrated on his spirituality, or his education. Bill swotted away in the same class as myself for several years, and then in the class behind me, as he had to repeat his Leaving Certificate. He commenced his course through the seminary system at the age of fifteen, in his third year of secondary school. Although I had two years start on him in handball, he and I seemed to meet regularly in the finals of the A Grade handball competition, both at Springwood and Manly.

At Springwood, the students could not submit as many clothes as they liked to the weekly wash-up. Our ration was severely limited, and washing clothes was not compulsory. A maximum quota was posted, though no minimum – two pairs of underpants, two shirts, four handkerchiefs, three pairs of socks each week, one sheet each month and two towels every two weeks. These restrictions developed in me a lifelong habit of stretching my clothes to the limit of cleanliness. I know how to make a shirt last two days in summer, three in winter.

Bill was the same, though we differed in that I wore my pyjamas only at night. He wore his, day and night throughout the winter. On the handball courts he sweated with his pyjamas under his long pants and lumber-jacket, practising his strokes before classes, before lunch and at every opportunity. When he woke in the freezing morning, Bill would tuck his pyjamas into his socks, and put his clothes over them. He was comfortable in the many layers of clothes.

Inflated on a diet of carbo-hydrates, Bill was a champion farter, and the wind he passed so secretly was trapped between the pyjama cord tightly drawn around his waist and the bottoms tucked into his socks. His pyjamas were washed once a fortnight, so by the time he had finished with them, they were pickled in personal odorant. No one could bear to sit beside him during study. Praying by his side in the chapel was pure agony. He felt the cold, while we suffered the foul draft. We complained bitterly, but Bill assumed we were joking. We were not. This was community living.

ONCE MORE TO THE CHAPEL

At the end of the study period, the bell summoned us again to chapel. As the bellman, who was appointed week by week, stepped out from one of the classrooms into the quadrangle, the clang of the large handbell echoed off the sandstone walls of the quadrangle, out into the lonely bush. In silence, we made our way to the chapel, arranging ourselves once more in six long rows. We were assembling for a lengthy visit to the Blessed Sacrament, or on solemn occasions, for benediction, before the pangs of hunger could be soothed in the refectory.

For any young teenager, fifteen minutes was an inordinate length of time to kneel silent and alone before the sacrament. There was no way I was able to fill this period from the meagre resources of my own head or heart. This was another spiritual exercise which demanded the Pelagian virtues of effort, concentration and determination. No wise counsellor had encouraged me to float free, relax, to drift away or be content to rest easy in the presence of the Lord. Such indulgent idleness was seriously discouraged. To waste time was sinful. Minds had to be perpetually at work and focused, otherwise at my weekly confession, I would have to admit that I had been distracted at prayers. I dreamt about home, or about the move I should have made, could have made, perhaps did make on the football field. Or I ached for something to eat, or became aware of my loneliness, or in the public privacy of the crowded chapel I took the opportunity to sink into melancholy about the teasing or the rejection of my classmates.

The minutes ticked by, slowly. I tried the usual, slick prayer formula, chasing the letters of ALTAR through constructed prayers of Adoration, Love, Thanksgiving, Asking and Reparation. I did my best to fill in the time, but it was always too long. A minute or so may have been more productive. Perhaps I could have occupied two minutes, but fifteen was asking the impossible of a young boy. Perhaps prayer was not the aim of the exercise so much as a routinised habit.

In despair I would turn to a book for inspiration. Beneath the polished prayer ledge on which I rested my clasped hands, I had neatly arranged a number of pious books. After some years, my English daily missal had been replaced by a *Missale Romanum* which occupied pride of place. I had to hand my own slim meditation book, black-bound, with red edges, in case the community topic of meditation proved a barren field of reflection. I had invested my limited funds in a *Breviary of Piety*, and an *Imitation of Christ* by Thomas à Kempis which had been the fount of spirituality for Pius XII – and of course, the usual collection of holy cards could be shuffled. From my earliest years, I have found comfort in books and have surrounded myself with a collection of them wherever possible.

Benediction days were a relief. At least I was not left to my own inadequate private resources to take my mind off hunger before the evening meal. Benediction of the Blessed Sacrament was a ceremonial performance of pious solemnity, although its format was simple. The Eucharistic bread in the enlarged circular form consecrated by the priest at mass for his own use, was lifted gently from the tabernacle and placed reverently in a monstrance, which was an ornate stand with a glass container. The thin, white bread was displayed, splendidly surrounded by sun rays of gold or silver beams, sometimes enriched with fake jewels.

The Eucharistic bread was exhibited for a short period. Hymns were sung and prayers recited. Then at a critical moment, the richly-robed celebrant raised the monstrance over the congregation. He solemnly traced the sign of the cross over heads bowed in adoration and reverent devotion. This simple format was ennobled by extravagant ritual.

On benediction days, a gaggle of sacristans would already be at work in the chapel when the student body began arriving in waves of cassocks. The thurible (or flamethrower), containing a smouldering charcoal piece, belched scented smoke. Someone held up a long taper to light six stately candles on the main altar. Two branches of candlesticks were arranged on each side of the tabernacle. The six or eight candles in each branch were already flickering. The celebrant entered, draped in a long, floor-length, embroidered cape, with his hands joined solemnly on his breast, eyes reverently cast down. He was accompanied by a master of ceremonies, a thurifer swinging a silver charcoal container on four silver chains (the thurible) and a boatbearer who carried the container of incense (the boat). Six other seminarians followed, carrying candles on top of long, polished poles, like the Roman Praetorian guard bearing spears in procession before the emperor. All the attendants were dressed in black, full-length cassocks over which they wore half-length, starched, white garments called surplices with dainty lace around the bottom edge and the bottom of each sleeve.

Now the scene was set for the solemn benediction. The organ at the back of the chapel was switched on and was gathering wind. A few notes led us into the first hymn as we took up the slow, rhythmical tune of *Adoremus*. Scented smoke began to fill the sanctuary and drift down into the body of the chapel. Myriads of candles flickered and danced. The celebrant, vested like an Inca high priest, would bow profoundly, ascend the steps slowly to the altar and solemnly remove the fine, precious cloth covering the monstrance. He delivered it by its corners to the server. While the server moved to the side and draped it evenly over the wooden pew, the celebrant would proceed to place the sacred bread in the central glass area of the ostensorium.

When he was celebrant, Charlie Dunne's demeanour was a little unorthodox. He used to grab the silken cloth off the monstrance, screw it up into a little ball, and drop it for the server to catch. The server would unravel it, arrange it on the pew, and return it in its pristine state to the rector at the end of the ceremony when the monstrance was to be covered again. While Charlie was free to be slovenly, we still had to be exact and reverent, otherwise he would turn dirty.

We were shocked, and amused, to watch Charlie Mercieca attending Charlie Dunne on one occasion before the evening meal. The rector screwed the veil up into a small untidy ball and handed it to Mercieca who caught it, straightened it out, and proceeded to the pew where he arranged it neatly. At the end of the ceremony, little Charlie, with hands solemnly joined, approached the sacred veil, removed it from the pew, screwed it up in a ball as he went up the steps to the celebrant, and handed over the untidy mess for him to unravel and straighten. It was a hoot!

After the celebrant had exposed the sacrament, he descended the steps with his cloak floating lightly. He knelt, bowed and proceeded to smother the glowing charcoal with incense. Bowing profoundly again, he dangled the smoke-filled thurible nine times in front of the Eucharistic bread. Nine was a mystical number, as was three. The throb of the swinging thurible was made in three lots of threes, as if to mimic the square root of nine. We were signalling our worship of the Father, Son and Holy Ghost. The student body then began to chant the last two verses of a Latin hymn composed by St Thomas Aquinas to celebrate the medieval feast of Corpus Christi. The strains of *Tantum Ergo* reverberated in the chapel, and rolled out like an enveloping fog into the empty corridors of the college, floating out into darkness, into the emptiness of the surrounding bush.

The solemn moment arrived. It was nearly feeding time for the seminarians. Jimmy Salway's stomach began to rumble more violently. The teenager with the thurible positioned himself in the centre of the main altar. The master of ceremonies edged closer to the hand-held altar bells ready to give them a good, hard twirl at the magic moment. An attendant appeared from offstage and draped the celebrant's shoulders in a soft diaphanous silk cloth which he tied with soft ribbons across his chest. The celebrant pushed himself away from his kneeling position on the bottom step, and glided up to the main altar. He gathered his cape and silk cloth, grasped the stand in which the blessed bread was exposed, slowly turned to the hushed gathering and lifted the monstrance in a large, extended, cross-shaped blessing. The altar bells rang out from the hand of the master of ceremonies several times, at the moments when the monstrance reached the four extremities of the cross. Heads were bowed, ejaculatory prayers whispered as the thurifer moved his flamethrower rhythmically in front of him, covering all with sweet smelling incense.

The ceremony was almost complete. The zenith of the celebration had passed. The celebrant descended, divested himself of the shoulder wrapping, held out a red-covered altar book in front of him and proclaimed the short ritualistic words of praise, each repeated loudly by the gathering: 'Blessed be God. Blessed be his Holy Name. Blessed be Jesus Christ true God and true man. Blessed be the name of Jesus. Blessed be his most Sacred Heart. Blessed be his most Precious Blood. Blessed be the Mother of God.' The sacred moment had passed. The experience of transcendent power had been real, but fleeting. As the students joined in the proclamation of the praises, the magic of the moment slowly began to disappear. The moment of mysticism had passed. We were back in the world of phenomena.

FOOD, BUT NEVER ENOUGH

As the pungent haze cleared and the waxy smoke drifted away from the extinguished candles, a mass exodus was in progress. A battalion of cassocks, marching again in a column two-abreast, made its way down the shadowy corridor to the refectory. Even in winter, the evening meal was light, often insubstantial. In the days before I had advanced to cassock status, my more senior friend, John 'Sausage' Hogan, would secrete a half-loaf of bread in one of the deep pockets of his cassock and deliver it to me in the darkness of the grounds after the meal had finished.

John and I have remained friends for over forty, nearly fifty years. He spent only a year and a bit at Springwood and now often comments that he left because they would not make him a bishop immediately. There is some truth in his complaint. John always loved ceremony and dressing up, whether in army uniform, barristers' robes or as a Master of the Supreme Court. He is a type of Gilbert and Sullivan character, an officer from Dad's Army. There have been a few outstanding features of John Hogan's post-seminary life – his studied pomposity, his uncanny ability to change jobs, the keg-like stomach that 'cost more than my education', and his deep loyalty to his friends.

After five years in secular clothes while most others enjoyed the status and convenience of a black, coverall cassock, I was finally at the stage of dressing up as a true cleric. I had of course worn the red cassock and white surplice of the altar boy since the age of eight, but I had grown well beyond that rank of service. I had also been privileged to wear the black soutane and pure white and laced surplice for a week in 1953, during the National Eucharistic Congress held in Sydney, when Norman Gilroy, the cardinal, welcomed serious dignitaries from around the world. There was Cardinal Agagianian, the Patriarch of the Armenians in communion with Rome, with his headgear and funny, neat, grey beard, the stately Cardinal Gracias from the slums of India, looking like a rajah, and various archbishops and bishops from around the world and all parts of Australia. The three cardinals and their retinues had visited the minor seminary at Springwood for a day, amid much pomp and ceremony.

The college was closed for the week of the congress. We were transported to Sydney by train to swell the numbers of Eucharistic worshippers who marched in procession and lined the footpaths, singing *'We Stand for God and for his Glory'*, and *'Faith of our Fathers, living still, in spite of dungeon, fire or sword.'* I processed, of course, with all the other seminarians, hands piously joined, eyes downcast (we had been trained to custody of the eyes). We moved at a reverent pace along Macquarie Street towards St Mary's Cathedral, preceding the religious float decorated with fake candles, real flowers and the cardinal in his heavy, embroidered cape holding the radiant monstrance which displayed the Lord in his most humble guise. Even the juniors were permitted to present themselves in black, clerical soutanes and chaste surplices – just for the occasion. I felt very important as I marched through the streets of Sydney, and thrilled to hear a lady on the footpath remark to her husband – 'look a those little priests in those long, black dresses.' She didn't even know they were called soutanes!

Another important stage of the long road to priesthood was reached when I moved from the mundane level of a secondary pupil, and was transmogrified into a philosophy student with the right to wear the cassock from morning to night. During the Christmas holidays, I visited Church Stores in the city (Pellegrini's was known to be unreasonably expensive). The tailor measured me from shoulder to shoes, and across the width of my shoulders, assured me I would have my order before the middle of February. He arranged for a final fitting, and delivered my new, clerical garment before my train ride back to the seminary early in 1956. I tried it on several times, in the privacy of my room at home (which was also Sean's room), looking approvingly in the mirror, back and front. I paraded up and down for the family. My parents were suitably impressed, though my siblings thought it was a bit of a joke. We were not so different to the family of Pius XII!

It was no joke. Another, important stage had been reached. I could dress more quickly, as the cassock could cover any combination of sartorial disorder. No tie. No shirt if it was hot. Football shorts instead of long pants, if I so wished. But it was not principally the convenience which pleased me. I was now dressed like a cleric. People could see I was a cleric and not merely a neophyte. I was well on my way. And I could at last convey extra supplies of bread from the refectory for myself, in my own deep, clerical pockets.

Before our eating concluded, another bell sounded. The reader fell silent, followed by a rumbling of chairs and a brief Latin prayer. A column of religious soldiers then marched on bloated stomachs, past their gallery of heroes, to the chapel for more prayers.

THE ROSARY

It was time for the rosary, only five decades, not the full fifteen. Five were as much as any mind could stand at one time. Sunday was the day allotted for the glorious mysteries, and as to the other six days of the week, we alternated between the joyful, the sorrowful and the glorious mysteries. Every student carried a string of beads in his cassock pocket. Some of the more pious aspirants would pass idle moments telling the beads privately in corridors or in dark corners of the grounds, but for the daily public recitation, the same deputised student would lead the rosary for seven days in a row. Like the other daily spiritual exercises, this ritual was repetitive, like a mantra.

For those who have never known or have forgotten, the complete rosary comprises fifteen mysteries, during which fifteen decades or series of ten *Ave Marias* are recited, each decade preceded by the *Pater noster*, and concluded by the *Gloria Patri* or a short prayer of praise to the Trinity.

When the five decades of the rosary were recited publicly, one lone voice said the first half of the Our Father or Hail Mary, and as the congregation we answered or took up the recitation. It was a perfect form of participatory prayer. It was a rather successful attempt to mingle reflective prayer with mantra-type recitation. Each participant was invited to meditate privately on one aspect of Christ's life, or on a central mystery of the Christian faith – the announcement of the coming of Christ to his mother Mary, the Bethlehem birth, Christ's agony in the garden at Gethsemane, the way of the cross, or the crucifixion, his resurrection from the dead, the descent of the Spirit of Pentecost, or the glories of heaven. At the same time the formula prayer was recited over and over.

While the ten *Aves* were recited back and forth, beads spinning through my fingers to count the tens and identify the *Paters*, I was trying to meditate on the main mysteries of my faith. I had been doing this since my early primary school years. I had knelt in the lounge room at home, after the evening radio news, after the wireless serials had ended at eight o'clock, face hidden in the lounge, elbowing Sean or Maureen by my side, giggling as my father took his turn to recite a decade. We giggled because he was even then unable to recite accurately the words of the simple prayers. The giggling was mostly suppressed, but when it suddenly burst out into uncontrollable blubbering, my father would stop the prayers, erupt into momentary anger and, as heads were buried into cushions, the prayers went on. The Springwood version was far more serious.

The official presentation of the rosary in the seminary chapel, after the evening meal, was reserved for senior students as they took their turn, week by week, to lead us in prayer. It was good training for later on. Once we were all settled in the chapel, the leader would appear on the bottom step of the altar, a white surplice over his cassock, a large thin, red-bound book in one hand, his beads in the other. Each decade was introduced by a set text, summarising in antiquated language the historical facts mixed with devotional beliefs surrounding the particular mystery on which we were invited to meditate during the recitation of the decade of prayers. These set introductions became familiar, and then known by heart. At the end of each decade, the officer in charge would recite a prayer formula by way of a general summing up, before a community 'Amen', and on to the next decade.

The public recitation would not be complete without lengthy trimmings, or prayers which were recited at the end of the rosary. The 'Hail Holy Queen', shouted out with gusto, since it signified the end of the exercise. Not quite the end – on Saturdays and during the month of Our Lady, the month of May, we did a litany in her honour. An extravagant title was announced, followed, like rapid gunfire, with 'Pray for us'. There may have been fifty or sixty such exchanges, run off like a rattle-gun from a bomb-shelter in the First World War. Tower of Ivory, Morning Star, House of Gold, Ark of the Covenant, Mystic Rose, Help of Christians, Root of Jesse, Queen of Angels. Mysterious, exotic titles.

The litany of Our Lady was the most popular, but there were several others, such as the litany of the saints, or to St Joseph, or the one to the Precious Blood or to the Sacred Heart, both of which were extravagantly pious, verging on the effeminate, on the psychotic. In recent years these types of prayers have become unfashionable. The spiritual exercises of the forties and fifties, the hierarchy of good works and the multiple superstitions surrounding Fatima and Lourdes, the nine First Fridays, devotion to the Sacred Heart, the plenary indulgences to be gained in their hundreds on the feast of the Holy Souls, the three *Hail Marys* for the conversion of Russia, or for purity, the accumulation of ejaculations, seem to have disappeared into the Otto bin of the sixties – benediction, the rosary, litanies, the devotional life of the Church, which used to run parallel to the liturgy, are only memories shared by those dying of old age.

More Study, and other Activities

But the day had not yet ended. On ordinary days, more study time was scheduled. But before the silence and supervised discipline of the study halls commenced, the built-up tension of silence, listening and praying was relieved by another brief interlude.

Some super-pious students remained in the chapel to snatch another ten minutes for their private devotions, maybe to stroll leisurely round the stations of the cross one more time, perhaps to shuffle holy cards, or push on with another few pages of spiritual reading. Others adjourned to the library, especially on chilly, wet evenings. The place was not heated, but it was warmer than the cold wind blowing round the sandstone walls. The library enjoyed a relaxed silence, to facilitate freely selected reading – from the Catholic Weekly published by the Sydney Archdiocese for example, or the Advocate from Melbourne, or an article in the Catholic Encyclopaedia. This was, after a fashion, a self-imposed silence because while in theory the librarians policed the area and placed offenders on report, prefect Milton Lonard was a friend. Despite his huffing and puffing, pretending to be cross, he could not bring himself to utter the magic words: 'See the dean.' Milton lacked the charisma of authority. He liked his friends too much and we exploited his softness. He is dead now. May he rest in peace.

Small groups of boys frequented the library to whisper and giggle. Others scanned the religious press, or pretended to read some spiritual book, a life of one of the saints, perhaps a little church history, a religious novel of Robert Hugh Benson, even some neo-scholastic philosophy. The books in our library were not very catholic. Dr Joiner, the professor in charge of the library, had conducted a wholesale clearance of superfluous, unnecessary books by throwing entire shelves of volumes into clothes baskets and burning them gleefully in a bonfire. George loved fires, and like a true inquisitor, he was able to discard hundreds of volumes without even glancing at the title on the binding. It didn't matter much as most of the books had come to Springwood from the estates of dead clergymen. Their interest in history, spirituality, philosophy, if it ever existed, had died years before their passage to heaven, or hell.

In my senior years I sometimes visited the library, especially on windy winter nights when walking in the grounds was unpleasant and we were forbidden to warm even our hands by plunging them into trouser pockets. The library was warm and protected.

One evening, thirsty for knowledge, I was browsing among the mysterious tomes on the upper shelves at the back of the library. I pulled down an old volume which had been printed on soft, rather absorbent, heavy grained paper. The author had even then disappeared into the earth.

I began to read. The heroes of the world, the great men of history, generals, gifted poets such as Lord Byron or Oscar Wilde, prime ministers, presidents and popes were to be judged by standards altogether different from those which governed the lives of ordinary men. It appeared that the all-seeing, just judge of heaven and earth would scrutinise the great and important members of the race through some special prism. Power and position sometimes demanded a man to ignore the commandments. Leaders could tell lies with impunity, or distribute largesse, order discreet taking of life, bomb or torture. Sometimes these things were necessary for the well-being of society or for the good of a religious institution.

I was horrified. What was this seditious book doing in our library? I was young and simple. I did not yet know how complicated life could be. I was still living in a black and white world in which all men were born equal and the commandments (which were to be interpreted literally), were meant for all. My reaction was a neat mixture of natural egalitarianism and moral rigorism.

Here was an opportunity for growth. I was on the verge of discovery. I climbed the stairs to Dr Joiner's study to discuss this weird world view with my teacher. He was the librarian, the dean of discipline, my lecturer in Greek, Latin, Psychology and Epistomology. We stood facing each other in his dimly lit, untidy room. He listened impatiently as I tried to give expression to my dilemma. He puffed furiously on his cigarette and tried to hurry me up.

'Anyway, anyway where is this book now?'

'In the library, Doctor.'

'Well, anyway, we had better deal with this straight away.'

He thundered out of the room onto the balcony, with me following, down the stairs, and burst into the library. I identified the book which he examined cursorily and tore it up there on the spot.

There was no further discussion. He and I went about our separate business. He was certainly not interested in ideas.

Juniors were not permitted in the library. The powers assumed young men of thirteen and fourteen would not be interested in reading, or might get up to some mischief. So we were herded once more onto the front drive, where we walked up and down in the middle of winter, under the supervision of two trusted senior prefects. An energetic walk all the way down the drive to the convent and back again, produced a warm glow on hands and face, at least for the beginning of the evening study period. Though seniors were permitted to visit the library after the evening meal, most did not engage much in reading. Any interest which may have existed was greatly reduced by the narrow band of books on our dark, wooden shelves. Most philosophers took off for a stroll round the ghost track before dawdling to the classroom to commence study.

The bellman rang the warning bell, echoing through the grounds. Five minutes later, the final study bell sounded. Everyone was expected to be seated at his desk, silent again for an hour, if he was a junior, an hour and a half if a senior. Once more, a prefect was prominent in every study hall. He positioned himself with his books and pencil case under the crucifix, at the top of the classroom, seated on an elevated desk (the tub) from which the professors used to deliver their lectures. He maintained the silence, ensured no one wasted his precious time reading novels, surveyed the assembled students from time to time in between doing his own work, and dispensed permission to leave the classroom to go to the toilets.

A large toilet block, built in solid sandstone near the recreation hall just past the belltower, included a stall of black urinals, each separated by a solid divide, and a stable of cubicles. Each dormitory was serviced by shower and toilet facilities close by. Just past the top of the zig-zag flight of external stairs, close to Saint Columba's dormitory, was a damp and mossy shower block which also featured four toilet cubicles. The area was shadowy by day, dark as a deep hole at night, creepy even with the pale lights on, with rows of doors down each side of a narrow, duckboarded passage lit by two mean bulbs.

When I left the study halls at night to go to the toilet, alone, I would feel my way in the dark to the toilets near the recreation hall, or up the shadowy stairs, along the enclosed verandah, into the damp darkness of St Columba's facilities. Wandering around the college, away from the concentrated lights of the study hall, I was edgy in the darkness, ready to be startled by any sudden noise or movement. I was conscious of the shadows, and ready to spring into flight at the least warning. Darkness has always flooded me with a sense of foreboding.

I remember one particular occasion when I wanted a break from study, to have a little wander before starting on another subject. With the permission of the prefect, I walked along the covered, quadrangle pathway, down the dark main corridor, past the photo portraits of bishops and the pope, up the external staircase. I fingered my way along the rough sandstone wall which separated the enclosed verandah from St Columba's dormitory. It was dark. I was cold.

Before I could switch on the dull lights in the shower block, some large, cassocked figure enveloped me from behind. It struggled with me. It turned me round and pressed itself against me. It was strong and taut like a wrestler. Perhaps I had disturbed him. Maybe he was waiting for someone, or anyone who was searching his way in the darkness as he stood motionless in one of the cubicles. He began pressing himself to me, rhythmically, hard against me, as though to crush me, with ever increasing, short bursts of energy.

What's that under his cassock? A poker? Something hard and rigid. Why is he rubbing up and down on me? Why does he hold me so tightly? I wondered whether he wanted to wrestle. But why did he want to wrestle so late at night, here in the toilet, in the dark. This was weird. He was not talking. Why was he squeezing so hard? That iron bar under his clothes was strange. I couldn't breathe properly. Why was he hugging me. I wrestled, pushed, struggled until he set me free.

It was all over within a few seconds. As he hurried away in the half-darkness, I recognised him, half man, half boy. He was older than me, though not much. A country boy. I had played cricket with him. Although later, I realised what this teenage boy had been doing, even then I sensed his feeling of desperation and wondered at his spontaneous demonstration of unnatural strength. Puzzled, I passed water and returned to my study hall for the final burst of work.

On reflection, after I was armed with more knowledge from the dairy and the college pigsty, I wondered why a young seminarian who had dedicated his life to God, would, could gamble his eternal salvation on a few frantic seconds with a stranger in the darkness of the toilet block. Hell. Fire. Torment. But age has softened my puzzlement. It was a hard God that we were serving.

THE SOLEMN SILENCE

Springwood was cold, and in winter the trees shook and the wind howled around the buildings. Some nights we ran the ghost track. Sometimes we huddled in sandstone corners out of the wind before bells rang to gather us in the chapel one last time, for one last series of prayers. The prayerman read at full throat the evening prayers, acts of thanksgiving, words of sorrow and contrition, a verbal nudge to the guardian angel, a prayer for purity, the *Memorare* to the Blessed Virgin. Then a rustle of black cassocks signified the movement of a hundred men from knees to bottoms on seats. A second prayerman announced the points of meditation for the next morning. These passages were composed in archaic, super-devotional verbiage, but it was of no consequence. Only the scrupulous listened, while the majority dreamt of bed.

Study finished earlier for juniors. Senior students studied until 9.15 p.m. while the juniors were programmed to finish at nine o'clock, so that, as growing lads, they could enjoy an extra half-hour of sleep. The young ones finished study, walked again on the front drive for a short time, recited night prayers in common in the chapel, and crept off to bed by

9.30 p.m. As a junior, I was asleep when the others came up to the dormitory, thirty minutes or so later. The day had been long, and full to exhaustion.

The chapel emptied in a rush as the senior students hurried up the stairs to the dormitories. Some poked around, cleaning teeth, sitting on the side of their beds looking into space, changing into long-leg pyjamas under cover of their dressing-gowns. As if we had not done enough, some students knelt by their bed for the final, but now personal, night prayers. A five-minute warning bell, and then the last bell of the day. The senior prefect in the dormitory shouted 'Benedicamus Domino', 'Deo gratias', echoed back. When the lights were extinguished the day was complete. The dormitory was in darkness, except when the full moon flooded the space, right up into the rafters, with its half-light. In those pious days, rosary beads, packed in a small leather pouch, were hidden under my pillow. Drifting off to sleep to the sound of music on the radio, or dozing off halfway through a chapter read by the light of a bed lamp, was unimaginable. Sleep was a friend, and I was out within minutes. Under the cover of several blankets, my hand drifted under the pillow to track my way through one final decade of the rosary before sleep removed me from the burden of the day.

This was the solemn silence, known to us as the *summum silentium*, which would conclude after breakfast the next day. Like death, this was a period of deep sleep, of dreams, a time to meditate and pray, to unravel the mysteries and converse with the Lord and his saints. Not a word would pass, or a wink. Not a smile or a nudge. I was alone with God, through the night, in the darkness, like Samuel, listening for the call, ready to respond.

But there may have also been a more mundane, hidden agenda. This period of imposed silence may have been a crafty mechanism to control an army of rowdy, spirited young men. Though not everyone obeyed the rule of silence (and those who were caught in breach were punished severely), the mystery was that most of us accepted it as our bounded religious duty. The solemn silence controlled the conversations, the laughter and horseplay of a hundred and fifty stallions!

High points and celebrations

TAME AMUSEMENTS

Not every night in the seminary was ruled by the same routine. Saturdays were different, as were the nights of Holy Week. On Saturday evenings, after the rosary, the juniors would gather in their own exclusive debating society (of which I was a member for five years), while the seniors congregated in the sandstone recreation hall. It had a proper stage, a piano and a rogues' gallery of all the Springwood football teams which had been successful against the rampaging Manly men. There were not many team photographs in the collection.

Each meeting would begin with general business, motions, speeches, amendments, voting, the whole proceedings conducted according to proper parliamentary system. Students often became unruly, points of order flew every which way, and sometimes a loud, outraged seminarian would be ejected by the president, to cool off outside. Motions of dissent, motions of no confidence in the chair, or about sporting facilities, a levy for a new tennis net. We were not in charge of our lives, so there was not much to discuss or argue about.

We were served by office-bearers, a president, a vice-president, a secretary, a treasurer, and multiple committees elected for six-monthly periods. There were committees for everything – tennis, handball, football, picnics, entertainment. From time to time, though rarely, I managed to be elected to one or other of these committees, but never to a more prestigious office. Nor was I ever appointed a prefect to control and supervise the troops. My fellow students and the authorities must have known I was no leader of men. I was a loner, a dreamer, and perhaps even then, I was showing signs of respectful dissent.

Despite my best endeavour, my constant obedience, my submission to authority, my years of service and cooperation, I realised late in my life that I have never been an unquestioning, enthusiastic member of the A-grade team. I was never entrusted with a position of real responsibility. Some time ago, after I had turned sixty, I observed to my friend Neil that from an early age I had tried hard to be accepted as 'one of them'. I had kept the rules conscientiously, rarely spoke during periods of silence, worked hard during study period, performed my spiritual exercises even during the Christmas holidays, reciting prayers, learning formulae by heart, and yet 'they' had never really trusted me.

> 'They used to elevate some strange people to prefectship, but never inducted me into their policing ranks. Why? Why didn't they make me one of them , Neil?'

He smiled knowingly. He reflected for a moment, perhaps judging whether he really wanted to enter this dangerous territory. As serious as a judge, Neil answered my query -

> 'Because you've always been a person with attitude. You did not have to do or say anything. They could smell anarchy on you'.

I have never realised this. Rebellion must have been oozing from the pores of my skin. My mouth always said the right thing, and my steps always marched to the official tune. They had known something I did not know: that I was destined to think my own thoughts; that I was unreliable, untrustworthy, because I would eventually be my own man. The spirit of revolt was like the smell of liquor on an alcoholic's breath, like garlic on a hot day in a crowded train. It was unmistakable. When they looked beneath the conformity, the years of discipline, the impressive obedience, they saw in me those mad, Celtic, unpredictable, rebellious character traits of which the English and the Papacy have always been so fearful.

The juniors would organise something different each Saturday, for special business. Once for example, Flack, Bach, English, probably Mansour, and I read the radio play *Fire on the Snow*. Often someone would organise a quiz, like Bob Dyer or Jack Davey's radio shows, but without the double entendres. Once every six months, an amateur hour would be staged and some boys would sing, or recite poetry, play the mouth organ and perform a few basic tricks. Debates were frequent but not popular, and we would organise for one of the seniors to attend as an adjudicator.

The seniors seemed to have more fun. There were more of them, they were older and somehow more imaginative and crazy, and their facilities were far better. When I advanced to the senior years, the students staged concerts and projected acceptably modest movies often starring Sir Alex Guinness. They produced Shakespearean plays after months of rehearsals (*Julius Caesar, Macbeth, The Merchant of Venice*), building and painting scenery, sewing costumes. Most years we were entertained by at least one of the Gilbert and Sullivan mock musicals (*Pirates of Penzance, Trial by Jury, The Mikado*). I played in the chorus of *HMS Pinafore* in 1956, and *The Pirates of Penzance* the year before. John Hogan swung the baton and ordered us around as the musical director for *The Pirates*, and later for *The Mikado*. A major feast day, such as that of SS Peter and Paul, or of St Columba, was celebrated by a concert with a full range of items – the mouth organ choir, several soloists, a piano recital, Ed Kenny scraping on a violin, Professor Neville's failed magic tricks, a few sketches and a poetic recital. One year, under the baton of Neil Collins, a group of us recited a poem entitled *A Racing Eight*, almost in unison. They were innocent days.

I was well cast to play Rod Steiger as the square, regulated, sensible brother of Terry Malloy in *On the Waterfront*. Mick Harfield had worked as an usher at the Marrickville cinema during his Christmas holidays. He had collected tickets, shown patrons to their seats, and shone a torch in the darkness, while watching Marlon Brando play Terry Malloy. Marlon talked out of the side of his mouth, biceps ballooning like rock-hard breasts in his Chesty Bond singlet. Mick had seen the movie over eighty times – which might explain why he used to spit out of the side of his mouth, why he used to scratch his bum before moving in to kick the football, and why he knew the script by heart.

Pat Martin took Lee J. Cobb's role as Johnny Friendly. No one was allowed to dress up as Eve Marie Saint playing the luscious Eddie Doyle, so that part had to be written out, and Harfield himself played Karl Malden as Father Barry. Little, cheeky Charlie Mercieca was the New York taxi driver who refused to look where he was driving and who had an opinion on everything. And I was Terry's older brother, Charlie Malloy. Charlie Mercieca brought the house down as he sat on the stage, legs over the side smoking a pretend cigar, peering through his spectacles and driving a make-believe taxi, with me and Harfield in the back. Together on a low lounge seat, we argued the familiar script written out by heart by Harfield. My performance that night culminated when I was seen hanging from a meat hook at the back of the stage in my heavy overcoat. I was perched precariously on a fruit box placed strategically behind the back curtain. The audience rose to applaud my dramatic exit.

While I also played a minor part in the cavalry in an extravagant production of *Around the World in Eighty Days*, and as the chief inspector of police in *James Ryan*, my contribution over the years to Saturday night entertainment was modest. I was stiff and nervous, rather self-conscious in public and unable to cast myself into any other role than the one I was playing as myself.

Memories of the different Saturday night performances over the years conjure up a passing parade of clerics and fellow students for the priesthood. One of the great performances was that of Tom Keneally as Julius Caesar. Later John Cootes played the same role. He could also play the piano, strum a guitar and sing, and he performed *Gypsy Rover* in a quartet with his mates Lex Johnson, who later became a monsignor, Terry Quinn who skipped off after ordination, and Clem Hill who later lectured in Liturgical Studies at Manly and inherited my valuable, liturgical library. John Cootes was a man of ten talents. He was ordained in Rome by Pope Paul VI, played centre for Australia in our national Rugby League team, and scored prolifically. He entertained smiling crowds in clubs with his music and patter, left the priesthood, worked at Channel 10 where he was allowed to do whatever he wished on the sports team, and finally set himself up in the retail furniture business which proved successful.

Sean Flood played an old man in *Macbeth*. Michael Green was in the same production as an apparition, and in the orchestra, alongside the excruciating violin of Ed Kenny, in *HMS Pinafore*. Sean and Michael later worked together as public defenders in Sydney, where they acted for people accused of criminal offences who could not afford their own private barristers. Both have married, and remarried. Michael became a Queen's Counsel and has fought hard for fathers' rights in the Family Law Courts. Sean had been a rebellious larrikin in the Sydney law scene. He sat for a while on a tribunal which dealt with Aboriginal land claims before he was sworn in as a judicial magistrate.

Flea Foley also became an occasional barrister in Sydney. He was cast out of Manly into exterior darkness after he had been ordained to the deaconate because Toto Murphy, our dean of discipline, had considered him unsuitable, even after he had been awarded the Roman collar and the Latin breviary. When he left, he went into the law and lived at Mascot for a time with Mrs Gingles, John Hogan's mother, before moving out to the eastern suburbs, to live in the fast lane with Wilbur Wilson who had left the priesthood and the Bathurst diocese. He later became the senior partner at Clayton Utz.

Foley has travelled far, and though he is grey and a little more paunchy, he still has a touch of that fatal charm, a twinkle in his eye, patent leather shoes, an eye for any opportunity and a happy, larrikin streak. He had learnt a great deal as the producer of *The Pirates of Penzance* and as a gentleman of Japan in *The Mikado*. Toto Murphy had been right to move him on. Foley would himself agree that he would not have made a good cleric. Pity Toto didn't take the gun to many more!

Michael Hogan had also been a gentleman of Japan, and a policeman in Flea Foley's *Pirates* production. Ordained in 1960, as priest No.1185, he later studied politics at Sydney University, and was eventually appointed associate professor of government at his alma mater. Ron Flack was ordained as priest No.1242, in the same year as myself. He played a banker in the *Round the World* play and performed as an attendant at the manger in an early Christmas pageant, but the highlight of his stage career was as Katisha in *The Mikado*. Ron is now wearing someone else's heart in the diocese of Canberra-Goulburn, and prays for his donor each Sunday. Ron was luckier than some of his fellows. A few of the Saturday night performers, Peter Ryan, Bernie Callachor, Bruce Heaps (who nailed his shoes to the stage floor so he could sway about like a giddy drunk), are dead and gone.

The college parade of amateur actors also included a few future bishops. Kevin Manning, our inflexible head prefect, was, like me, too stiff and serious to perform in public in any role other than his own. The years have changed us all. Geoffrey Robinson played the soft, feminine role of Pish-Tush in *The Mikado* and then disappeared to Rome. Later, as auxiliary bishop to the cardinal in Sydney, he proved resolute and courageous in the scandalous sexual crisis which hit the Church in the 1990s. He led his brother bishops, protesting and feet-dragging, into some face-saving, public acknowledgment of fault. Bishop Peter Ingham, the future bishop of Wollongong, always smiling, played Lucius in *Julius Caesar*, while, rather ominously, the future bishop of Newcastle, Michael Malone, assumed the role of Soothsayer in the same performance. Since his enthronement in the Hunter Valley, he has had some painful messages to deliver, especially about Father Vince Ryan who played Portia, the wife of Brutus the traitor, on the same night. There was much foreboding then, and since.

David Walker became the bishop of Broken Bay. He was ordained with me, as priest No. 1258. We laboured for our doctorate together. As seminarians we packed into the same sweaty scrums, and walked through London together as wide-eyed clerics. Neil Brown and I were then doubled up with stomach cramps after being in Bombay. At Springwood, David showed both sides of his personality in our Saturday night dramas. He played a nobleman in *Macbeth*, on the side of the angels, and a cardsharp in *Around the World*.

The darker element of clergy life was also represented on the seminary stage. One of our old boys has been awarded a prison sentence for a history of serious breaches of trust over many years against innocent young boys. He was ordered, by two judges, to serve a total of twenty-two years penal servitude. Another served his prison sentence for entertaining schoolboys in his presbytery, and complicating their young lives. When he was removed from his parish, he was replaced by another old boy, later awarded a few years himself in gaol for misappropriating the parish funds to feed a gambling habit. The next one in charge of the flock summoned a meeting of the remaining parishioners in an attempt to get the parish back on the orthodox tracks, to tidy up the planned giving and increase the second collection which seemed to have fallen away. One of these priests as a seminarian at St Columba's, had acted as an attendant at the manger during a Christmas liturgical drama. At one stage he journeyed far away from the eastern star.

Father Vince Kiss is one of the college's more notorious old boys. He was invited to officiate in Venice at the wedding of Primrose Dunlop to a gay count who failed to show up for the ceremony. Vince was one of those high-profile clergymen. He lived in wealth among jewelled socialites. He dressed well, skied, ate in expensive restaurants, and used his easy charm and good looks to extend his social contacts. People loved him, including Monsignor Tommy Veech when he was rector at Springwood. Vince used to visit us there with presents for Tommy, gossip and laughter for us professors, and to remain in contact with those young men he had encouraged to follow his path.

Vince went to prison in Melbourne, for fraud. He misappropriated the trust funds of a charity which was dear to his heart. Vince had played many parts in the seminary. As well as being a champion runner and playing on the wing in our Rugby League team, he was the Mikado in one performance of Gilbert and Sullivan. He sang the *Magnificat* solo at our annual concert and played the leading role of the angel in a liturgical drama. He was a man of many guises.

On some important occasions, we would publish a programme for the performance, with a summary of the plot, a list of actors and the names of the producer, the director of music, the man in charge of lighting, or scenery, or costumes. The programme was run off on a Roneo machine and handed out as the patrons entered the hall. The rector and his team would enter the hall, and on major occasions, His Eminence Cardinal Norman Gilroy would grace us with his regal presence and fixed grin. It was not the State Theatre, The Tivoli or Capital Theatre, but we had to create some fun, occasionally, to relieve the tension of stressful formation.

Holy Week

Holy Week created a buzz of activity at Springwood. Classes ceased for a few days. When we were not in the chapel immersed in a lengthy Latin ceremony, those of us who could hold a note were practising medieval chants. These were generally mournful tunes. They set the tone for sin, suffering and death, though some were stirring and ecstatic and would herald new creation.

Just before Holy Thursday, there was a flurry in the chapel. Parquet floors had to be polished, marble sanctuaries washed, brass candlesticks rubbed to a golden sheen. There was general spring cleaning for Easter. For almost four days we occupied the chapel day and night. On Holy Thursday, Good Friday, Saturday and Easter Sunday, we were up and down, kneeling, genuflecting, singing, and standing for interminable periods for the singing of the Passion narratives from the various gospels. We recited the breviary, or the liturgy of the hours, with much bowing, sitting, and processing to and fro. We reproduced the ritual prayer every Roman priest recited privately daily, and which monks chanted night and day throughout the year. One side of the chapel against the other, verse after verse of what was for a teenager, mumbo-jumbo chanted in a sleepy monotone. The observances were sometimes in purple and without music, at other times in white ornate vestments, with bells tingling, perfumed smoke from thurible rising, candles burning, and the organ working overtime to fill the sacred space with thunderous life.

The matin prayers were the long haul. These were the prayers which monastics have recited for centuries in the dark morning hours – nine psalms, chanted reading of passages from St Augustine, St Thomas Aquinas, Gregory Nazianzus, John Chrysostom, or Theodore of Mopsuestia. Then the morning prayers of lauds and prime, terce after breakfast, sext at midday and none in the afternoons. This was followed by evening prayers or vespers, and night prayers or compline. The day was stuffed with plainchant and Latin prayers, rattled off at pace, and which none of us could understand. In later life I came to relish the beauty, the earthiness, the grandeur, the gutsiness of the psalms which our religious tradition had preserved for me. At the time, however, I used to watch the ceremony of the candles, longing for the end.

At night, to keep count through the readings, a cassocked figure would solemnly extinguish one candle at a time from the twelve-branch Paschal candelabrum at the top of the chapel, until all candles were exhausted and we were in darkness. On cue, each student would slam the pew in front of him with his *Liber Usualis*, the thick red ruby-leafed book, full of colourful ribbons containing the Gregorian chants. This ritual outburst of thunder and racket symbolised the discontent of the souls of the dead. We worked the moment with added enthusiasm since the rector usually insisted on absolute silence in the chapel. Suddenly, the lights would be switched on and we were back with the angels. These Holy Week ceremonies were known as *Tenebrae* (the Shadows).

To add to the religious strains of Holy Week, the programme demanded continued adoration of the Blessed Sacrament from the afternoon of Good Friday until the evening of Holy Saturday, a thirty-hour period lasting throughout the night. Each seminarian, in cassock and starched, lace surplice, was scheduled to take his turn before the Eucharistic bread which was entombed in the tabernacle, awaiting the liturgical re-appearance during the Easter Vigil ceremonies. Masses of candles and floods of flowers surrounded the tabernacle while six attendants kept their watch, as though near the tomb of Christ, kneeling on wooden prie-dieux, moving from one knee to the other, trying to pray. By the time Monday arrived, we were ready for rest, and recreation.

DISCIPLINE WAS PARAMOUNT

Monsignor Charles Dunne adopted the practice of reading aloud, at his public Sunday conferences, selected sections of the little green college rule book. These occasions were scheduled for fifteen minutes in the chapel, after the High Mass. When we had gathered once more in the chapel, the rector would announce any special happening, inform us of any important personages who planned to visit the college, or deal with any particularly scandalous situation which had come to his attention. On rare occasions he even named and publicly humiliated senior students for some particularly evil act, such as smoking, or raiding the freezer, or possession of food. He would always drill the assembled students. His exercises were performed until all hundred and fifty of us could move as one, sitting, standing and kneeling like angels, in total silence.

The college rule book was a thin, green, pocket-sized booklet delivered to each student on his induction into the college. Its contents were to be committed to memory since these detailed rules governed his life. He was obliged, for example, to attend punctually each and every exercise throughout the day. Reprimanded for placing his hands in his pockets, he was required to be dressed neatly at all times and directed to be polite, and charitable, without having any particular friends. He was forbidden to leave the college grounds without permission and to have contact with anyone from outside. Required to obey every command from lawful authorities, he was never to enter another student's room, to confess sins at least once a week, attend daily mass, meditate for half an hour each day, participate in morning and night prayers, do spiritual reading and two examinations of conscience during the annual holidays at home, and at all times to dress as a seminarian might be expected to dress. We thought we knew what that meant. Conservatively. Modestly. Not like Johnny O'Keefe.

These rules were considered to be so important that one of our spiritual directors, in answer to a scrupulous question from an especially innocent student, had advised that to deliberately and perhaps consistently break one of the college rules, could amount to a mortal sin. A mortal sin! An utterance like that could only further undermine the tenuous credit of a director, at least for any sane seminarian. His advice served only to unsettle the lives of the spiritually neurotic seminarians, of which there were always a good number. Those were the days when mortal sins multiplied like flies.

Only a new student would be dense enough to blow his nose during the rector's conference. Those who offended, only sinned once as the monsignor had a fetish against nose-blowing in public places. He would explode in anger, demand the student stand, castigate him in public, and forbid him ever to blow his nose in the chapel again. It was such fun for us. Each year we would wait for the same performance, and he would never let us down. Charlie must have loved the chance to traumatise and teach the new recruits how the system worked.

Charlie stood at the front of the chapel, a broad, red sash around his ample waist, addressing us in a lazy, nasal twang, as we all sat in silence, rigid in anticipation of what might be about to occur. At least once each year, he announced the names of the two or three blessed students who had been chosen by some secret process to study at Propaganda College in Rome. These were the special ones. They could reasonably expect to be bishops once they had completed their time in the centre of Vaticanised Christianity. These were the gifted students who showed signs of leadership. None who showed initiative or personal flair were chosen.

A steady stream of two or three seminarians moved on from Springwood (sometimes, though rarely, from Manly), to the Eternal City where they would be trained to be Rome's men in the provinces. Finishing touches would be made to their formation. They were expected to drink deeply at the wells of Roman learning. They would assume the dress, the manners, the mode of speech, the bearing, the mind-set of a Roman dignitary (*sub specie aeternitatis*). This special quality was known by us as 'Romanità'. Jack Moroney, Bruce McPherson, Geoffrey Robinson, Paul Mulconry, Hilton Roberts, Bill Brennan, Dick Hazlitt, Kevin Manning – these were the students of my time who followed such Roman personages as Con Keogh, Harry Davis, Grove Johnson, Dick Connolly, Roger Pryke, Guilford Young.

I remember one of the names announced by Charlie during his Sunday conference in my first year was that of the senior sacristan, and one of the more gifted members of the senior year which was made up of people like Colin Rice, Hos Dryden, Happy Byron, Brian Larkey, George Connolly. They were the really senior men, much admired by the lower ranks. Peter occupied the chapel pew immediately in front of the master of ceremonies, George Connolly, close to the sacristy, where he was able to dart in and out. He was forever supervising the neat arrangement of vestments for the various priests who wished to celebrate each morning, lighting candles and filling cruets. His eyes flashed while the rest of us were struggling to keep awake, wrestling with distractions in prayer, and struggling with our contemplation.

Peter was on his way to Rome, and all the students knew it. He had accepted our congratulations with bright eyes and obvious satisfaction. His diligent work and study had paid dividends. He had become one of the darlings of Dr Cornelius Keogh. Peter's intellect would be fully exploited in the centre of Christendom. Con Keogh was a Propaganda man himself. Armed with a Roman doctorate in theology, he had continued his brilliant career at Louvain, where he had been awarded a second doctorate in

Philosophy. He too had been a gifted student, energetic, enthusiastic, bubbling with personality and ideas. Smilingly he used to communicate his fascination with learning in refreshing, original insights.

In 1951 Keogh had returned to the Springwood seminary where he had begun his boyhood journey to the priesthood. He arrived with a removalist van full of European literature, books on philosophy, religion, poetry, literature, all paperbacks with soft, paper covers, many with pages still uncut. His liberating studies in Europe were to be exploited by the diocese in the seclusion of our Blue Mountains retreat where he became the dean of discipline.

Con sang in the corridors, and entertained the seniors in his study. His reading lamp burned into the early hours of the morning. His energy, carefree spirit and depth of scholarship captivated students like Peter, who listened attentively well after the lights went out in the dormitories and the solemn silence had begun. The senior students who had been privileged to share Con Keogh's new life, would creep back to their beds in the darkness, brimful of ideas, thrilled to have spent private hours in Con's den. His enthusiasm was disruptive. His institutional recklessness, his insouciance for the regulatory *vox Dei* was infectious.

Dr Keogh was an impressive man. Springwood was only an interlude on his journey. We all knew he would go far (to the university, to the cathedral) but he drove himself too hard. He deprived himself of sleep and pushed himself beyond the limits of endurance. Suddenly, our dean of discipline was no longer in the college, singing in the corridors, burning the midnight oil. He had been spirited away, late at night, without explanation.

Our Philosophy professor recovered from his episodes of mental illness, but only after many years of struggle and loneliness. He has recounted his terrible story many times. Feelings of desperation, his sense of profound loneliness brought him at last, by accident, in from the cold, to a meeting of members of the Alcoholics Anonymous. He was as debilitated by his illness as they by their alcohol. Both were suffering rejection, loneliness, failure and hopelessness.

From that netherworld experience, Con created something noble - a program of self-help for the mentally afflicted. Over the years he has established groups of the organisation called 'Grow' in many corners and suburbs of the globe.

When Con Keogh was lecturing Peter and his fellows at Springwood, both were at the top of their form. But Peter's triumph, which promised overseas, Roman studies, did not last as long as Con's promising career. Within weeks his ecstacy had turned to chocking resentment. Another member of the senior class of 1951 went in his place. This was someone educated at St Joseph's College, Hunter's Hill, and the son of a leading King's Counsel, an acclaimed Sydney advocate making his way at common law at the same time as Norman Jenkyn, Conybeare, Amsberg, Le Gay Brereton, Clive Evatt, Hugh Maguire, John Ferrari, Jock McClemens, Alf Rainbow, Colman-Wall and John Kerr, all names now known to me. The KC was a leading Catholic figure in Sydney at a time when it was not fashionable for Catholics to number members among the professional elite. The Church of England was still in the ascendant and its members made up the Establishment in Australia. The Masons were also powerful, even in the police force, and Catholics, by and large, made up the uneducated working class. But there were a few exceptions, doctors and barristers and the like, well known to His Eminence Cardinal Norman Thomas Gilroy, who undoubtedly often called on them for advice and support. Who you were and whom you knew were important even to the Church.

This King's Counsel had apparently been instructed by the cardinal to visit Jimmy Carlton (father of Michael Carlton, the ex-ABC journalist and more recently disc jockey on the infamous 2UE) on the very day of his wedding, to threaten him with hell and damnation. Michael's notorious father, also an old boy of St Joseph's, an athletic superstar, was leaving the priesthood to marry a Protestant, and the Catholic community was facing down a major, public scandal. The cardinal's man visited Father Jimmy Carlton as he was dressing for his own wedding. He frightened the groom so much that he did not front up at the church until sometime later, thereby puzzling the guests and causing tearful consternation for the bride. Jimmy Carlton later reported that the King's Counsel had informed him that if he went through with the sinful wedding, he would personally see to it that he would never find employment anywhere in Australia. Oh what power! The cardinal had sent a member of the Catholic Mafia on an errand of evangelical kindness.

If anything needed to be said to His Eminence, it would only have been a wink and a nudge. In any institution, the first will be first, and the last, last. Though the selection had already been finalised for 1951, perhaps the choice had been too hasty, plans could be changed. Peter's name was withdrawn, and his position on the team taken by another worthy candidate, who for a time brought glory on the Church. He was himself an intelligent, liberal, urbane man, a popular second choice.

Peter never made the journey to Rome. The selection committee had chosen him, but when the gift had been withdrawn, his disappointment, humiliation, and anger were unbearable. He left Springwood at the end of the year. His youthful desire to consecrate himself to God turned to a load of dry dust across his back. Like so many of us, neither candidate now walks the path he had originally chosen. Perhaps in the end, the wrong man went to Rome. Maybe, if the selection process had been more worldly-wise, neither would have gone to Rome, and both could have lived their lives without the unnecessary clerical complications visited on them. But who was to know? Each life, as it unfolds, is a surprise.

Holidays

In December we were released from the seminary for a few weeks of rest and relaxation with the estranged members of our families. I would work for a few weeks before Christmas in the delicatessen department at David Jones for Mr Bannon. My first job each day in the old George Street store was changing the dates on oyster bottles for fussy shoppers who demanded fresh produce. I worked also at the post office, sorting or delivering mail, and at Shelleys factory with Neil Brown and other seminarians, making soft drinks and trying to pretend that I was not a little shocked by what real workers said and did. After Christmas, I would go away with a few of my mates, travelling up and down the coastline, camping, cooking, driving, surfing, lazing in the sun.

The system expected us to maintain our routine of religious observance. There could be no holiday from the interior life. We were bound by rule to attend mass each day, to examine consciences, to set aside a regular period for reflection, to visit the Blessed Sacrament, to read some spiritually uplifting book (and of course to avoid the other kind of uplifting material) even during our holidays. To make sure of my conformity, I had to arrange for my parish priest to write a report for the rector about my spiritual practice during the vacation.

I had some trouble extracting a suitable letter from 'Mad' Mick O'Dea, the new parish priest of Neutral Bay. He had been known as Mad Mick since his days in the seminary and was a big disappointment to the loyal folk of Neutral Bay who were so accustomed to the smooth, gentle touch of Eris O'Brien. Instead of persuasion, we had infallible decrees. Rather than soft preaching from the Sunday pulpit, we endured loud, abrasive abuse, insulting diatribes and petulant, crazy displays of authority. A feeling of well-being and optimism gave way to alienation and puzzlement. He would order people about, ignore them, or abuse them from the pulpit. 'Mrs Mac, if you come to mass late again, you can take the fruitcake you gave me for Christmas and get out of the parish.'

To save parish finances, he would switch off the electricity at the mains at exactly 9 p.m. even in the middle of a parish dance or a theatre performance. Charlie Dunne asked me only once why he had not received a report card from my parish priest. When I told him who my parish priest was, he nodded, and never asked again. He obviously knew more than I did. He never chased me up again. Even though I reminded Father O'Dea to send off a report every time, he always failed to do so.

I was a touch scrupulous even during holidays. I attended daily mass without fail, and tried to set aside a period, an all too brief period, for meditation. I dressed like a seminarian, always conscious of my special vocation. I related to people, even to members of my family, in the role of a teenage priest. Though we had no transport, I used to try to visit the church at Neutral Bay a second time during the day for private prayer. The church was several kilometres away from home. I was often too lazy to walk there and back, but I was still plagued with the knowledge that I was bound. The burden of the routine was heavy for a young boy.

My drive to obey the demands of the rule would sometimes amuse my travelling companions, and sometimes annoy the hell out of them. I would insist on daily mass attendance even if it meant driving a long distance from our camp site, leaving without breakfast or a cup of tea, perhaps breaking the speed limit to arrive breathless in the pew on time. They would go along just to keep me happy.

The prize-giving

But before the holidays, after all the praying and swotting for examinations, in an atmosphere of excitement and anticipation, the college would enter a frenzy of cleaning and packing up. The wooden floors of the dormitories were scrubbed and swept. The college grounds were mowed and cleaned. I visited the loft under the belltower to retrieve my old, tan-coloured suitcase and packed my few possessions ready for a speedy getaway.

One ceremony remained before we pushed into the familiar buses for the ride between the Twins, down the drive into Springwood station and out into the world. Cardinal Norman Thomas Gilroy was driven from Sydney in his secretary's simple, bottom-of-the-market car. Mr Resch had not yet bequeathed his Darling Point mansion and his stock of Bentleys to His Eminence. His Eminence would prise himself out of the front passenger's seat, all smiles and grins, oily voice and platitudes, intending to stay the night and graciously distribute prizes the next day before taking the train back to Sydney. The cardinal was usually joined by several bishops, a group of monsignors and a retinue of local clergy, all adding colour to the occasion.

The choir had been practising for weeks – several pieces of rarefied polyphony, under the baton of Brother Kevin, or Valerius, or Gregory. We were on our best behaviour. We were dressed in cassocks and ruby-red sashes, though for my first few years, with a few other boys, I stood out for comment with my knees bare.

Prizes were distributed to the worthy, though no rewards or recognition were given for the most improved or for outstanding effort. We were all expected to make an outstanding effort. The rector announced names in Latin, and the cardinal distributed books, or sometimes money, for winners in Latin, Greek, Logic, Psychology or even Metaphysics. I sat for years hearing these announcements without any earthly idea of what they meant. Students clapped. The rector passed the book to His Eminence, who handed it on, toothy smile, throaty,

HIGH POINTS AND CELEBRATIONS

exaggerated congratulations, a limp hand shake, an awkward genuflection and a reverent kiss of the episcopal ruby. Next please.

On one occasion at Springwood, our final prize-giving was almost interrupted by a major bushfire which enveloped the lower Blue Mountains and which had surrounded the college. At night, I watched sparks floating on the hot breeze across the quadrangle, high up, between heaven and earth. Homes had been threatened – some destroyed. The district was covered with smoke on the move. It had permeated classrooms, dormitories and the chapel. Emergency rescue teams were on day and night shifts. Fire-engines could be heard wailing in the distance, as we packed for our Christmas holidays.

On another occasion, when the fires were raging on all sides, under instructions, the students had left the classrooms to join the locals. This was an emergency which put the examinations at year's end on hold. The mysterious men whom the locals hardly ever saw, were commissioned by the monsignor in the name of God to fight shoulder to shoulder with volunteers to save property. With bags and branches, rakes and shovels, they laboured. A group of blackened seminarians came upon a hut, a hall in the bush which was being threatened. It was the Communist Eureka Youth League building – the property of atheists, the focus of anarchy, the place of meetings for those who would undermine the faith, against whom Pius XII had spoken so convincingly. There was no time for a crisis of conscience. Defeating the enemy was a luxury to be reserved for later. They moved in rapidly, energetically, and saved the enemy's bush hideaway.

Some years later, with another fire raging, God's high-ranking representative, the cardinal, arrived with his secretary, not to lend a hand or even to rally the troops, but to distribute the prizes to the seminarians, and continue the tradition as though all was bliss under heaven. Multiple messages went unheard. Newspaper articles about bushfires went unread, radio warnings unheeded. In a hall full of smoke, students in cassocks, with shiny shoes and red sashes, received prizes (for Greek, Epistemology, Metaphysics), and kissed a gemmed ring on a soft dainty hand. Instead of rushing to the aid of distressed locals, thumping sparks with wet bags and extinguishing brush fires with dry branches of eucalypts, an army of young men sang polyphony in perfect unison. Salvador Dali could not have imagined a scene more bizarre. The students suppressed coughs from smoke-filled lungs and wiped tears from stinging eyes, as they sang and genuflected. Then they unbuttoned their cassocks, closed their suitcases and drove through the smoke, passing the fire-engines, to Springwood railway station. They were out of there, and on holidays, leaving behind the blackened gums, the stiff rock wallabies, the fried lizards, the charcoaled snakes. Truly in the world, but certainly not of the world!

J.M.J.

XM 5611

Marist Brothers' High School,
Cardinal Street,
Mosman.

Nov. 13th   19

CERTIFICATE OF CHARACTER.

This is to certify that

Christopher GERAGHTY,
of 16 Florence Street, Cremorne,

has been a pupil of the above School for two years, and is now in 6th Class. (He is 12 years old.) His teachers during his time here testify to his excellent character and conduct, both in and out of school. In class he works well, although he has not won very high positions in the Term Tests; out of class he takes full part in all the usual school sports.

I am pleased to be able to add my personal testimony to his character and conduct, which I have observed during the past twelve months.

Br. Gregory
Director.

Epilogue

A LIFE BEYOND

My boys have sometimes asked me why I stayed. My wife Adele has sometimes expressed her wonderment. I too have puzzled over why I willingly, sometimes happily, endured so much.

The simple explanation is that I believed I had a vocation – whatever that might have meant. From tender years I had come to accept that I had a calling to be a priest like Father Lander, Justin McGlynn, and that maybe I could aspire to be like Monsignor (later Archbishop) Eris O'Brien who seemed wise, learned and gentlemanly. I was challenged to set my sights high, to aim for the heavens, and in trust and docile faith I believed Springwood was the sweaty road to tread, the small price to pay.

Then after seven years I was promoted to Manly, to the major seminary, and after twelve years, ordained to priesthood. I was ambitious, ecclesiastically, and welcomed the invitations to undertake postgraduate studies. It was important, or so I thought, to build an elevated plinth from which I could effectively proclaim the message. I was eventually awarded a doctorate in theology and, although I served some time in the sun and on the beaches of the parishes of Cronulla and Avalon, I quickly returned to the hothouse at Springwood where I lectured, five or six years, to the continuing flood of youthful vocations. Those years were different but no happier than the earlier ones. I was still a junior, and forever anxious to please.

From Springwood, I escaped overseas. I spent two years studying with the Dominicans and Jesuits in Paris, with Congar, Chenu, and Danielou S.J., finding the confidence to be free.

I was trouble when I returned home to Sydney, to lecturing duties in the major seminary at Manly. All their suspicions suddenly turned into real fears. I had my own thoughts and my own, private inner life. The Gospel and the religious mysteries of the ages did not belong to them. They were mine as much as the property of others, and I could learn to cherish them for myself.

I took some time to find my way. While I drove a shuddering taxi cab, or pretended to advance the public image of the Health Department as its public relations officer, or pontificated on commercial television as a show pony for channel 10, I studied law at night and on weekends. For some perverse reason a mega legal firm in Sydney employed me for a few years while I practised and practised to forge a new career. Then I practised law some more, but at the Bar, before I concluded my second career on the Bench, hearing cases and judging, not so as to determine some poor sinners' eternal future, but only to circulate money throughout the community of injured workers.

I began to record this early period of my life so that my two boys might have some appreciation of who their father is, and why. I am pleased to record that what began so painfully, is ending so happily. And I have learnt so much.

Over the years I have learnt to speak up for myself, that 'no one's piss is port wine'; that some colours clash and should not be worn together; that it is a rare leader who will tell you the truth; that most problems have no simple solution; that despite my aspirations and some eighteen years of ministry, the priesthood was never really for me; that I am not, that I was never meant to be an organisation man; that a loving wife is a precious gift.

It took years for me to discover the beauty, the goodness of God's glorious creation. I learnt to dance late in life, and badly. Slowly, painfully, I learnt that intimacy was splendid and enriching, that it was permissible to be spontaneous, that sex was meant to be fun and a powerful means of communication with the person one loves beyond words. The warnings, the restrictions and terrible prohibitions slowly evaporated under the simple gaze of a happy creator who loved me.

For the past twenty five years, I have had the blessing of living with a friend whom I met in Germany, with whom I have given life to, and educated two sons, and who accepts my tendency to woof my food, cleaning my plate almost before others have begun. She knows I have a damaged digestive system from the seminary and that I should eat bland food, and slowly, though I cannot resist the urge to eat whatever is available. She accepts my contempt for cant and my love of rant. There is never any complaint from her that I want to attend the Eucharist each Sunday (though the boys have bucked as they have grown older and now attend only from time to time). She accepts that I cherish a faith-view of the world which she does not share, that I have an insatiable desire to catch up on my education, to read, attend lectures, to listen to hourly news bulletins, but only on the ABC!

Adele smiles knowingly at my advanced innocence, my incurable unworldliness. She frowns at my terrifying dress sense. I am often sent back to change my tie or a shirt, ordered to pull my shorts down from under my armpits. I am a creature of my past, and no willing or wishing will change this, so what's the point?

> 'Everyone's been young sometime, you know Chris - everyone except you. You don't have the benefit of the usual youthful mistakes or experiences', she told me.

And Adele was right. She knows I am reticent to discuss my clerical past on social occasions. There is too much to explain before people can begin to understand.

For this reason, and mostly while I was on circuit, I embarked on the recording of my memories for my boys, so that eventually they might come to understand the curious journey in which their father had participated. My world would be strange to them. They had not left their family at an early age, or attended boarding school, or learnt a book of Catechism by heart, or been governed by inflexible rules. Despite their Jesuit education, they had not spent long periods each day in silence, or at prayer, or in a chapel. Their world was not cluttered with dogmas and devotions, with nuns and priests in long, serge habits, with pious hymns and prayer formulae. I had had to fight my way out of that mess, out into the open spaces where God could be experienced and his creation celebrated. Patrice and Pascal had both lived in a warm, accepting home, with parents who had taken a daily interest in their education, who were anxious that they be happy, that they experience a tender mercy, some caring guidance, maternal and paternal love, where they could receive medical attention as soon as they fractured a limb and their stomachs were never twisted in hunger. They would never understand that in my previous life I could not visit the refrigerator whenever I felt peckish, that I had to eat whatever was provided, or that I had never laid in bed till ten or eleven, that I had hit the cold deck under orders at 6.30, or 7 a.m. on Sundays. How could they understand?

But I know that people can enter the world of others. By the power of the imagination, when invited and when ready, friends, lovers, readers can step into someone else's shoes and walk around in his world for a time. Otherwise there would never be a just judge, or a merciful confessor, or an understanding friend, or a compassionate wife, or a knowing son.

AND WHAT ABOUT THE OTHERS?

As a resident at Springwood, how was I to know what the others were thinking? How am I to know now whether they too have been haunted over the years by memories of their confinement? Whether they judge others harshly, or gently? Whether they regret their years of formation, or look back in gratitude? Do they too recall some youthful faces, some events with a nostalgic smile, some bullies, some tight-arsed prefects, some serious and obsessional clerics whose emotional and spiritual development had been poisoned, recalling them with forgiveness, or with bitterness?

How am I to know whether others felt enriched, or deprived, ground down or nourished? We were bound by a divisive silence. We were obedient. We accepted in faith what was provided without question, in the hope that one day we would be chosen. There were no questions to be asked, no criticisms to be welcomed, no exchange of ideas, no opportunity to open up to a fellow seminarian or to an authority figure.

I did not know what was happening in the head or heart of any of my teachers or confreres. I was a boy, then a teenager, cocooned in a small world. To begin with, what was happening elsewhere, even to those around me, was of no concern to me. I did not ask myself why they did what they did, or said what they said. I was concerned with what was happening to me. Though the priests who policed the corridors of the seminary had brothers and sisters, and friends, and each his own private life, his needs, his doubts, his times of laughter, his dreams, I knew none of this. We were expected to remain alone. While we shared the same faith, the same way of life, the same God, in another sense we shared nothing. No one opened up to another, sharing his deepest longings, his puerile fears in trust. There was no time! We were too busy. There was no forum, no space in which to share. We were too regulated and friendless.

What were my companions making of the incessant lectures? What did they do to fill up the tedious periods of prayer? How did they occupy the long hours of silence? Were some persecuted by doubts? How did a boy with a scrupulous conscience survive? How did those hungry young men cope with their lives as clerics in the wilderness, at a time when their hormones were multiplying and swelling their loins? I did not know. I could not even guess. We were all alone, and in training to remain so all the days of our lives. '*Noli me tangere*' was a dictate to govern our lives.

Like the trees of the Blue Mountains, the Sydney Archdiocese had vocations to burn in the fifties and sixties. Boys were coming from everywhere, from Cronulla, Henty, Dubbo, Campbelltown, Bourke, Willow Tree, Guyra, Lewisham, to volunteer for heavenly service. Busloads arrived at the steps. Many of them survived a selection process which in truth amounted only to their determination to persevere to the end. While pretending to scrutinise and choose, it failed to encourage the talented and reject the dross, but accepted almost anyone in its unreflective drive to clericalise the world. By chance, I happened to arrive at Springwood during a wasteful period, when the system as a whole was suffering the contagious disease of infallibility.

Many of my confreres are now dead. Some are in gaol, or lost the faith, or divorced, perhaps again and again. Some are generous priests whose lives are filled with faith and hope. Others have families who love them, a mortgage to service, a circle of friends, a mass to attend on Sundays. Springwood is empty, though the birds, the rock wallabies and the bush remain.

TELEPHONE: SPRINGWOOD 8

ST. COLUMBA'S COLLEGE,
SPRINGWOOD,
N.S.W.

LIST OF STUDENTS 1951.

1st PHILOSOPHY

- J. SHANAHAN (SYD)
- J. SATTERTHWAITE (ARM)
- S. McDONALD (CAN-G)
- J. KELLETT (SYD)
- T. CROKE (SYD)
- W. FULTON (WAGGA)
- K. COMER (WIL-F)
- P. CURRAN (BATH)
- B. RYAN (ARM)
- R. LACEY (SYD)
- W. MORONEY (WIL-F)
- B. DRINAN (SYD)
- J. MORIARTY (LIS)
- C. RICE (SYD)
- B. LARKEY (SYD)
- J. JENKINS (SYD)
- B. GALLERY (SYD)
- P. CLOHESSY (SYD)
- B. BYRON (SYD)
- R. MALLYON (WIL-F)
- F. BRADY (SYD)
- J. DUCK (SYD)
- P. LONG (SYD)
- G. CONNOLLY (SYD)
- T. MARTLAND (SYD)
- J. RILEY (LIS)
- J. MILLER (SYD)

3rd YEAR

- M. STEMMING (SYD)
- W. DUNN (SYD)
- P. DRISCOLL (JYD)
- G. DICK (LIS)
- R. BROWN (LIS)
- C. LENNON (ARM)
- D. LENNOX (ARM)
- J. SWANEY (ARM)
- T. SHARPE (SYD)
- F. JOSEPH (SYD)
- G. ROBINSON (SYD)
- M. HOGAN (SYD)
- J. MAHER (SYD)

5th YEAR

- J. GRIFFIN
- M. McNAMARA (SYD)
- J. CONWAY (SYD)
- N. TAIG (SYD)
- K. PENDERGAST (SYD)
- D. DAVIS (SYD)
- M. SINCLAIR (SYD)
- J. TIMBS (SYD)
- K. O'GRADY (MAIT)
- J. WALSH ((SYD)
- B. TITMUSS (SYD)
- L. HUNT (SYD)
- W. MEACHAM (SYD)
- R. BALDWIN (SYD)
- J. BLANCHFIELD (LIS)
- T. O'CONNOR (SYD)
- D. WILLOUGHBY (SYD)
- G. MATTHEWS (SYD)
- A TURNER (MAIT)
- J. LOWE (ARM)
- KYMES (WIL-FO)
- K. STOCKTON (SYD)
- R. BAKER (LIS)
- K. SARGENT (SYD)
- J. CAREY (ARM)
- M. KELLY (SYD)
- Paul RYAN (SYD)
- J. KELLEHER (SYD)
- B. BAILEY (MAIT)
- B. O'NEILL (MAIT)
- J. HEAPS (SYD)
- J. FORD (SYD)
- A. MURPHY (SYD)
- B. YATES (SYD)
- T. YOUNG (SYD)

2nd YEAR

- L. TOOHEY (SYD)
- M. FASSLOW (LIS)
- P. LEHMANN (WAGGA)
- F. DAVIS (SYD)
- W. CHALLONER (SYD)
- T. HYNES (SYD)
- J. LANGTRY (SYD)
- E. LEARY (CAN-G)
- D. McCARTHY (LIS)
- J. PEMBLE (WAGGA)

4th YEAR

- A. LANGTRY (SYD)
- T. McCARTHY (SYD)
- P. FOLEY (SYD)
- R. RHEINBERGER (CAN-G)
- C. HOLDSWORTH (WAGGA)
- R. LEAVER (WAGGA)
- B. SHADY (SYD)
- P. COFFEY (SYD)
- W. DOUGHERTY (SYD)
- K. BAYADA (SYD)
- T. BRIEN (SYD)
- N. GRANT (SYD)
- M. CONDON (SYD)
- J. PORTER (SYD)
- V. DOYLE (LI)
- M. LONARD (SYD)
- S. THOMPSON (SYD)
- P. CRITTENDON (SYD)
- M. MURPHY (SYD)
- P. LAW (SYD)
- L. PURCELL (SYD)
- B. CARROLL (SYD)
- G. McMAHON (CAN-G)
- T. INGRAM (CAN-G)
- H. ROBERTS (CAN-G)
- F. BURG (MAIT)
- F. BAROHMAN (CAN-G)
- A. SHARAH (SYD)

SPECIAL CLASS

- J. DONNELLY (SYD)
- P. TAYLOR (SYD)
- G. HILDER (SY)
- P. HARRINGTON (SYD)
- J. KENNEDY (WAGG)
- T. DOUGHERTY (LIS)
- A. McPHERSON (MAIT)
- W. KENNEDY (CAN-)
- Pat RYAN (MAIT)
- B. HEAPS (SY)

1st YEAR

- D. SHERRY (SY)
- K. ENGLISH (SY)
- C. GERAGHTY (SY)
- J. GALWAY (CAN-)
- R. SPECKMAN (CAN-)
- A. STARR (L)

LIST OF STUDENTS   ST. COLUMBA'S COLLEGE   1952

SCHOOL OF PHILOSOPHY

2nd PHILOSOPHY

C. RICE	(SYD)
B. DRINAN	(SYD)
B. BYRON	(SYD)
P. LONG	(SYD)
J. MORIARTY	(LIS)
T. CROWE	(SYD)
P. BRADY	(SYD)
J. JENKINS	(SYD)
J. DUCK	(SYD)
B. GALLWEY	(SYD)
G. CONNOLLY	(SYD)
K. COLMER	(WIL-F)
B. RYAN	(ARM)
J. SHANAHAN	(SYD)
B. LARKEY	(SYD)
P. CURRAN	(BATH)
J. KELLETT	(SYD)
R. LACEY	(SYD)
T. MARTLAND	(SYD)
J. SATTERTHWAITE	(ARM)
W. FULTON	(WAG)
W. MORONEY	(WIL-F)
J. RILEY	(LIS)
J. MILLER	(SYD)

1st PHILOSOPHY

J. CONWAY	(SYD)
N. TAIG	(SYD)
K. PENDERGAST	(SYD)
D. DAVIS	(SYD)
J. BLANCHFIELD	(SYD)
J. TIMBS	(MAIT)
G. MATTHEWS	(MAIT)
A. TURNER	(ARM)
J. GRIFFIN	(SYD)
M. McNAMARA	(SYD)
D. WILLOUGHBY	(SYD)
K. O'GRADY	(SYD)
J. WALSH	(SYD)
B. TITMUSS	(SYD)
L. HUNT	(SYD)
W. MEACHAM	(SYD)
E. STOCKTON	(SYD)
R. BAKER	(LIS)
M. KELLY	(SYD)
Paul RYAN	(SYD)
K. SARGENT	(SYD)
B. BAILEY	(MAIT)
R. O'NEILL	(MAIT)

J. HEAPS	(SYD)
J. FORD	(SYD)
A. MURPHY	(SYD)
B. YATES	(SYD)
P. YOUNG	(SYD)
P. TAYLOR	(SYD)
P. HARRINGTON	(SYD)
T. DOUGHERTY	(LIS)
A. McPHERSON	(MAIT)
Pat. RYAN	(MAIT)
J. TOOMEY	(SYD)
T. SULLIVAN	(SYD)
J. TUFFY	(SYD)
N. CLIFT	(SYD)
D. COFFEY	(SYD)
W. JOHNS	(SYD)
J. McRAE	(SYD)
N. COLLINS	(SYD)
F. MULCAHY	(LIS)
M. BURGESS	(WAG)
P. MURPHY	(LIS)
J. MORONEY	(WIL-F)
M. CLARKE	(BATH)
P. Nelson	(C-G)

SECONDARY SCHOOL

5th YEAR

W. DOUGHERTY	(SYD)
K. BAYADA	(SYD)
T. BRIEN	(SYD)
N. GRANT	(SYD)
M. CONDON	(SYD)
J. PORTER	(SYD)
P. FOLEY	(SYD)
B. SHEEDY	(SYD)
P. COFFEY	(SYD)
P. RHEINBERGER	(CAN-G)
C. HOLDSWORTH	(WAG)
R. LEAVER	(WAG)
V. DOYLE	(LIS)
J. KELLEHER	(SYD)
P. CRITTENDEN	(SYD)
M. MURPHY	(SYD)
P. LAW	(SYD)
L. PURCELL	(SYD)
T. PIGRAM	(CAN-G)
H. ROBERTS	(CAN-G)
P. BURG	(MAIT)
A. SHARAH	(SYD)
B. HEAPS	(SYD)
T. CROWLEY	(SYD)
G. AGNEW	(SYD)
D. RHEINBERGER	(SYD)
F. BURDETT	(SYD)
N. ARMSTRONG	(SYD)
K. FITZGERALD	(WAG)
T. HORNERY	(MAIT)

4th YEAR

M. STENNING	(SYD)
W. DUNN	(SYD)
P. DRISCOLL	(SYD)
G. DICK	(LIS)
R. BROWN	(LIS)
C. LENNON	(ARM)
D. LENNOX	(ARM)
T. SHARPE	(SYD)
P. JOSEPH	(SYD)
G. ROBINSON	(SYD)
J. DONNELLY	(SYD)
M. LONARD	(SYD)
W. KENNEDY	(CAN-G)
M. HOGAN	(SYD)
J. MAHER	(SYD)
E. LEARY	(CAN-G)
D. McCARTHY	(LIS)
B. CARROLL	(SYD)
D. HORAN	(SYD)
P. BELLHOUSE	(SYD)
M. JOYCE	(MAIT)

SPECIALS

J. SPALDING	(SYD)
P. NORTON	(SYD)
P. SIMMONS	(WIL-F)
E. LIUGA	(MAIT)

3rd YEAR

L. TOOHEY	(SYD)
M. PASSLOW	(LIS)
P. LEHMANN	(WAG)
P. DAVIS	(SYD)
W. CHALLENOR	(SYD)
J. LANGTRY	(SYD)
J. PEMBLE	(WAG)
J. SALWAY	(CAN-G)
R. BRAY	(SYD)
C. HASSETT	(MAIT)

2nd YEAR

T. HYNES	(SYD)
K. ENGLISH	(SYD)
C. GERAGHTY	(SYD)
R. SPACKMAN	(CAN-G)
A. STARR	(LIS)
K. MANNING	(BATH)
D. CARROLL	(SYD)

```
LIST OF STUDENTS        ST. COLUMBA'S COLLEGE                        1953

                        SCHOOL OF PHILOSOPHY
                             2nd PHILOSOPHY
    J. CONWAY      (SYD)    R. BAKER(Ireland)(LIS)  T. SULLIVAN    (SYD)
    D. DAVIS       (SYD)    M. KELLY        (SYD)   J. TUFFY       (SYD)
    J. TIMBS       (MAIT)   Paul RYAN       (SYD)   N. CLIFT       (SYD)
    A. TURNER      (ARM)    K. SARGENT      (SYD)   D. COFFEY      (SYD)
    J. GRIFFIN     (SYD)    R. O'NEILL      (MAIT)  W. JOHNS (Rome)(SYD)
    M. McNAMARA    (SYD)    J. HEAPS        (SYD)   J. McRAE       (SYD)
    D. WILLOUGHBY  (SYD)    J. FORD         (SYD)   N. COLLINS     (SYD)
    K. O'GRADY     (SYD)    B. YATES        (SYD)   F. MULCAHY     (LIS)
    J. WALSH       (SYD)    P. YOUNG        (SYD)   M. BURGESS     (WAG)
    B. TITMUSS     (SYD)    P. TAYLOR       (SYD)   D. MURPHY(Ireland)(LIS)
    L. HUNT        (SYD)    P. HARRINGTON   (SYD)   J. MORONEY     (WIL-F)
    W. MEACHAM     (SYD)    T. DOUGHERTY    (LIS)   M. CLARKE      (ARM)
    E. STOCKTON    (SYD)    A. MACPHERSON   (MAIT)  P. NELSON(Rome)(CAN-G)
                            Patrick RYAN    (MAIT)

                             1st PHILOSOPHY
    W. DOUGHERTY   (SYD)    F. BURG         (MAIT)  Anthony RYAN   (SYD)
    T. O'BRIEN     (SYD)    A. SHIRAH       (SYD)   D. LIEVESLEY   (SYD)
    N. GRANT       (SYD)    D. HEAPS        (SYD)   P. GILCHRIST   (SYD)
    M. CONDON      (SYD)    T. CROWLEY      (SYD)   D. O'NEILL     (SYD)
    J. PORTER      (SYD)    G. AGNEW        (SYD)   K. HOMANN      (SYD)
    P. FOLEY       (SYD)    D. RHEINDERGER  (SYD)   M. SCOTT       (SYD)
    B. SHEEDY      (SYD)    T. HORNERY      (MAIT)  W. ALIPRANDI   (SYD)
    P. COFFEY      (SYD)    J. SPALDING     (SYD)   T. KENEALLY    (SYD)
    P. RHEINDERGER (CAN-G)  J. NORTON       (SYD)   P. FRANCIS     (SYD)
    V. DOYLE       (LIS)    P. SIMMONS      (WIL-F) J. NESBITT     (SYD)
    P. CRITTENDEN  (SYD)    E. LUGA         (MAIT)  J. MACKINNON   (SYD)
    M. MURPHY      (SYD)    A. WILKINSON    (CAN-G) B. MACPHERSON  (ARM)
    L. PURCELL     (SYD)    E. BARRY        (SYD)   J. McGEE       (WAG)
    T. PIGRAM      (CAN-G)  L. CASHEN       (SYD)   B. HUNT        (WAG)
    H. ROBERTS     (CAN-G)  Brian RYAN      (SYD)   A. PARSONS     (MAIT)
                            P. MURRAY       (SYD)

                        SECONDARY SCHOOL
    5th YEAR                4th YEAR                SPECIAL CLASS
    K. BAYADA      (SYD)    L. TOOHEY       (SYD)   P. LAW         (SYD)
    C. HOLDSWORTH  (WAG)    P. LENEHAN      (WAG)   J. NAGYS       (---)
    R. LEAVER      (WAG)    P. DAVIS        (SYD)   F. WARHAM      (SYD)
    B. BURDETT     (SYD)    W. CHALLENOR    (SYD)   F. JANOVSKY    (SYD)
    H. STENNING    (SYD)                            J. MASTERS     (SYD)
    W. DUNN        (SYD)    J. LANGTRY      (SYD)   J. HICKEY      (SYD)
    P. DRISCOLL    (WLG)    J. SALWAY       (WLG)   D. FLETCHER    (SYD)
    G. DICK        (LIS)    R. BRAY         (SYD)   A. CASTELLI    (ARM)
    R. BROWN       (LIS)    C. HASSETT      (MAIT)  R. STAPLETON   (BATH)
    D. LENNOX      (ARM)    J. KENNEDY      (CAN-G) W. HEFFERNAN   (WAG)
    T. SHARPE      (SYD)    G. MONAGHAN     (CAN-G) J. KELLY       (LIS)
    P. JOSEPH      (SYD)    D. GIBBONS      (MAIT)  B. JOHNS       (WLG)
    G. ROBINSON    (SYD)    W.              (SYD)   R. FLACK       (CAN-G)
    J. DONNELLY    (SYD)    D. PEGREM       (SYD)
    M. LONARD      (SYD)
    W. KENNEDY     (CAN-G)  3rd YEAR
    K. HOGAN       (SYD)
    J. MAHER       (SYD)    T. HYNES        (SYD)
    E. LEARY       (CAN-G)  K. ENGLISH      (SYD)
    D. McCARTHY    (LIS)    C. GERAGHTY     (SYD)
    D. HORAN       (SYD)    R. SPACKMAN     (CAN-G)
    P. BELLHOUSE   (SYD)    K. MANNING      (BATH)
    M. JOYCE       (MAIT)   D. CARROLL      (SYD)
    Peter RYAN     (SYD)    W. ALLPORT      (SYD)
    H. KIRBEN      (WAG)    W. Rohan
    H. CHAPMAN     (MAIT)
    T. BRENNAN     (MAIT)
```

LIST OF STUDENTS ST. COLUMBA'S COLLEGE 1954

SCHOOL OF PHILOSOPHY

SECOND YEAR PHILOSOPHY

W. DOUGHERTY	(SYD)	T. PIGRAM	(CAN-G)	D. O'NEILL	(SYD)
N. GRANT	(SYD)	H. ROBERTS	(CAN-G)	K. HOMANN	(SYD)
M. CONDON	(SYD)	P. BURG	(MAIT)	M. SCOTT	(SYD)
P. FOLEY	(SYD)	T. CROWLEY	(SYD)	W. ALIPRANDI	(SYD)
B. SHEEDY	(SYD)	G. AGNEW	(SYD)	T. KENEALLY	(SYD)
P. COFFEY	(SYD)	D. RHEINBERGER	(SYD)	P. FRANCIS	(SYD)
D. RHEINBERGER	(CAN-G)	T. HORNERY	(MAIT)	J. NESBITT	(SYD)
V. DOYLE	(LIS)	J. SPALDING	(SYD)	J. MACKINNON	(SYD)
P. CRITTENDEN	(SYD)	J. NORTON	(SYD)	B. MACPHERSON	(ARM)
M. MURPHY	(SYD)	P. SIMMONS	(WIL-F)	J. McGEE	(WAG)
L. PURCELL	(SYD)	E. BARRY	(SYD)	A. PARSONS	(MAIT)
		D. LIEVESLEY	(SYD)		

FIRST YEAR PHILOSOPHY

J. KELLEHER	(SYD)	D. McCARTHY	(LIS)	J. DESMARCHELIER	(SYD)
K. BAYADA	(SYD)	P. BELLHOUSE	(SYD)	J. DAVOREN	(SYD)
C. HOLDSWORTH	(WAG)	M. JOYCE	(MAIT)	R. BROGAN	(SYD)
R. LEAVER	(WAG)	T. BRENNAN	(MAIT)	E. CAMPION	(SYD)
F. BURDETT	(SYD)	B. HEAPS	(SYD)	T. HUNT	(CAN-G)
M. STENNING	(SYD)	P. LAW	(SYD)	C. NAUGHTON	(CAN-G)
W. DUNN	(SYD)	F. JANOVSKY	(SYD)	P. BRYANT	(CAN-G)
P. DRISCOLL	(W'GONG)	J. MASTERS	(SYD)	J. McCARTHY	(CAN-G)
G. DICK	(LIS)	B. FLETCHER	(SYD)	J. RHEINBERGER	(CAN-G)
R. BROWN	(LIS)	A. CASTELLI	(ARM)	R. BUCKHORN	(ARM)
G. ROBINSON	(SYD)	R. STAPLETON	(BATH)	Thos. CROWLEY	(ARM)
J. DONELLY	(SYD)	J. KELLY	(LIS)	W. SHIEL	(MAIT)
M. LONARD	(SYD)	B. JOHNS	(W'GONG)	A. MAYES	(MAIT)
W. KENNEDY	(CAN-G)	F. DENDEICH	(SYD)	G. MULLINS	(CAN-G)
M. HOGAN	(SYD)	J. GINMAN	(SYD)	G. IVERSON	(WAG)
J. MAHER	(SYD)			R. BARTLETT	(WAG)

SECONDARY SCHOOL

5th YEAR

D. HORAN	(SYD)
L. TOOHEY	(SYD)
P. LEHMANN	(WAG)
P. DAVIS	(SYD)
W. CHALLENOR	(SYD)
J. LANGTRY	(SYD)
J. SALWAY	(W'GONG)
R. BRAY	(SYD)
C. HASSETT	(MAIT)
G. MONAGHAN	(CAN-G)
D. PEGREM	(SYD)
L. McDONALD	(BATH)
D. DOYLE	(W-F)

3rd YEAR

W. ALLPORT	(SYD)
A. ADAMS	(MAIT)
B. HART	(SYD)
P. HODGSON	(W'GONG)
J. WALL	(ARM)

4th YEAR

Peter RYAN	(SYD)
R. FLACK	(CAN-G)
J. KENNEDY	(CAN-G)
B. GIBBONS	(MAIT)
W. ROHAN	(SYD)
T. HYNES	(SYD)
K. ENGLISH	(SYD)
C. GERAGHTY	(SYD)
R. SPACKMAN	(CAN-G)
K. MANNING	(BATH)
B. CALLACHOR	(SYD)
J. GILES	(SYD)
B. DOOLAN	(SYD)
M. O'NEILL	(SYD)
T. HART	(SYD)
B. DWYER	(SYD)
G. TURLEY	(SYD)
J. BRYANT	(CAN-G)
P. SMYTH	(WAG)
M. BACH	(W'GONG)
P. MANSOUR	(ARM)

SPECIAL LATIN CLASS

M. CHAPMAN	(MAIT)
W. HEFFERNAN	(WAG)
J. McCAFFERY	(SYD)
P. PINEL	(SYD)
F. ALLSOPP	(SYD)
J. BROWNE	(Can-G)
C. CROESE	(WAG)
N. HUGHES	(CAN-G)
T. O'BRIEN	(ARM)
B. SINCLAIR	(LIS)
J. WOODS	(MAIT)
P. QUINN	(WAG)
K. BARRY-COTTER	(CAN-G)

SECOND YEAR PHILOSOPHY

J. KELLEHER	(SYD)	D. McCARTHY	(LIS)	J. DESMARCHELIER	(SYD)
K. BAYADA	(SYD)	P. BELLHOUSE	(SYD)	J. DAVOREN	(SYD)
C. HOLDSWORTH	(WAG)	M. JOYCE	(MAIT)	R. BROGAN	(SYD)
R. LEAVER	(WAG)	T. BRENNAN	(MAIT)	E. CAMPION	(SYD)
T. BURDETT	(SYD)	B. HEAPS	(SYD)	T. HUNT	(CAN-G)
M. STENNING	(SYD)	P. LAW	(SYD)	P. BRYANT	(CAN-G)
W. DUNN	(SYD)	~~P. JANOVSKY~~ 14/8/5 (SYD)		J. McCARTHY	(CAN-G)
G. DICK 22/8/55	(LIS)	J. MASTERS	(SYD)	J. RHEINBERGER	(CAN-G)
~~R. BROWN~~	(LIS)	B. FLETCHER	(SYD)	R. BUCKHORN	(ARM)
~~G. ROBINSON~~ 22/8/55	(SYD)	~~R. STAPLETON~~ CASTELLI 19/8/55	(ARM)	T. CROWLEY	(ARM)
J. DONELLY	(SYD)		(BATH)	W. SHIEL	(MAIT)
M. BONARD	(SYD)	J. KELLY	(LIS)	A. HAYES	(MAIT)
W. KENNEDY	(CAN-G)	B. JOHNS	(W'GONG)	G. IVERSON	(WAG)
M. HOGAN July 6, 55	(SYD)	F. BENDEICH	(SYD)	R. BARTLETT	(WAG)
~~J. MAHER~~	(SYD)	J. GINMAN	(SYD)		

44/39

FIRST YEAR PHILOSOPHY

M. CHAPMAN	(MAIT)	J. LANGTRY	(SYD)	J. SAUNDERS	(MAIT)
W. HEFFERNAN	(WAG)	R. BRAY	(SYD)	J. McGEE	(WAG)
J. McCAFFERY	(SYD)	D. PEGREM	(SYD)	B. COLLINS	(SYD)
~~P. PINE~~ 4/5/55	(SYD)	J. SALWAY	(W'GONG)	J. ALT	(SYD)
F. ALLSOPP	(SYD)	C. HASSETT	(MAIT)	~~P. TITMUSS~~ 26/8/5	(SYD)
J. BROWNE	(CAN-G)	G. MONAGHAN	(CAN-G)	T. DAVEY	(SYD)
~~C. CROESE~~	(WAG)	L. McDONALD	(BATH)	V. REDDEN	(SYD)
P. QUINN	(WAG)	F. WARHAM	(SYD)	W. STENNING	(SYD)
R. O'BRIEN	(ARM)	J. DARGAN	(MAIT)	K. MURPHY	(WIL-F)
~~D. SINCLAIR~~ 22/8/55	(LIS)	T. O'CONNOR	(SYD)	K. CALLINAN	(MAIT)
J. WOODS	(MAIT)	G. RUTLEDGE	(WIL-F)	J. FOLEY	(WAG)
K. BARRY-COTTER	(CAN-G)	F. LE FEVRE	(SYD)	D. PERRETT	(ARM)
D. DOYLE	(WIL-F)	~~J. O'DONNELL~~	(MAIT)	W. BRENNAN	(WIL-F)
M. DARGAN	(MAIT)	T. MEAGHER	(CAN-G)	C. DICK	(LIS)
D. COATES	(WIL-F)	J. SPORA	(SYD)	M. MULLANE	(ARM)
D. HORAN	(SYD)	P. QUILTY	(SYD)	~~M. CLIFFORD~~	(CAN-G)
L. TOOHEY	(SYD)	G. KINGS	(SYD)	~~F. MOBBS~~ 7/2/55	(ARM)
W. CHALLENOR	(SYD)	J. HOGAN	(SYD)	def. 24/5/55	

SPECIAL LATIN

L. O'NEILL	(CAN-G)
P. ALAM	(MAIT)
J. PERIERA	(SAMOA)
P. MAY	(SYD)
R. LAWLER	(SYD)
M. BELL	(SYD)
P. DAY	(SYD)
R. RYAN	(SYD)
P. NEVILLE	(SYD)
B. WILLIS	(SYD)
J. STACE	(MAIT)
J. TINKLER	(WIL-F)
B. PIERCE	(SYD)
~~B. SADLIER~~ 25/7/55	(SYD)
~~P. HEFFER~~ 3/8/55	(ARM)
A. LEVEY	(MAIT)
N. HUGHES	(CAN-G)
T. SCHREIBER	(LIS)
P. Martin 18/4/55	

FIFTH YEAR

P. RYAN	(SYD)
R. FLACK	(CAN-G)
J. KENNEDY	(CAN-G)
B. GIBBONS	(MAIT)
W. ROHAN	(SYD)
T. HYNES	(SYD)
K. ENGLISH	(SYD)
C. GERAGHTY	(SYD)
R. SPACKMAN	(CAN-G)
K. MANNING	(BATH)
B. CALLACHOR	(SYD)
J. GILES	(SYD)
B. DWYER	(SYD)
G. TURLEY	(SYD)
M. BACH	(W'GONG)
P. MANSOUR	(ARM)
J. O'NEILL	(SYD)
R. CHIVERS	(SYD)

18

FOURTH YEAR

~~T. DOOLAN~~ 10/8/55	(SYD)
M. O'NEILL	(SYD)
~~T. HART~~ 3/8/55	(SYD)
A. ADAMS	(MAIT)
P. HODGSON	(W'GONG)
J. R. BEAVEN	(BATH)
N. SLOAN	(CAN-G)
P. REES	(MAIT)
~~P. IRVING~~ 12/4/55	(SYD)
R. SYNOTT	(SYD)
R. GRANT	(SYD)
J. ANDERSON	(SYD)
B. INNIS	(SYD)
F. WILKINSON	(MAIT)
~~L. BRUGG~~ 30/9/55	(LIS)

17

149 Started
134 Finished
Dismissed

10/8/55 14
15/8/55 140
19/8/55 139
22/8/55 136
27/8/55 135
F. Meloork 1/10/55 134
NOT returning

12/4/55
148
11/5/55 147
7/55 146
29/7/55 144
3/8/55 142

LIST OF STUDENTS   ST. COLUMBA'S COLLEGE   1956

SECOND YEAR PHILOSOPHY

M. CHAPMAN 5/7/56	(MAIT)	R. BRAY	(SYD)	J. HOGAN	(SYD)
W. HEFFERNAN	(WAG)	D. PEGREM	(SYD)	J. SAUNDERS	(MAIT)
J. McCAFFERY	(SYD)	J. SALTAY	(W'GONG)	J. McGEE	(WAG)
J. BROWNE	(CAN-G)	C. HASSETT	(MAIT)	B. COLLINS	(SYD)
C. CROESE	(WAG)	G. MONAGHAN	(CAN-G)	J. ALT	(SYD)
P. QUINN	(WAG)	D. McDONALD 14/9/56	(BATH)	T. DAVEY	(SYD)
R. O'BRIEN	(ARM)	F. WARHAM	(SYD)	V. REDDEN	(SYD)
J. WOODS	(MAIT)	J. DARGAN	(MAIT)	W. STENNING	(SYD)
K. BARRY-COTTER	(CAN-G)	T. O'CONNOR 14/9/56	(SYD)	K. MURPHY	(WIL-F)
D. DOYLE	(WIL-F)	G. RUTLIDGE	(WIL-F)	K. CALLINAN	(MAIT)
M. DARGAN	(MAIT)	F. LE FEVRE	(SYD)	J. FOLEY	(WAG)
D. COATES	(WIL-F)	J. O'DONNELL	(MAIT)	D. PERRETT	(ARM)
D. HORAN	(SYD)	T. MEAGHER	(CAN-G)	W. BRENNAN	(WIL-F)
L. TOOHEY 29/3/56	(SYD)	J. SPORA	(SYD)	C. DICK	(LIS)
W. CHALLONER	(SYD)	P. QUILTY	(SYD)	M. MULLANE	(ARM)
J. LANGTRY	(SYD)	G. KINGS	(SYD)		

FIRST YEAR PHILOSOPHY

P. RYAN	(SYD)	K. ENGLISH	(SYD)	M. HARFIELD	(SYD)
R. FLACK	(CAN-G)	C. GERAGHTY	(SYD)	S. HYNDES	(SYD)
J. KENNEDY	(CAN-G)	R. Spackman 19/3/	(CAN-G)	P. DELANEY	(SYD)
K. MANNING	(BATH)	B. CALLAGHOR	(SYD)	D. WALKER	(SYD)
L. O'NEILL	(CAN-G)	J. GILES 22/10/56	(SYD)	B. NOBBS	(SYD)
J. PERIERA	(SAM)	D. DWYER 15/4/	(SYD)	N. BROWN	(SYD)
P. MAY	(SYD)	M. BACH	(W'GONG)	E. KENNY	(ARM)
R. LAWLER	(SYD)	P. MANSOUR	(ARM)	J. FLOOD	(ARM)
R. RYAN	(SYD)	J. O'NEILL	(SYD)	M. WILLIAMS	(ARM)
P. NEVILLE	(SYD)	J. PHELAN	(ARM)	P. CAIN	(BATH)
B. WILLIS	(SYD)	A. WOOLLADER 5/6/	(WAG)	P. MULCONRY	(MAIT)
J. STACE	(MAIT)	R. HAZLITT 17/6/	(W'GONG)	J. DREWE	(SYD)
J. TINKLER	(WIL-F)	K. HISCOX 3/4/	(MAIT)	D. FOLEY	(SYD)
B. PIERCE	(SYD)	P. LAWLER	(SYD)	B. FRASER	(SYD)
A. LEVEY	(MAIT)	J. ASHTON	(SYD)	R. PERRETT	(ARM)
P. MARTIN	(MAIT)	R. WEAVER	(SYD)	G. MULHEARN	(MAIT)
B. GIBBONS	(MAIT)	J. WALTER	(SYD)	C. MERCIECA	(WIL-F)
T. HYNES	(SYD)	K. O'BRIEN	(SYD)	A. CASEY	(MAIT)

SPECIAL LATIN

P. ALAM	(MAIT)
R. CHIVERS	(SYD)
K. FLANAGAN 1/2/56	(WAG)
B. ROONEY	(SYD)
J. KENNY	(BATH)
B. BURKE	(MAIT)
G. JACKSON	(MAIT)
J. BATES	(MAIT)
A. DOHERTY	(SYD)
J. KEARNEY	(SYD)
V. WHITEMAN	(W'GONG)
A. BRESLIN	(SYD)
B. MITCHELL	(SYD)
J. SHEEHY	(SYD)
B. FRIZE 26/2/56	(ARM)
S. FLOOD	(ARM)
G. HANNAN	(CAN-G)
L. BLAKE	(CAN-G)
M. CRITTENDEN	(MAIT)
A. LENNON 19/6/	(WAG)
P. CHRISTIE	(SYD)
B. Ebert 26/7/56	(WIL-F)

FIFTH YEAR

W. ROHAN	(SYD)
G. THURLEY 26/3/56	(SYD)
M. O'NEILL 13/9/56	(SYD)
A. ADAMS	(MAIT)
P. HODGSON	(W'GONG)
R. BEAVEN	(BATH)
N. SLOAN	(CAN-G)
P. REES	(MAIT)
R. SYNOTT	(SYD)
R. GRANT	(SYD)
J. ANDERSON 6/5/	(SYD)
B. INNIS	(SYD)
F. WILKINSON	(MAIT)
S. OCZYNSKI 19/2/16	(SYD)
C. ANDERSON	(LIS)
A. HAYES 18/9/56	(LIS)
H. KENNEDY	(SYD)
C. SCIBBERAS 2/4/56	(SYD)

FOURTH YEAR

N. HUGHES	(CAN-G)
T. SCHREIBER	(LIS)
J. DUCK 31/7/56	(SYD)
P. KINGSLEY	(SYD)
P. INGHAM	(SYD)
A. DONNELLY	(CAN-G)
K. HAZELL	(MAIT)
P. JACOBS	(SYD)
B. JONES	(W'GONG)

LIST OF STUDENTS   ST. COLUMBA'S COLLEGE   1957

SECOND YEAR PHILOSOPHY

J. McCAFFERY	(SYD)	T. HYNES	(SYD)	D. WALKER	(SYD)
R. RYAN	(SYD)	K. ENGLISH	(SYD)	B. NOBBS	(SYD)
R. FLACK	(C-G)	C. GERAGHTY	(SYD)	N. BROWN	(SYD)
~~J. KENNEDY~~	(C-G)	B. CALLACHOR	(SYD)	~~E. KENNY~~	(ARM)
~~K. MANNING~~ Rome 11/5/57	(BATH)	M. BACH	(W'GONG)	J. FLOOD	(ARM)
L. O'NEILL	(C-G)	P. MANSOUR	(ARM)	M. WILLIAMS	(ARM)
R. LAWLER	(SYD)	J. O'NEILL	(SYD)	P. CAIN 15/4/57	(BATH)
R. RYAN	(SYD)	R. HAZLITT	(W'GONG)	P. MULCONRY	(MAIT)
P. NEVILLE	(SYD)	~~P. LAWLER~~ 15/5/57	(SYD)	~~J. DRUWE~~	(SYD)
B. WILLIS	(SYD)	J. ASHTON	(SYD)	D. FOLEY	(SYD)
J. STACE	(MAIT)	R. WEAVER	(SYD)	B. FRASER	(SYD)
J. TINKLER	(W-F)	J. WALTER	(SYD)	R. PERRETT	(ARM)
B. PIERCE	(SYD)	K. O'BRIEN	(SYD)	G. MULHEARN	(MAIT)
A. LEVEY	(MAIT)	M. HARFIELD	(SYD)	C. MERCICA	(W-F)
P. MARTIN	(MAIT)	S. HYNDES	(SYD)	A. CASEY	(MAIT)
B. GIBBONS	(MAIT)	P. DELANEY	(SYD)		

FIRST YEAR PHILOSOPHY

~~R. CHIVERS~~ 27.4.57	(SYD)	A. ADAMS	(MAIT)	P. O'KEEFE	(SYD)
K. FLANAGAN	(WAG)	R. BEAVEN	(BATH)	P. TOSI	(SYD)
B. ROONEY	(SYD)	N. SLOAN	(C-G)	C. MADDEN	(SYD)
J. KENNY	(BATH)	P. REES	(MAIT)	~~R. COOPER~~	(SYD)
B. BURKE	(MAIT)	R. SYNOTT	(SYD)	~~A. DIXON~~	(SYD)
G. JACKSON	(MAIT)	D. INNIS	(SYD)	J. McEWAN	(SYD)
~~J. BATES~~ 26.8.57	(MAIT)	F. WILKINSON	(MAIT)	A. NELSON	(SYD)
A. DOHERTY	(SYD)	~~BLOCZYNSKI~~	(SYD)	~~FITZGERALD~~	(ARM)
J. KEARNEY	(SYD)	C. ANDERSON	(LIS)	M. GREEN	(ARM)
V. WHITEMAN	(W'GONG)	H. KENNEDY	(SYD)	J. FITZGERALD	(C-G)
~~J. SHEEHY~~	(SYD)	J. RIVETT Rome 11/8/57	(SYD)	~~S. NOLAN~~ Rome 11/8/57	(LIS)
B. FRIZE	(ARM)	B. WRIGHT 14/8/57	(SYD)	T. WILLIAMS	(MAIT)
~~S. FLOOD~~	(ARM)	P. BAYNES	(SYD)	F. COOLAHAN	(MAIT)
G. HANNAN	(C-G)	M. CRITTENDEN	(SYD)	~~J. SULLIVAN~~	(MAIT)
M. CRITTENDEN	(MAIT)	T. BELL	(SYD)	R. PACKER	(WAG)
P. CHRISTIE	(SYD)	P. DENNETT	(SYD)	B. CONNELL	(WAG)
W. ROHAN	(SYD)	J. McCULLOCH	(SYD)	~~C. MULLINS~~	(W'GONG)

B. Hassett (C. and G.)

SPECIAL LATIN

B. MITCHELL	(SYD)	M. FLANAGAN	(SYD)	G. SING	(WAG)
L. BLAKE	(C-G)	K. CRUIKSHANK	(SYD)	A. CURRY	(W-F)
B. EBERT	(W-F)	F. CREWS	(BATH)	M. ROSA	(W'GONG)
D. McGEE	(SYD)	A. LAVIS	(LIS)	L. STEVENS	(W'GONG)
R. ANDERSON	(SYD)	P. TRISLEY	(LIS)	E. ATKINSON	(W'GONG)
B. GRAVES	(SYD)	L. HOLZ	(MAIT)	S. OCZYNSKI	(SYD)
A. SINARI	(SYD)	A. BURGESS	(MAIT)		

20

FIFTH YEAR

N. HUGHES	(C-G)	M. DONNELLY	(C-G)	C. SCIBBERAS	(SYD)
~~P. SCHREIBER~~	(LIS)	K. HAZELL	(MAIT)	~~B. WHITEHEAD~~	(SYD)
P. KINGSLEY	(SYD)	P. JACOBS	(SYD)		
P. INGHAM	(SYD)	B. JONES	(W'GONG)		

www.ingramcontent.com/pod-product-compliance
Lightning Source LLC
Chambersburg PA
CBHW050634300426
44112CB00012B/1792